AXEL'S CASTLE

AXEL'S CASTLE

A STUDY IN THE IMAGINATIVE LITERATURE
OF 1870–1930

By
EDMUND WILSON

CHARLES SCRIBNER'S SONS
NEW YORK

Dear Christian Gauss:

You will see how these essays have grown out of your lectures of fifteen years ago. But it is not merely on that account that I have felt I owe you a debt in connection with them. It was principally from you that I acquired then my idea of what literary criticism ought to be—a history of man's ideas and imaginings in the setting of the conditions which have shaped them. And though this book is only a very limited and a very incomplete attempt at that sort of history, I have wanted to dedicate it to you in acknowledgment of the kindness and instruction which, beginning when I was at college, have continued ever since, and as a tribute to a master of criticism who has taught much in insisting little.

Yours as ever,

Edmund Wilson.

CONTENTS

AXEL'S CASTLE

I

SYMBOLISM

IT is my purpose in this book to try to trace the origins of certain tendencies in contemporary literature and to show their development in the work of six contemporary writers. To persons already familiar with the field, my explanations in this first chapter will seem rudimentary; but I believe that it is still true in general, for reasons which I shall suggest, that the sources and fundamental principles of many of the books which have excited most discussion during the period since the War are singularly little understood. It is not usually recognized that writers such as W. B. Yeats, James Joyce, T. S. Eliot, Gertrude Stein, Marcel Proust and Paul Valéry represent the culmination of a self-conscious and very important literary movement; and even when we have become aware that these writers have something in common, that they belong to a common school, we are likely to be rather vague as to what its distinguishing features are.

We do, however, to-day as a rule have a pretty clear idea of the issues which were raised by the Romantic Movement of the beginning of the nineteenth century. We still debate Classicism and Romanticism, and when we attempt to deal with contemporary literary problems, we often tend to discuss them in those terms. Yet the movement of which in our own day we are witnessing the mature development is not merely a degeneration or an elaboration of Romanticism, but rather a counterpart to it, a second flood of the same tide. And even the metaphor of a tide is misleading: what we have to-day is an entirely distinct movement, which has arisen from different conditions and must be dealt with in different terms.

Romanticism, as everyone has heard, was a revolt of the individual. The "Classicism" against which it was a reaction meant, in the domain of politics and morals, a preoccupation with society as a whole; and, in art, an ideal of objectivity. In "Le Misanthrope," in "Bérénice," in "The Way of the World," in "Gulliver's Travels," the artist is out of the picture: he would consider it artistic bad taste to identify his hero with himself and to glorify himself with his hero, or to intrude between the reader and the story and give vent to his personal emotions. But in "René," in "Rolla," in "Childe Harold," in "The Prelude," the writer is either his own hero, or unmistakably identified with his hero, and the personality and emotions of the writer are presented as the principal subject of interest. Racine, Molière, Congreve and Swift ask us to be interested in what they have made; but Chateaubriand, Musset, Byron and Wordsworth ask us to be interested in themselves. And they ask us to be interested in themselves by virtue of the intrinsic value of the individual: they vindicate the rights of the individual against the claims of society as a whole—against government, morals, conventions, academy or church. The Romantic is nearly always a rebel.

In this connection, it is illuminating to consider the explanation of the Romantic Movement given by A. N. Whitehead in his "Science and the Modern World." The Romantic Movement, Whitehead says, was really a re-action against scientific ideas, or rather against the mechanistic ideas to which certain scientific discoveries gave rise. The seventeenth and eighteenth centuries were in Europe the great period of the development of mathematical and physical theory; and in the literature of the so-called Classical period, Descartes and Newton were influences as important as those of the classics themselves. The poets, like the astronomers and mathematicians, had come to regard the universe as a machine, obeying logical laws and susceptible of reasonable explanation: God figured merely as the clockmaker who must have existed to make the clock. People applied this conception also to society, which, from the point of view of Louis XIV and of the American Constitution alike, had the character of a planetary system or a well-regulated machine; and they examined human nature dispassionately, in the same lucid and reasonable spirit, to find the principles on which it worked. Thus the theorems of the physicist were matched by the geometrical plays of Racine and the balanced couplets of Pope.

But this conception of a fixed mechanical order came eventually to be felt as a constraint: it excluded too much of life—or rather, the description it supplied did not correspond to actual experience. The Romantics had become acutely conscious of aspects of their experience which it was impossible to analyze or explain on the theory of a world run by clockwork. The universe was not a machine, after all, but something more mysterious and less rational.

> "The atoms of Democritus,
>   And Newton's particles of light
> Are sands upon the Red Sea shore,
>   Where Israel's tents do shine so bright!"

Blake had already contradicted contemptuously the physical theory of the eighteenth century. And to Wordsworth, the countryside of his boyhood meant neither agriculture nor neo-classic idylls, but a light never seen on land or sea. When the poet looked into his own soul, he beheld something which did not seem to him reducible to a set of principles of human nature such, for example, as La Rochefoucauld's "Maxims": he saw fantasy, conflict, confusion. And he either set himself, like Wordsworth and Blake, to affirm the superior truth of this vision as compared to the mechanical universe of the physicists; or, accepting this mechanical universe, like Byron or Alfred de Vigny, as external to and indifferent to man, he pitted against it, in defiance, his own turbulent insubordinate soul.

In any case, it is always, as in Wordsworth, the individual sensibility, or, as in Byron, the individual will, with which the Romantic poet is preoccupied; and he has invented a new language for the expression of its mystery, its conflict and confusion. The arena of literature has been transferred from the universe conceived as a machine, from society conceived as an organization, to the individual soul.

What has really taken place, says Whitehead, is a philosophical revolution. The scientists of the seventeenth century who presented the universe as a mechanism had caused people to draw the conclusion that man was something apart from nature, something introduced into the universe from outside and remaining alien to all that he found. But a Romantic poet like Wordsworth has come to feel the falsity of this assumption: he has perceived that the world is an organism, that nature includes planets, mountains, vegetation and people alike, that what we are and what we see, what we hear, what we feel and what we smell, are inextricably related, that all are involved in the same great entity. Those who make fun of the Romantics are mistaken in supposing that there is no intimate connection between the landscape and the poet's emotions. There is no real dualism, says Whitehead, between external lakes and hills, on the one hand, and personal feelings, on the other: human feelings and inanimate objects are interdependent and developing together in some fashion of which our traditional notions of laws of cause and effect, of dualities of mind and matter or of body and soul, can give us no true idea. The Romantic poet, then, with his turbid or opalescent language, his sympathies and passions which cause him to seem to merge with his surroundings, is the prophet of a new insight into nature: he is describing things as they really are; and a revolution in the imagery of poetry is in reality a revolution in metaphysics.

Whitehead drops the story at this point; but he has provided the key to what follows. In the middle of the nineteenth century, science made new advances, and mechanistic ideas were brought back into fashion again. But they came this time from a different quarter—not from physics and mathematics, but from biology. It was the effect of the theory of Evolution to reduce man from the heroic stature to which the Romantics had tried to exalt him, to the semblance of a helpless animal, again very small in the universe and at the mercy of the forces about him. Humanity was the accidental product of heredity and environment, and capable of being explained in terms of these. This doctrine in literature was called Naturalism, and it was put into practice by novelists like Zola, who believed that composing a novel was like performing a laboratory experiment: you had only to supply your characters with a specific environment and heredity and then watch their automatic reactions; and by historians and critics like Taine, who asserted that virtue and vice were as much the products of automatic processes as alkalis and acids, and who attempted to account for masterpieces by studying the geographical and climatic conditions of the countries in which they had been produced.

Not, however, that the movement known as Naturalism arose directly from "The Origin of Species." There had already set in, about the middle of the century, quite independent of the theory of Evolution, a reaction against the sentimentality and the looseness of Romanticism, and in the direction of the objectivity and the severity of Classicism again; and this reaction had already been char. acterized by a kind of scientific observation which closely corresponded to that of biological science. This reaction is seen most clearly in France. The Parnassian group of poets, who made their first appearance in the fifties— Gautier, Leconte de Lisle, Hérédia—seemed to have taken it for their aim merely to picture historical incidents and natural phenomena as objectively and accurately as possible in impassive perfect verse. Leconte de Lisle's elephants crossing the desert is a celebrated example: the elephants appear and disappear with a certain classical dignity and grandeur, and the poet leaves it at that.

It is less easy, in English poetry, to give clear examples of the reaction toward Naturalism: the English did not, after the Romantic Movement, take much interest in literary methods till toward the end of the nineteenth century. But the tendency toward what we call realism had set in, none the less: Browning, though he had, of course, nothing of the classical form of the Parnassians, was addicted to historical reconstruction of a kind more pedantic and less flamboyant than that of the true Romantics, and when he dealt with contemporary life, did so at least as realistically as any of the Victorian novelists—themselves going in Zola's direction without quite being aware of the fact. And we can see very plainly in Tennyson, who was much preoccupied with the doctrines of Evolution, something of the same exactitude of description combined with something of the same severity of verse—though with less hardness and more grace—that we find in the French poets.

> "Nor wilt thou snare him in the white ravine,
> Nor find him dropt upon the firths of ice,
> That huddling slant in furrow-cloven fells
> To roll the torrent out of dusky doors:
> But follow; let the torrent dance thee down
> To find him in the valley; let the wild
> Lean-headed eagles yelp alone."

And it is interesting to compare Tennyson, in this connection, with Pope on the rare occasions (though not so rare as people sometimes suppose) when he is describing natural objects:

> "The silver eel, in shining volumes roll'd,
> The yellow carp, in scales bedropp'd with gold."

These lines have the technical perfection and the precise observation of Tennyson, but they are heavier and more metallic. Pope is often, as a matter of fact, very close to the French Parnassians. The latter represent, in reality, a second classical-scientific movement, the counterpart to that represented by Pope.

But the highest developments of Naturalism took place, not in poetry, but in prose. The plays of Ibsen and the novels of Flaubert are the masterpieces of this second period of modern classicism, as Racine and Swift are of the first. The art of Flaubert and Ibsen is again, like the art of the seventeenth-century writers, scrupulously non-personal and objective, and it insists upon precision of language and economy of form. Compare the lucidity, the logic and the limited number of characters of such a tragedy of Ibsen's as "Rosmersholm" with the rigorous conventions of Racine; or compare "Gulliver's Travels" with "Bouvard et Pécuchet" or "L'Education Sentimentale." Yet, though the earlier works resemble the later ones in many obvious ways, they differ from them in this: where a seventeenth-century moralist like La Rochefoucauld would have sought to discover and set forth the universal principles of human behavior, a nineteenth-century writer like Ibsen or Flaubert has begun to study man in relation to his particular environment and time. The method of approach in both cases, however, may be described as "scientific," and it tends to lead us to mechanistic conclusions.

Now Flaubert and Ibsen both had been suckled on Romanticism. Flaubert had begun by writing a Romantic "Saint-Antoine" before he chastened it and cut it down to the more sober one which he published; and Ibsen had written in verse his Faustian "Brand" and "Peer Gynt" before he arrived at his realistic plays in prose. Each, beginning in Romanticism, had evolved for himself a new discipline and developed a new point of view. For "Madame Bovary" is not merely arranged and written differently from a novel by Victor Hugo: it also constitutes an objective criticism of a case of Romantic personality; and Ibsen was occupied all his life with situations produced by the conflict of the essentially Romantic conception of one's duty to one's own personality with the conception of one's duty to society.

But in the later prose plays of Ibsen, the trolls and ghosts of his early dramatic poems have begun to creep back into the bourgeois drawing-rooms: the Naturalist has been finally compelled to make cracks in his own mold. All that vaporous, confused and grandiose world of Romanticism had been resolutely ordered and compressed; but now the objective point of view of Naturalism, the machine-like technique which went with it, begin to cramp the poet's imagination, to prove inadequate to convey what he feels. The reader begins to chafe at the strain, and the artist begins to betray it. Huysmans described Leconte de Lisle as "the sonorous hardware man": we remember Wordsworth's strictures on Pope. Literature is rebounding again from the scientific-classical pole to the poetic-romantic one. And this second reaction at the end of the century, this counterpart to the Romantic reaction of the end of the century before, was known in France as Symbolism.

Now in attempting to write literary history, one must guard against giving the impression that these movements and counter-movements necessarily follow one another in a punctual and well-generalled fashion—as if eighteenth-century reason had been cleanly put to rout by nineteenth-century Romanticism, which then proceeded to hold the field till it was laid by the heels by Naturalism, and as if Mallarmé and Rimbaud had then blown up Naturalism with bombs. What really happens, of course, is that one set of methods and ideas is not completely superseded by another; but that, on the contrary, it thrives in its teeth—so that, on the one hand, Flaubert's prose has learned to hear, see and feel with the delicate senses of Romanticism at the same time that Flaubert is disciplining and criticizing the Romantic temperament; and so that, on the other hand, certain members of a school, unaffected by new influences abroad, will continue to practise its methods and to exploit its possibilities further and further, when nearly everybody else has abandoned it.

I have here purposely been selecting writers who seemed to represent some tendency or school in its purest or most highly developed form. We must, however, now consider some Romantics who, in certain ways, carried Romanticism further than even Chateaubriand or Musset, or than Wordsworth or Byron, and who became the first precursors of Symbolism and were afterwards placed among its saints.

One of these was the French writer who called himself Gérard de Nerval. Gérard de Nerval suffered from spells of insanity; and, partly no doubt as a result of this, habitually confused his own fancies and feelings with external reality. He believed, even in his lucid periods—and no doubt Whitehead would approve his metaphysics—that the world which we see about us is involved in some more intimate fashion than is ordinarily supposed with the things that go on in our minds, that even our dreams and hallucinations are somehow bound up with reality. And in one of his sonnets he outdoes Wordsworth, with his "Presences of Nature in the sky" and his "Souls of lonely places," by imagining shuttered eyes coming to life in the very walls and "a pure spirit under the bark of stones."

But a more important prophet of Symbolism was Edgar Allan Poe. It was in general true that, by the middle of the century, the Romantic writers in the United States—Poe, Hawthorne, Melville, Whitman and even Emerson—were, for reasons which it would be interesting to determine, developing in the direction of Symbolism; and one of the events of prime importance in the early history of the Symbolist Movement was the discovery of Poe by Baudelaire. When Baudelaire, a late Romantic, first read Poe in 1847, he "experienced a strange commotion." When he began to look up Poe's writings in the files of American magazines, he found among them stories and poems which he said that he himself had already "thought vaguely and confusedly" of writing, and his interest became a veritable passion. In 1852, Baudelaire published a volume of translations of Poe's tales; and from then on the influence of Poe played an important part in French literature. Poe's critical writings provided the first scriptures of the Symbolist Movement, for he had formulated what amounted to a new literary programme which corrected the Romantic looseness and lopped away the Romantic extravagance, at the same time that it aimed, not at Naturalistic, but at ultra-Romantic effects. There was, of course, a good deal in common between Poe's poetry and such Romantic poetry as Coleridge's "Kubla Khan," as there was between his poems in prose and such Romantic prose as that of De Quincey. But Poe, by insisting on and specially cultivating certain aspects of Romanticism, helped to transform it into something different. "I *know*," we find Poe writing, for example, "that indefiniteness is an element of the true music [of poetry]—I mean of the true musical expression . . . a suggestive indefiniteness of vague and therefore of spiritual *effect*." And to approximate the indefiniteness of music was to become one of the principal aims of Symbolism.

This effect of indefiniteness was produced not merely by the confusion I have mentioned between the imaginary world and the real; but also by means of a further confusion between the perceptions of the different senses.

"Comme de longs échos qui de loin se confondent . . .
Les parfums, les couleurs et les sons se répondent,"

wrote Baudelaire. And we find Poe, in one of his poems, *hearing* the approach of the darkness, or writing such a description as the following of the sensations which follow death: "Night arrived; and with its shadows a heavy discomfort. It oppressed my limbs with the oppression of some dull weight, and was palpable. There was also a moaning sound, not unlike the distant reverberation of surf, but more continuous, which beginning with the first twilight, had grown in strength with the darkness. Suddenly lights were brought into the room . . . and issuing from the flame of each lamp, there flowed unbrokenly into my ears a strain of melodious monotone."

13

This notation of super-rational sensations was a novelty in the forties of the last century—as was the dreamlike irrational musical poetry of "Annabel Lee" and "Ulalume"; and they helped to effect a revolution in France. For an English-speaking reader of to-day, Poe's influence may be hard to understand; and even when such a reader comes to examine the productions of French Symbolism, it may surprise him that they should have caused amazement. The medley of images; the deliberately mixed metaphors; the combination of passion and wit—of the grand and the prosaic manners; the bold amalgamation of material with spiritual—all these may seem to him quite proper and familiar. He has always known them in the English poetry of the sixteenth and seventeenth centuries—Shakespeare and the other Elizabethans did all these things without theorizing about them. Is this not the natural language of poetry? Is it not the norm against which, in English literature, the eighteenth century was a heresy and to which the Romantics did their best to return?

But we must remember that the development of French poetry has been quite different from that of English. Michelet says that in the sixteenth century the future of French literature had hung in the balance between Rabelais and Ronsard, and he regrets that it was Ronsard who triumphed. For Rabelais in France was a sort of equivalent to our own Elizabethans, whereas Ronsard, who represented to Michelet all that was poorest, dryest and most conventional in the French genius, was one of the fathers

of that classical tradition of lucidity, sobriety and purity
which culminated in Molière and Racine. In comparison
with the Classicism of the French, which has dominated
their whole literature since the Renaissance, the English
Classicism of the eighteenth century, the age of Dr.
Johnson and Pope, was a brief ineffective deviation. And
from the point of view of English readers, the most daring innovations of the Romantic revolution in France,
in spite of all the excitement which accompanied them,
must appear of an astonishingly moderate character. But
the age and the rigor of the tradition were the measure of
the difficulty of breaking out of it. After all, Coleridge,
Shelley and Keats—in spite of Pope and Dr. Johnson—
had only to look back to Milton and Shakespeare, whose
dense forests had all along been in view beyond the formal
eighteenth-century gardens. But to an eighteenth-century
Frenchman like Voltaire, Shakespeare was incomprehen-
sible; and to the Frenchman of the classical tradition of
the beginning of the nineteenth century, the rhetoric of
Hugo was a scandal: the French were not used to such
rich colors or to so free a vocabulary; moreover, the Romantics broke metrical rules far stricter than any we have
had in English. Yet Victor Hugo was still very far from
the variety and freedom of Shakespeare. It is enlightening
to compare Shelley's lyric which begins, "O World! O
Life! O Time!" with the poem of Alfred de Musset's which
begins, "J'ai perdu ma force et ma vie." These two
lyrics are in some ways curiously similar: each is the
breath of a Romantic sigh over the passing of the pride

of youth. Yet the French poet, even in his wistfulness, makes epigrammatic points: his language is always logical and precise; whereas the English poet is vague and gives us images unrelated by logic. And it will not be till the advent of the Symbolists that French poetry will really become capable of the fantasy and fluidity of English.

The Symbolist Movement broke those rules of French metrics which the Romantics had left intact, and it finally succeeded in throwing overboard completely the clarity and logic of the French classical tradition, which the Romantics had still to a great extent respected. It was nourished from many alien sources—German, Flemish, modern Greek—and especially, precisely, from English. Verlaine had lived in England, and knew English well; Mallarmé was a professor of English; and Baudelaire, as I have said, had provided the movement with its first programmes by translating the essays of Poe. Two of the Symbolist poets, Stuart Merrill and Francis Vielé-Griffin, were Americans who lived in Paris and wrote French; and an American, reading to-day the latter's "Chevauchée d'Yeldis," for example, may wonder how, when Symbolism was new, such a poem could ever have been regarded as one of the movement's acknowledged masterpieces: to us, it seems merely agreeable, not in the least revolutionary or novel, but like something which might not impossibly have been written by Thomas Bailey Aldrich if he had been influenced by Browning. We are surprised to learn that Vielé-Griffin is still considered an important poet.

But the point was that he had performed a feat which astonished and impressed the French and of which it is probable that no Frenchman was capable: he had succeeded in wrecking once for all the classical Alexandrine, hitherto the basis of French poetry—or rather, as an English reader at once recognizes, he had dispensed with it altogether and begun writing English metres in French. The French called this *"vers libre,"* but it is "free" only in the sense of being irregular, like many poems of Matthew Arnold and Browning.

What made Poe particularly acceptable to the French, however, was what had distinguished him from most of the other Romantics of the English-speaking countries: his interest in æsthetic theory. The French have always reasoned about literature far more than the English have; they always want to know what they are doing and why they are doing it: their literary criticism has acted as a constant interpreter and guide to the rest of their literature. And it was in France that Poe's literary theory, to which no one seems to have paid much attention elsewhere, was first studied and elucidated. So that, though the effects and devices of Symbolism were of a kind that was familiar in English, and though the Symbolists were sometimes indebted to English literature directly—the Symbolist Movement itself, by reason of its origin in France, had a deliberate self-conscious æsthetic which made it different from anything in English. One must go back to Coleridge to find in English a figure comparable to the Symbolist leader, Stéphane Mallarmé. Paul Valéry says of Mallarmé that, as he was the greatest French poet of his time, he could also have been one of the most popular. But Mallarmé was an unpopular poet: he taught English for a living, and wrote little and published less. Yet, ridiculed and denounced by the public, who reiterated that his poetry was nonsense and yet were irritated by his seriousness and obstinacy, he exercised, from his little Paris apartment, where he held Tuesday receptions, an influence curiously far-reaching over the young writers—English and French alike—of the end of the century. There in the sitting-room which was also the dining-room on the fourth floor in the Rue de Rome, where the whistle of locomotives came in through the windows to mingle with the literary conversation, Mallarmé, with his shining pensive gaze from under his long lashes and always smoking a cigarette "to put some smoke," as he used to say, "between the world and himself," would talk about the theory of poetry in a "mild, musical and unforgettable voice." There was an atmosphere "calm and almost religious." Mallarmé had "the pride of the inner life," said one of his friends; his nature was "patient, disdainful and imperiously gentle." He always reflected before he spoke and always put what he said in the form of a question. His wife sat beside him embroidering; his daughter answered the door. Here came Huysmans, Whistler, Degas, Moréas, Laforgue, Vielé-Griffin, Paul Valéry, Henri de Régnier, Pierre Louys, Paul Claudel, Remy de Gourmont, André Gide, Oscar Wilde, Arthur Symons, George Moore and W. B. Yeats. For Mallarmé was a true saint of literature:

he had proposed to himself an almost impossible object, and he pursued it without compromise or distraction. His whole life was dedicated to the effort to do something with the language of poetry which had never been done before. "Donner un sens plus pur," he had written in a sonnet on Poe, "aux mots de la tribu." He was, as Albert Thibaudet has said, engaged in "a disinterested experiment on the confines of poetry, at a limit where other lungs would find the air unbreathable."

What, then, was this purer sense which Mallarmé believed he was following Poe in wishing to give to the words of the tribe? What, precisely, was the nature of this experiment on the confines of poetry which Mallarmé found so absorbing and which so many other writers tried to repeat? What, precisely, did the Symbolists propose? I have called attention, in speaking of Poe, to the confusion between the perceptions of the different senses, and to the attempt to make the effects of poetry approximate to those of music. And I should add, in this latter connection, that the influence on Symbolist poetry of Wagner was as important as that of any poet: at the time when Romantic music had come closest to literature, literature was attracted toward music. I have also spoken, in connection with Gérard de Nerval, of the confusion between the imaginary and the real, between our sensations and fancies, on the one hand, and what we actually do and see, on the other. It was the tendency of Symbolism—that second swing of the pendulum away from a mechanistic view of nature and from a social conception of man—to make poetry even more a matter of the sensations and emotions of the individual than had been the case with Romanticism: Symbolism, indeed, sometimes had the result of making poetry so much a private concern of the poet's that it turned out to be incommunicable to the reader. The peculiar subtlety and difficulty of Symbolism is indicated by the name itself. This name has often been complained of as being inadequate for the movement to which it was given and inappropriate to certain of its aspects; and it may prove misleading to English readers. For the symbols of Symbolism have to be defined a little differently from symbols in the ordinary sense—the sense in which the Cross is the symbol of Christianity or the Stars and Stripes the symbol of the United States. This symbolism differs even from such symbolism as Dante's. For the familiar kind of symbolism is conventional and fixed; the symbolism of the Divine Comedy is conventional, logical and definite. But the symbols of the Symbolist school are usually chosen arbitrarily by the poet to stand for special ideas of his own—they are a sort of disguise for these ideas. "The Parnassians, for their part," wrote Mallarmé, "take the thing just as it is and put it before us—and consequently they are deficient in mystery: they deprive the mind of the delicious joy of believing that it is creating. To name an object is to do away with the three-quarters of the enjoyment of the poem which is derived from the satisfaction of guessing little by little: to suggest it, to evoke it—that is what charms the imagination."

To intimate things rather than state them plainly was thus one of the primary aims of the Symbolists. But there was more involved in their point of view than Mallarmé here explains. The assumptions which underlay Symbolism lead us to formulate some such doctrine as the following: Every feeling or sensation we have, every moment of consciousness, is different from every other; and it is, in consequence, impossible to render our sensations as we actually experience them through the conventional and universal language of ordinary literature. Each poet has his unique personality; each of his moments has its special tone, its special combination of elements. And it is the poet's task to find, to invent, the special language which will alone be capable of expressing his personality and feelings. Such a language must make use of symbols: what is so special, so fleeting and so vague cannot be conveyed by direct statement or description, but only by a succession of words, of images, which will serve to suggest it to the reader. The Symbolists themselves, full of the idea of producing with poetry effects like those of music, tended to think of these images as possessing an abstract value like musical notes and chords. But the words of our speech are not musical notation, and what the symbols of Symbolism really were, were metaphors detached from their subjects—for one cannot, beyond a certain point, in poetry, merely enjoy color and sound for their own sake: one has to guess what the images are being applied to. And Symbolism may be defined as an attempt by carefully studied means—a complicated association of ideas represented by a medley of metaphors—to communicate unique personal feelings.

The Symbolist Movement proper was first largely confined to France and principally limited to poetry of rather an esoteric kind; but it was destined, as time went on, to spread to the whole western world and its principles to be applied on a scale which the most enthusiastic of its founders could scarcely have foreseen. Remy de Gourmont, who was eventually to become the most distinguished critical champion of the movement, tells of his excitement, one afternoon in the eighties, at discovering the new poetry in a little magazine which he had picked up at a book-stall in the Odéon: "As I looked through it, I experienced the little æsthetic thrill and that exquisite impression of novelty which has so much charm for youth. I seem to myself to have been dreaming rather than reading. The Luxembourg was pink with early April: I crossed it toward the Rue d'Assas, thinking a great deal more about the new literature which was coinciding for me that day with the renewal of the world than about the business which had brought me to that part of Paris. All that I had written up to that time inspired me with profound disgust. . . . In less than an hour my literary orientation was radically modified." And Yeats wrote in 1897: "The reaction against the rationalism of the eighteenth century has mingled with a reaction against the materialism of the nineteenth century, and the symbolical movement, which has come to perfection in Germany in Wagner, in England in the Pre-Raphaelites, and in France in Villiers de L'Isle-

Adam and Mallarmé and Maeterlinck, and has stirred the imagination of Ibsen and D'Annunzio, is certainly the only movement that is saying new things."

We do not talk about Symbolism to-day in dealing with English literature; we do not even, as Yeats did at the end of the last century, think of the writers whom he mentions as all belonging to a "symbolical movement"; yet the influence of Mallarmé and his fellow poets was felt widely and deeply outside of France, and it is difficult to understand certain of the things which have been happening lately in English literature without some knowledge of the Symbolist school. I believe, in fact, that if English and American criticism have sometimes shown themselves at a loss when confronted with the work of certain recent writers, it is partly because the work of these writers is the result of a literary revolution which occurred outside English literature. The case of the Romantic Movement was different: Wordsworth's prefaces were English manifestoes; Lockhart's attack on Keats and Byron's attack on Jeffrey were blows struck in an English civil war. But in spite of the Pre-Raphaelites, who were launched by an impulse somewhat similar to that of the Symbolists, and in spite of the English "æsthetics" and "decadents," who for the most part imitated the French without very much originality, the battle of Symbolism has never properly been fought out in English. So that whereas French writers like Valéry and Proust who have grown out of the Symbolist Movement, are well understood and appreciated by French literary criticism, the critics of the English-speaking countries have often seemed not to know how to deal with writers such as Eliot and Joyce. Even when these writers have brought back into English qualities which are natural to it and resources which it originally possessed, these elements have returned by way of France and have taken on the complexion of the French mind—critical, philosophical, much occupied with æsthetic theory and tending always to aim self-consciously at particular effects and to study scrupulously appropriate means.

It has perhaps been peculiarly easy for certain of the leaders of contemporary English literature—that is, of the literature since the War—to profit by the example of Paris, because they have themselves not been English. Of the writers in English I shall discuss in this book, Yeats is an Irishman who turns almost as easily toward Paris as toward London; Joyce an Irishman who has done most of his work on the Continent and who has scarcely lived in England at all; and T. S. Eliot and Gertrude Stein are Americans living abroad. The work of these writers has been largely a continuance or extension of Symbolism. Yeats, the ablest of the *fin de siècle* group who tried in London to emulate the French, managed to make Symbolism flourish triumphantly by transplanting it to the more favorable soil of Ireland. T. S. Eliot in his earliest poems seems to have been as susceptible to the influence of the Symbolists as to that of the English Elizabethans. Joyce, a master of Naturalism as great as Flaubert, has at the same time succeeded in dramatizing Symbolism by making use of its methods for differentiating between his various characters and their varying states of mind. And Gertrude Stein has carried Mallarmé's principles so far in the direction of that limit where other lungs find the air unbreathable as perhaps finally to reduce them to absurdity. It is true, however, that under proper conditions, these principles remain valid; and both the strength and the weaknesses characteristic of much of the literature since the War derive naturally from the Symbolist poets and may already be studied in their work. The literary history of our time is to a great extent that of the development of Symbolism and of its fusion or conflict with Naturalism.

II

W. B. YEATS

BORN in Dublin in 1865, William Butler Yeats was the son of an Irish Pre-Raphaelite painter, who had given him, at "fifteen or sixteen," Rossetti and Blake to read. Yeats's earliest verse was Pre-Raphaelite and Romantic: his long poem, "The Wanderings of Oisin" (1889), on a subject from Irish mythology, stains a kind of Shelleyan fluidity with a Keatsian richness of color. But, during the nineties, Yeats met Mallarmé in Paris, and though he knew at that time little French, was instructed in the doctrines of Symbolism by his friend Arthur Symons. "I think," he says, "that Symons's translations from Mallarmé may have given elaborate form to my verses of those years, to the latter poems of 'The Wind among the Reeds,' to 'The Shadowy Waters.'" And we have seen that he wrote of Symbolism as "the only movement that is saying new things."

If we do not ordinarily think of Yeats as primarily a Symbolist poet, it is because, in taking Symbolism to Ireland, he fed it with new resources and gave it a special accent which lead us to think of his poetry from the point of view of its national qualities rather than from the point of view of its relation to the rest of European literature.

It is easy, however, to see how close Yeats is, even in his later years, to the French poetry of the end of the century, in such a comparatively recent poem as "On a Picture of a Black Centaur":

"Your hooves have stamped at the black margin of the wood,
Even where horrible green parrots call and swing.
My works are all stamped down into the sultry mud.
I knew that horse play, knew it for a murderous thing.
What wholesome sun has ripened is wholesome food to eat
And that alone; yet I, being driven half insane
Because of some green wing, gathered old mummy wheat
In the mad abstract dark and ground it grain by grain
And after baked it slowly in an oven; but now
I bring full flavoured wine out of a barrel found
Where seven Ephesian topers slept and never knew
When Alexander's empire past, they slept so sound.
Stretch out your limbs and sleep a long Saturnian sleep;
I have loved you better than my soul for all my words,
And there is none so fit to keep a watch and keep
Unwearied eyes upon those horrible green birds."

Compare this with a characteristic sonnet of Mallarmé's:

"Le vierge, le vivace et le bel aujourd'hui
Va-t-il nous déchirer avec un coup d'aile ivre
Ce lac dur oublié que hante sous le givre
Le transparent glacier des vols qui n'ont pas fui?

Un cygne d'autrefois se souvient que c'est lui
Magnifique mais qui sans espoir se délivre
Pour n'avoir pas chanté la région où vivre
Quand du stérile hiver a resplendi l'ennui.

Tout son col secouera cette blanche agonie
Par l'espace infligée à l'oiseau qui le nie,
Mais non l'horreur du sol où le plumage est pris.

Fantôme qu'à ce lieu son pur éclat assigne,
Il s'immobilise au songe froid de mépris
Que vêt parmi l'exil inutile le Cygne."

The centaur, the parrots, the wheat and the wine are, like the swan, the lake and the frost, not real things (except that the centaur is something Yeats has seen in a picture), but merely accidental images which, by an association of ideas, have come to stand for the poet's emotion. But where the French poets were obliged to depend almost exclusively upon such symbols, which tended to become more bewildering as they became more heterogeneous, Yeats found in Irish mythology, unfamiliar even to Irish readers, and in itself rather cloudy and vague, a treasury of symbols ready to his hand. He had thus perhaps a special advantage. The Danaan children, the Shadowy Horses and Fergus with his brazen cars—those mysterious and magical beings who play so large a part in Yeats's verse—have little more objective reality than the images of Mallarmé: they are the elements and the moods of Yeats's complex sensibility. But they have a more satisfactory character than such a French Symbolist mythology as Mallarmé's—though Mallarmé does occasionally draw on the Old Testament or the classics for a Salome or a faun—because they constitute a world of which one can to some extent get the hang, where one can at least partly find one's way about.

And, as we follow the progress of Yeats's poetry, this world becomes less dim and iridescent. In "The Wind among the Reeds," which appeared in 1899, we still find "the flaming lute-thronged angelic door" and "the heaven's embroidered cloths—enwrought with golden and silver light" of the earlier Pre-Raphaelite Yeats. But sometime about the beginning of the century, the poet became dissatisfied, he tells us, and set out rigorously to eliminate from his poetry both Romantic rhetoric and Symbolistic mistiness.

The development of Yeats's later style seems to coincide with a disillusionment. The younger Yeats has lived much in fairyland: the heroes of his short stories and poems— Oisin, Red Hanrahan, the Man Who Dreamed of Fairyland—are always deserting the real world for the world of the Sidhe, the fairies. The real world is a sad unsatisfactory place: in one of the very first of Yeats's poems, the fairies warn the child they are stealing away—

"Come away, O human child!
  To the waters and the wild
  With a faery, hand in hand,
  For the world's more full of weeping than you can understand."

And the mortals who escape to fairyland find eternal lovemaking and laughter: they dance on twilit lawns to strange music. The Irish fairies of Yeats are not, like the fairies of the ordinary fairy-story, merely smaller human beings like ourselves, possessed of special supernatural powers: they are a different order of beings altogether, existing, as it were, in different dimensions. This strangeness, this real other-worldliness of the fairyland of Yeats's poetry, derives partly, no doubt, it would appear from the fascinating anthology of Irish fairy-tales which Yeats compiled and edited, from Irish folk-lore itself. The Sidhe were the natural creation of the dreaming and mocking

Irish mind amid the illusory uncertain lights and mists of
the Irish countryside. But Yeats has made of this Irish
fairyland something which puts upon us a stronger spell
than the spell even of the folk-tales in his anthology.
Yeats's fairyland has become a symbol for the imagination
itself. The world of the imagination is shown us in Yeats's
early poetry as something infinitely delightful, infinitely
seductive, as something to which one becomes addicted,
with which one becomes delirious and drunken—and as
something which is somehow incompatible with, and fatal
to, the good life of that actual world which is so full of
weeping and from which it is so sweet to withdraw.
There is nothing sinister about the Sidhe in themselves:
they are non-moral and relieved of mortal cares; for
them, there is not even time; and from our human point
of view, their fairy point of view is unseizable. But to the
mortal who has lived among the fairies, who has lost the
sense of human laws in their world, the consequences may
be terrible—for he has preferred something else to reality
—he has escaped the responsibilities of human life and he
must fail of its satisfactions. The Man Who Dreamed of
Fairyland, in one of the most beautiful of Yeats's early
poems, had

> ". . . stood among a crowd at Drumahair;
> His heart hung all upon a silken dress,
> And he had known at last some tenderness,
> Before Earth made of him her sleepy care;
> But when a man poured fish into a pile,
> It seemed they raised their little silver heads,
> And sang how day a Druid twilight sheds

Upon a dim, green, well-beloved isle,
Where people love beside star-laden seas;
How Time may never mar their faery vows
Under the woven roofs of quicken boughs:
The singing shook him out of his new ease.

He wandered by the sands of Lisadill;
His mind ran all on money cares and fears,
And he had known at last some prudent years
Before they heaped his grave under the hill;
But while he passed before a plashy place,
A lug-worm with its gray and muddy mouth
Sang how somewhere to north or west or south,
There dwelt a gay, exulting, gentle race;
And how beneath those three times blessed skies
A Danaan fruitage makes a shower of moons,
And as it falls awakens leafy tunes:
And at that singing he was no more wise."

And so with all our human needs and passions—the man who dreamed of fairyland is always being distracted from them by intimations of a world outside our world; and even when he is dead, he can find "no comfort in the grave." So in another poem, the joys of the "Happy Townland" where "boughs have their fruit and blossom at all times of the year," where "rivers are running over with red beer and brown beer" and where "queens, their eyes blue like the ice, are dancing in a crowd," are irreconcilable with real life: the enchanted Happy Townland is also "the world's bane."

In the prose stories of Yeats's early period, this fairyland appears under its real aspect as the life of revery and imagination—and of solitude. The narrator of "Rosa Alchemica" exiles himself from the world in a house where tapestries, "full of the blue and bronze of peacocks . . . shut out all history and activity untouched with beauty and peace," and where he is able to find in "antique bronze gods and goddesses . . . all a pagan's delight in various beauty . . . without his terror at sleepless destiny and his labor with many sacrifices." Another solitary, Michael Robartes, lives on the lonely Irish coast in a house which he calls "the Temple of the Alchemical Rose" and where by night the immortal spirits of beautiful long-dead men and women from Egypt and from Greece come to dance in a mosaic-lined room, with a great rose in mosaic on the ceiling. It was characteristic of the *fin de siècle* writers to want to stand apart from the common life and live only in the imagination. I have said that the battle of Symbolism was never properly fought out in English; but there was one writer in England who played a rôle somewhat similar to that of Mallarmé in France. Walter Pater was, like Mallarmé, a man of much intellectual originality who, living quietly and writing little, had a profound influence on the literature of his time. More nearly than anyone else, he supplied, in his literary criticism, an English equivalent to the Symbolist theory of the French. When Pater says that experience gives us, "not the truth of eternal outlines, ascertained once for all, but a world of fine gradations and subtly linked conditions, shifting intricately as we ourselves change," he is stating a point of view exactly similar to that of the Symbolists. But it was less in the field of æsthetic theory than in that of the appreciation of life that Pater developed this point of view. The famous conclusion to "The Renaissance" fixed the ideal of a whole generation: "To regard all things and principles of things as inconstant modes or fashions has more and more become the fashion of modern thought. . . . The service of philosophy, of speculative culture, towards the human spirit, is to rouse, to startle it to a life of constant and eager observation. Every moment some form grows perfect in hand or face; some tone on the hills or the sea is choicer than the rest; some mood of passion or insight or intellectual excitement is irresistibly real and attractive to us—for that moment only. Not the fruit of experience, but experience itself, is the end. A counted number of pulses only is given to us of a variegated, dramatic life. How may we see in them all that is to be seen in them by the finest senses?" "We looked consciously to Pater for our philosophy," Yeats wrote of himself and his friends; and the tapestried house, the Alchemical Temple, had been invented as ideal abodes where this philosophy might be put into practice—as Yeats's fairyland itself had been but one of the imaginary domains of the *fin de siècle* mind.

But just as Yeats's early poetry presents the fascination of fairyland as something inimical to life in the real world, so these stories of the life of ecstatic revery, unlike the typical writings of the *fin de siècle* æsthetes, are edged with a consciousness of dangers and temptations inescapably involved in such a life. In Yeats, we find the æstheticism of Pater carried through to its consequences.

What *is* the consequence of living for beauty, as beauty was then understood, of cultivating the imagination, the enjoyment of æsthetic sensations, as a supreme end in itself? We shall be thrown fatally out of key with reality— we shall incur penalties which are not to be taken lightly. There is a conflict here which cannot be evaded; and Yeats, even in his earliest period, is unceasingly aware of this conflict. But still he prefers to dwell most of the time in fairyland or among the dancers of the Alchemical Temple. He would even transport his human love, his human desire, into the climate of that immortal world, where nothing that is ugly can jar and where nothing that is beautiful fades:

"All things uncomely and broken, all things worn out and old,
The cry of a child by the roadway, the creak of a lumbering cart,
The heavy steps of the ploughman, splashing the wintry mould,
Are wronging your image that blossoms a rose in the deeps of my
    heart.
The wrong of unshapely things is a wrong too great to be told;
I hunger to build them anew and sit on a green knoll apart,
With the earth and the sky and the water, remade, like a casket
    of gold
For my dreams of your image that blossoms a rose in the deeps of
    my heart."

But now, in the period inaugurated by "The Green Helmet" (published in 1912), the balance is to dip on the other side. In the frustration of early love, apparently, he has paid the price of escaping to fairyland, and the memory of it is bitter: he still champions, he still puts above everything, the nobility and splendor of the imagination;

but he must face life's hard conditions. And the consciousness of inexorable limits has brought his art to a sharper
focus—the unbinding of "youth's dreamy load" has made
him a better poet. No longer content with the ice-eyed
queens of fairyland at the same time that he no longer
hopes from real life any satisfaction other than the triumph of imagination through art, he applies to poetry
all the vigor of his intellect and all the energy of his
passion. He would reduce his verse to something definite
and hard—at the same time more severe and more passionate. Now the soap-bubble colors vanish; the music of
fairyland dies away; we behold only, earthly and clear,
the bare outlines of "cold Clare rock and Galway rock and
thorn."

In a poem which is at once a description of this style
and an admirable example of it, he tells how,

> "Maybe a twelvemonth since
> Suddenly I began
> In scorn of this audience
> Imagining a man,
> And his sun-freckled face,
> And gray Connemara cloth,
> Climbing up to a place
> Where stone is dark under froth,
> And the down turn of his wrist
> When the flies drop in the stream:
> A man who does not exist,
> A man who is but a dream;
> And cried, 'Before I am old
> I shall have written him one
> Poem maybe as cold
> And passionate as the dawn.'"

Yeats inhabits, in this phase, a world of pure intense emotions expressed in distinct fine images. His words, no matter how prosaic, are always somehow luminous and noble, as if pale pebbles smoothed by the sea were to take on some mysterious value and become more precious than jewels or gold. He is less prodigal now of symbols and names, and his visions have a new austerity:

> "I call to the eye of the mind
> A well long choked up and dry
> And boughs long stripped by the wind,
> And I call to the mind's eye
> Pallor of an ivory face,
> Its lofty dissolute air,
> A man climbing up to a place
> The salt sea wind has swept bare."

When he returns to the heroic world of Irish mythology, he describes it with a new homeliness of detail. And more and more steadily he fixes his attention upon the actual world about him. He has come to desire above everything, as he says in another part of the poem about the fisherman,

> "To write for my own race
> And for the reality."

And again, in another poem:

> "Through all the lying days of my youth
> I swayed my leaves and flowers in the sun;
> Now I may wither into the truth."

He finds his subjects now in the events of his own life,

no longer transposed into romantic convention, and in the
public affairs of Ireland. And he succeeds in dignifying
such subjects, as perhaps no other contemporary poet has
done, at the same time that he never ceases to deal with
them without sentimentality and in the plainest language.
He can even challenge comparison with Dante—whom he
now describes as "the chief imagination of Christendom"
—by his ability to sustain a grand manner through sheer
intensity without rhetorical heightening. He assumes, indeed, a kind of Dantesque mask. How he suggests the
compactness and point of Dante's two- or three-line allusions in such a passage as,

> "Traders or soldiers who have left me blood
> That has not passed through any huxter's loin,
> Pardon, and you that did not weigh the cost,
> Old Butlers when you took to horse and stood
> Beside the brackish waters of the Boyne
> Till your bad master blenched and all was lost" . . .

and Dante's epigrammatic bitterness in,

> "Why should I blame her that she filled my days
> With misery, or that she would of late
> Have taught to ignorant men most violent ways,
> Or hurled the little streets against the great,
> Had they but courage equal to desire?"

And he has also a Dantesque exaltation—an exaltation no
longer the opium dream of fairyland, but such as life has
to offer within its limits: the admiration for ancestor or

friend, the pride in honor kept or work well done, the wild memory of early love:

> "And what of her that took
> All till my youth was gone
> With scarce a pitying look?
> How should I praise that one?
> When day begins to break
> I count my good and bad,
> Being wakeful for her sake,
> Remembering what she had,
> What eagle look still shows,
> While up from my heart's root
> So great a sweetness flows
> I shake from head to foot."

II

With the development of this maturer style, it became impossible any longer to regard Yeats merely as one of the best of the English lyric poets of the nineties. The author of "The Lake of Innisfree," which had so delighted Robert Louis Stevenson, had grown, in an interval of ten years during which nobody outside of Ireland had apparently paid much attention to him, to the unmistakable stature of a master. No other poet writing English in our time has been able to deal with supreme artistic success with such interesting and such varied experience. No other writer has been able to sustain the traditional grand manner of the poet with so little effect of self-consciousness.

And in spite of the immense amount of poetry published and read to-day, the personality truly and naturally poetic seems to be becoming rarer and rarer. It may be true that the kind of dignity and distinction which have been characteristic of the poet in the past are becoming more and more impossible in our modern democratic society and during a period when the ascendancy of scientific ideas has made man conscious of his kinship with the other animals and of his subjection to biological and physical laws rather than of his relation to the gods. It was easy for the lyric poet, from Wyatt's age to Waller's, to express himself both directly and elegantly, because he was a courtier, or, in any case, a member of a comparatively small educated class, whose speech combined the candor and naturalness of conversation among equals with the grace of a courtly society. It was possible for him honestly to take up a residence in an intellectual world where poetic images stood for actualities because the scientific language and technique for dealing with these actualities had not yet come to permeate thought. But the modern poet who would follow this tradition, and who would yet deal with life in any large way, must create for himself a special personality, must maintain a state of mind, which shall shut out or remain indifferent to many aspects of the contemporary world. This necessity accounts partly, I suppose, for Yeats's preoccupation in his prose writings with what he calls the Mask or Anti-Self, a sort of imaginary personality, quite antagonistic to other elements of one's nature, which the poet must impose upon himself. It is hard to imagine a seventeenth-century poet being driven to such a theory—a theory which makes

one's poetic self figure as one of the halves of a split personality; and it seems true that Yeats himself has not
been able to keep up his poetic rôle without a certain effort. We find, at any rate, in his criticism and his autobiographical writings a remarkably honest and illuminating account of the difficulties of remaining a poet during the age in which we live.

Yeats seems to be conscious from the first of an antagonism between the actual world of industry, politics
and science, on the one hand, and the imaginative poetic
life, on the other. He tells us, in his autobiography, that
a vital issue seemed to be raised for him, in his boyhood,
by the then popular and novel realism of Bastien-Lepage
and Carolus Durand as against the mysticism of the Pre-
Raphaelite painters. Bastien-Lepage's "clownish peasant
staring with vacant eyes at her great boots" represented
already to the young Yeats that Naturalistic, scientific
vision which contradicted and warred with his own. And
he takes up from the beginning, in his criticism, a definite and explicit position in regard to Naturalism: he will
stand apart from the democratic, the scientific, modern
world—his poetic life shall be independent of it; his art
shall owe nothing to its methods. His principles in literature are those of the Symbolists, but he formulates them
more clearly and defends them with more vigor than anyone else has yet done in English.

"There is," he asserts in his early essay on the symbolism of Shelley, "for every man some one scene, some one
adventure, some one picture, that is the image of his secret

life, for wisdom first speaks in images and . . . this one image, if he would but brood over it his whole life long, would lead his soul, disentangled from unmeaning circumstance and the ebb and flow of the world, into that far household, where the undying gods await all whose souls have become simple as flame, whose bodies have become quiet as an agate lamp." All great literature, says Yeats, is created out of symbols: observations and statistics mean nothing; works of art which depend upon them can have no enduring value. "There is something," he says, "of an old wives' tale in fine literature. The makers of it are like an old peasant telling stories of the great famine or the hangings of '98 or from his own memories. He has felt something in the depth of his mind and he wants to make it as visible and powerful to our senses as possible. He will use the most extravagant words or illustrations if they will suit his purpose. Or he will invent a wild parable, and the more his mind is on fire or the more creative it is, the less will he look at the outer world or value it for its own sake. It gives him metaphors and examples, and that is all. He is even a little scornful of it, for it seems to him while the fit is on that the fire has gone out of it and left it but white ashes. I cannot explain it, but I am certain that every high thing was invented in this way, between sleeping and waking, as it were, and that peering and peeping persons are but hawkers of stolen goods. How else could their noses have grown so ravenous or their eyes so sharp?"

And in all his activity as playwright and journalist in

connection with the Abbey Theatre, Yeats is leading a
reaction against Naturalism. This reaction, which, by way
of Germany and under the name of Expressionism, has
attracted so much more attention since the War, had not,
at the time of the founding of the Abbey Theatre, manifested itself very vigorously on the Continent. Symbolism
did not play yet in the theatre the rôle that it was playing in poetry. Yet its seeds had already sprouted here and
there. August Strindberg, returning from Paris to Sweden,
wrote between 1899 and 1902 the Symbolistic "To Damas-
cus" and "Dream Play," the prototypes of the German Ex-
pressionistic drama; and Maeterlinck, with vague, pale
and suave images, quite different from Strindberg's lively,
queer and dissonant ones, had created quite a little theatre
of Symbolism. Now Yeats, in his own dramatic works, has
produced a theatre somewhat similar to Maeterlinck's.
The productions of a greater poet, equipped with a richer
and more solid mythology, these plays do, however, take
place in the same sort of twilit world as Maeterlinck's—
a world in which the characters are less often dramatic
personalities than disembodied broodings and longings.
Yeats's plays have little dramatic importance because
Yeats himself has little sense of drama, and we think of
them primarily as a department of his poetry, with the
same sort of interest and beauty as the rest. But Yeats, the
director and propagandist of the Abbey Theatre, does have
considerable importance in the history of the modern
stage. The Abbey Theatre itself, of recent years, with the
Gorky-Chekhovesque plays of Sean O'Casey, has taken a

Naturalistic turn which Yeats never contemplated or desired; but his long and uncompromising campaign for a revival of poetic drama contributed much to contemporary efforts to break up the rigid technique and clear the stage of the realistic encumbrances of the Naturalistic drama. Yeats's greatest contribution to the theatre has been, not his own plays, but those of Synge, whom in 1896 he discovered stagnating in Paris and induced to return to Ireland. Synge succeeded, on a small scale, during the few years before he died, in creating for the Abbey Theatre perhaps the most authentic example of poetic drama which the modern stage has seen.

Yeats at this period, the period of the founding and the first battles of the Abbey Theatre, is both active and effective. There has always been more of the public figure and more of the pugnacious Irishman about him than his philosophy invites us to believe. But this philosophy never ceases to insist upon the irreconcilable opposition between the life of self-assertion in the practical world and the life consecrated to the recovery and contemplation of the precious symbol, which, "if he [the poet] would but brood over it his whole life long, would lead his soul, disentangled from unmeaning circumstance and the ebb and flow of the world," into the presence of the gods. Yeats recurs again and again to the necessity of mortifying the will: "Every visionary knows that the mind's eye soon comes to see a capricious and variable world, which the will cannot shape or change, though it can call it up and banish it again"; "We must find some place upon the Tree of Life

43

for the Phœnix nest, for the passion that is exaltation and the negation of the will"; the style of the dialogue in Synge's plays "blurs definition, clear edges, everything that comes from the will, it turns imagination from all that is of the present, like a gold background in a religious picture, and it strengthens in every emotion whatever comes to it from far off, from brooding memory and dangerous hope," etc.

For the rest, Yeats's prose, in its beginnings, when he is most under the influence of the Pre-Raphaelites and Pater, is a little self-consciously archaic—it has a Renaissance elaborateness and pomposity; and it is a little too close to the language of poetry—the meaning is often clotted by metaphor. But Yeats's prose, like his verse, has, with time, undergone a discipline and emerged with a clearer outline. Yeats is to-day a master of prose as well as a great poet. He was already magnificent in his intermediate period—the period of "Per Amica Silentia Lunae" (1917): "We make out of the quarrel with others rhetoric, but of the quarrel with ourselves, poetry. Unlike the rhetoricians, who get a confident voice from remembering the crowd they have won or may win, we sing amid our uncertainty; and, smitten even in the presence of the most high beauty by the knowledge of our solitude, our rhythm shudders. I think, too, that no fine poet, no matter how disordered his life, has ever, even in his mere life, had pleasure for his end. Johnson and Dowson, friends of my youth, were dissipated men, the one a drunkard, the other a drunkard and mad about women, and yet they had the

gravity of men who had found life out and were awakening from the dream; and both, one in life and art and
one in art and less in life, had a continual preoccupation
with religion. Nor has any poet I have read of or heard of
or met with been a sentimentalist. The other self, the anti-
self or the antithetical self, as one may choose to name it,
comes but to those who are no longer deceived, whose
passion is reality. The sentimentalists are practical men
who believe in money, in position, in a marriage bell, and
whose understanding of happiness is to be so busy whether
at work or at play, that all is forgotten but the momentary
aim. They find their pleasure in a cup that is filled from
Lethe's wharf, and for the awakening, for the vision, for
the revelation of reality, tradition offers us a different
word—ecstasy."

This is perhaps still a little *too* magnificent, still a little
too much like poetry. But in his autobiography, "The
Trembling of the Veil" (1922), Yeats has achieved a combination of grandeur with a certain pungency and homeliness which recalls the more lightly and swiftly moving
writers of the seventeenth century rather than the more
heavily upholstered ones of the earlier Renaissance. The
prose of Yeats, in our contemporary literature, is like the
product of some dying loomcraft brought to perfection
in the days before machinery. The qualities of a good
prose style in English to-day are likely to be those of a
sound intellectual currency, clipped out by a sharp cutter and stamped by a solvent mint; Rudyard Kipling,
Bernard Shaw and T. S. Eliot, however else they may

differ, have these characteristics in common. Of Samuel Butler, Shaw's master, Yeats has written that he was "the first Englishman to make the discovery that it is possible to write with great effect without music, without style, either good or bad, to eliminate from the mind all emotional implication and to prefer plain water to every vintage, so much metropolitan lead and solder to any tendril of the vine." The style of the seventeenth century, on the other hand—the style of Walton's "Lives" or Dryden's prefaces—was a much more personal thing: it fitted the author like a suit of clothes and molded itself to the natural contours of his temperament and mind; one is always aware that there is a man inside, whereas with Kipling, Eliot or Shaw, the style seems to aim at the effect of an inflexible impersonal instrument specially designed to perform special functions. Yeats's prose is, however, still a garment worn in the old-fashioned personal manner with a combination of elegance and ease, at the same time that it is unmistakably of our time by virtue of a certain modern terseness and of a characteristically modern trick—we shall encounter it later in Proust—of revealing by unexpected juxtapositions relations of which one had not been aware—"He had been almost poor," writes Yeats of Wilde in the period before his disaster, "and now, his head full of Flaubert, found himself with ten thousand a year"—or of effecting almost startling transitions from the particular to the general and back again. For Yeats has become a critic now not merely of literature, but of human life and society in general: compare the passage on

Johnson and Dowson which I have quoted above from "Per Amica Silentia Lunae," with the realistic and subtle analysis, in "The Trembling of the Veil," of the causes for the final breakdown of that "tragic generation."

III

Yeats has shown himself, in his prose writings, a man of both exceptionally wide information and exceptional intellectual curiosity; but, for all the variety of his interests and the versatility of his intelligence, he has, in rejecting the methods of modern science, cut himself off in a curious way from the general enlightened thought of his time. Yet his mind is so comprehensive and so active that he has felt the need of constructing a system: and, finding it impossible to admit the assumptions upon which most modern systems are based, he has had recourse to the only science which his position has allowed him to accept, the obsolete science of Astrology. As a young man, Yeats frequented clairvoyants and students of Astrology and Magic; Madame Blavatsky, the necromantic Theosophist, seems to have made upon him a considerable impression. And in 1901 he was led to formulate, in an essay on Magic, the following set of beliefs, to which he still apparently adheres:

"(1) That the borders of our mind are ever shifting, and that many minds can flow into one another, as it were, and create or reveal a single mind, a single energy.

"(2) That the borders of our memories are as shifting, and that our memories are a part of one great memory, the memory of Nature herself.

"(3) That this great mind and great memory can be evoked by symbols."

What Yeats was really approaching here was some such systematic study of the symbolism of myths, trances, dreams and other human visions as psychoanalysis and anthropology were attempting from a different direction. And despite the obvious charlatanism or naïveté of most of his instructors and fellow investigators, Yeats's account of his researches is interesting. For it is not merely that Yeats loves the marvellous: he is also intent upon discovering symbols which may stand for the elements of his own nature or which shall seem to possess some universal significance. The results of this research are very curious. When we read Yeats's account of his adventures among the mediums, it becomes plain that, in spite of his repudiation of science, he has always managed to leave himself a margin of scientific doubt. Like Huysmans, he betrays an instinct to scrutinize and check up on the supernatural which is disastrous to genuine mysticism. Just as in Huysmans's case, we always feel that the wistful student of Satanism has too much solid Dutch common sense really to deceive himself about his devils, so in Yeats— he himself has confessed it—the romantic amateur of Magic is always accompanied and restrained by the rationalistic modern man. "He and I often quarrelled," Yeats writes of himself and A. E., "because I wanted him to examine and question his visions, and write them out as they occurred; and still more because I thought symbolic what he thought real like the men and women that had passed him on the road." Yet Huysmans went so far as to claim—or at least to make one of his characters claim—as genuine examples of demoniacal possession those very hysteria cases of Charcot's which at that moment were leading Charcot's young pupil Freud to his first great discovery of the principle of emotional repression; and Yeats attributes to a sort of supernatural being designated as "Anima Mundi" precisely such universal symbols as are studied by such psychologists as Jung. What is most curious is that Yeats should at last have constructed out of these symbols an elaborate mystical-metaphysical system.

This system was set forth in "A Vision," a work which occupied Yeats for many years and which he published privately in 1926. "A Vision" presented an elaborate theory of the variation of human personality, of the vicissitudes of human history and of the transformations of the soul in this world and the next. This theory was worked out with geometrical diagrams and set forth in terms of such unfamiliar conceptions as *daimons, tinctures, cones, gyres, husks* and *passionate bodies.*

Yeats asserts that human personality follows the pattern of a "Great Wheel." That is, the types of personality possible constitute a kind of closed circle—they are regular stages in a circular journey to and fro between complete objectivity at one pole and complete subjectivity at the other; and this journey may be represented by the orbit of the moon, to which it corresponds. Let the moon represent subjectivity and the sun, objectivity: then the dark of the moon, when it is closest to the sun, is the phase of complete objectivity; and the full moon, which is farthest from the sun, is the phase of complete subjectivity. At these two opposite poles of the circle, human life is impossible: there exist only antipodal types of supernatural beings. But along the circumference of the circle, between these two ultra-human poles, there occur twenty-six phases which cover all possible types of human personality.

Yeats's theory of the variation of these types is extremely complicated. He begins by assigning to "incarnate man" four "Faculties": the Will, "by which is understood feeling that has not become desire . . . an energy as yet uninfluenced by thought, action or emotion"; the Mask, which means "the image of what we wish to become, or of that to which we give our reverence"; the Creative Mind, "the intellect . . . all the mind that is consciously constructive"; and the Body of Fate, "the physical and mental environment, the changing human body, the stream of Phenomena as this affects a particular individual, all that is forced upon us from without." The Will is always opposite the Mask: "it looks into a painted picture." The Creative Mind is opposite the Body of Fate: "it looks into a photograph; but both look into something which is the opposite of themselves." We follow the Will around the clock, and by combining it with the other

elements according to geometrical laws we calculate the
characters of the different phases. Starting at the right of
the objective pole, the soul passes first through varieties of
almost purely physical life—Yeats takes his examples here
from the Bacchuses and shepherds of the poets. It is moving toward subjectivity, however—Walt Whitman, Alex-
andre Dumas: it is seeking itself, and as it progresses, it
becomes more beautiful. The ultra-human subjective
phase, which apparently includes Christ, is described as
"a phase of complete beauty," where "Thought and Will
are indistinguishable, effort and attainment are indistinguishable—nothing is apparent but dreaming Will and
the Image that it dreams." This is preceded and followed
by phases which include Baudelaire and Beardsley; Keats
and Giorgione; Blake and Rabelais; Dante and Shelley;
and presumably Yeats himself: men who have withdrawn
from the life of the world in order to live in their dream.
But once the all-subjective phase is past, the soul

> ". . . would be the world's servant, and as it serves,
> Choosing whatever task's most difficult
> Among tasks not impossible, it takes
> Upon the body and upon the soul
> The coarseness of the drudge. Before the full
> It sought itself and afterwards the world."

And it is now leaving beauty behind and headed toward
deformity:

> "Reformer, merchant, statesman, learned man,
> Dutiful husband, honest wife by turn,

Cradle upon cradle, and all in flight and all
Deformed because there is no deformity
But saves us from a dream."

The soul has now come full circle: the three final human
phases before the phase of complete objectivity are the
Hunchback, the Saint and the Fool.

Yeats has worked all this out with great care and with
considerable ingenuity. He has described each of the
twenty-eight phases and supplied us with typical examples. What we find in this part of the book is Yeats's
familiar preoccupation with the conflict between action
and philosophy, reality and imagination. (It is amusing
and characteristic that, according to his system, the side
of humanity closest to the sun—that is, closest the objective nature—should be the side that is bathed in darkness,
whereas the side which is furthest from the sun—that is,
nearest the subjective nature—should be the side that is
bright!) Now this is a subject which has hitherto, in
Yeats's prose as well as in his verse, usually inspired him
well; the symbols of the Mask, the Sun and Moon, etc., if
they have sometimes been a little disconcerting when we
encountered them in his critical writings, have created just
the right impression of significance in mystery for Symbolistic poetry. And there are, to be sure, certain passages
of "A Vision" as brilliant as Yeats at his best. He writes,
for example, of the phase of "the Receptive Man," to
which he assigns Rembrandt and Synge: "The man wipes
his breath from the window pane, and laughs in his delight at all the varied scene." And of the phase of "the

Obsessed Man," to which he assigns Giorgione and Keats: "When we compare these images with those of any subsequent phase, each seems studied for its own sake; they float as in serene air, or lie hidden in some valley, and if they move it is to music that returns always to the same note, or in a dance that so returns upon itself that they seem immortal." And, in what is perhaps the most eloquent passage in the book, he returns to a certain type of beautiful uncontemplative woman who has already haunted his poetry: "Here are born those women who are most touching in their beauty. Helen was of this phase; and she comes before the mind's eye elaborating a delicate personal discipline as though she would make her whole life an image of a unified *antithetical* (that is, subjective) energy. While seeming an image of softness, and of quiet, she draws perpetually upon glass with a diamond. Yet she will not number among her sins anything that does not break that personal discipline, no matter what it may seem according to others' discipline; but if she fail in her own discipline she will not deceive herself, and for all the languor of her movements, and her indifference to the acts of others, her mind is never at peace. She will wander much alone as though she consciously meditated her masterpiece that shall be at the full moon, yet unseen by human eye, and when she returns to her house she will look upon her household with timid eyes, as though she knew that all power of self-protection had been taken away, and that of her once *primary Tincture* (that is, objective element) nothing remained but a strange irresponsible innocence. . . . Already perhaps, through weakness of desire, she understands nothing, while alone seeming of service. Is it not because she desires so little and gives so little that men will die and murder in her service?" And there is a strange imaginative power in the conception behind the final sequence of the Hunchback, the Saint and the Fool.

Yet "A Vision," when we try to read it, makes us impatient with Yeats. As a rule, he expounds his revelations as if he took them seriously—that is, as if he believed that *masks* and *husks* and *daimons* and *passionate bodies* were things which actually existed, as if they were as real as those visions of A. E.'s which had been as real to A. E. as the people in the street, but which Yeats had tried to induce him to question; and indeed one would think that to elaborate a mystical system so complicated and so tedious, it would be necessary to believe in it pretty strongly. Yet now and then the skeptical Yeats reasserts himself and we are startled by an unexpected suggestion that, after all, the whole thing may be merely "a background for my thought, a painted scene." If the whole thing, we ask ourselves, has been merely an invented mythology, in which Yeats himself does not believe, what right has he to bore us with it—what right has he to expect us to explore page after page of such stuff as the following description of the habits of the soul after death: "The *Spirit* first floats horizontally within the man's dead body, but then rises until it stands at his head. The *Celestial Body* is also horizontal at first but lies in the opposite position, its feet where the *Spirit's* head is, and then rising, as does the *Spirit,* stands up at last at the feet of the man's body. The *Passionate Body* rises straight up from the genitals and stands in the centre. The *Husk* remains in the body until the time for it to be separated and lost in *Anima Mundi."*

In "A Packet for Ezra Pound" (1929) a new light is thrown on "A Vision." We learn that Yeats's wife is a medium, and that the theories set forth in this book were communicated through her by supernatural beings. Yeats tells us how, four days after their marriage in 1917, Mrs. Yeats surprised him by attempting automatic writing. "What came in disjointed sentences, in almost illegible writing, was so exciting, sometimes so profound, that I persuaded her to give an hour or two day after day to the unknown writer, and after some half-dozen such hours offered to spend what remained of life explaining and piecing together those scattered sentences. 'No,' was the answer, 'we have come to give you metaphors for poetry.' The unknown writer took his theme at first from my just published 'Per Amica Silentia Lunae.' I had made a distinction between the perfection that is from a man's combat with himself and that which is from a combat with circumstances, and upon this simple distinction he built up an elaborate classification of men according to their more or less complete expression of one type or the other. He supported his classification by a series of geometrical symbols and put these symbols in an order that answered the question in my essay as to whether some prophet could not prick upon the calendar the birth of a Napoleon or a Christ." Yeats describes the manifestations which accompanied these revelations: the perfumes, whistlings, smells of burnt feathers, bursts of music, apparitions of great black birds and of "persons in clothes of the late sixteenth century and of the seventeenth." On one occasion, when an owl was hooting in the garden, the dictating spirit asked for a recess: "Sounds like that," the spirit explained, "give us great pleasure." And there were also mischievous obstructive spirits who attempted to mislead the Yeatses and who were designated as "Frustrators"; "the automatic script would deteriorate, grow sentimental or confused, and when I pointed this out the communicator would say 'from such and such an hour, on such and such a day, all is frustration.' I would spread out the script and he would cross all out back to the answer that began it, but had I not divined frustration he would have said nothing."

We learn also, by the way, a fact which might, for a psychologist, throw a good deal of light on the development of Yeats's personality. It appears that not only has Yeats always succeeded in steering clear of science: he has never till recently read philosophy. "Apart from two or three of the principal Platonic Dialogues I knew no philosophy. Arguments with my father, whose convictions had been formed by John Stuart Mill's attack upon Sir William Hamilton, had destroyed my confidence and driven me from speculation to the direct experience of the Mystics. I had once known Blake as thoroughly as his unfinished confused Prophetic Books permitted, and I had read Swedenborg and Boehme, and my initiation into the 'Hermetic Students' had filled my head with Cabalistic imagery." Now, however, he wants to study philosophy as an aid to understanding the "system." The spirits ask him to wait till they have finished. At the end of three years, when the supernatural revelations have ceased, and "A Vision" is actually in proof, Yeats takes down from Mrs. Yeats, who, it appears, did not share her husband's ignorance, a list of the philosophers she had read. For four years, Yeats applies himself to these, and what he finds makes him uneasy about "A Vision": he feels that he must partly have misinterpreted what the spirits have told him. But the spirits themselves intervene to put an end to this disquieting situation: they make him stop his philosophical studies.

As we read all this, we say to ourselves that Yeats, growing older, has grown more credulous. But we come, at the end, to the following passage: "Some will ask if I believe all that this book contains, and I will not know how to answer. Does the word belief, used as they will use it, belong to our age, can I think of the world as there and I here judging it?" And he intimates that, after all, his system may be only a set of symbols like another—a set of symbols, we recognize, like the Irish myths with which he began.

Into the personal situation suggested by Yeats's account of his revelations, it is inappropriate and unnecessary to go: the psychological situation seems plain. When Yeats, at the crucial period of his life, attempted to leave fairy-land behind, when he became aware of the unsatisfying character of the life of iridescent revery, when he completely recreated his style so as to make it solid, homely and exact where it had formerly been shimmering or florid—the need for dwelling with part of his mind—or with his mind for part of the time—in a world of pure imagination, where the necessities of the real world do not hold, had, none the less, not been conjured away by the new artistic and intellectual habits he was cultivating. Where the early Yeats had studied Irish folk-lore, collected and sorted Irish fairy tales, invented fairy tales for himself, the later Yeats worked out from the mediumistic communications of his wife the twenty-eight phases of the human personality and the transformations of the soul after death. Yeats's sense of reality to-day is inferior to that of no man alive—indeed, his greatness is partly due precisely to the vividness of that sense. In his poetry, in his criticism and in his memoirs, it is the world we all live in with which we are confronted—the world we know, with all its frustrations, its defeats, its antagonisms and its errors —the mind that sees is not naïve, as the heart that feels is not insensitive. They meet reality with comprehension and with passion—but they have phases, we are astonished to discover, when they do not seem to meet it at all. Yet the scientific criticism of supernatural phenomena is actually as much a part of the reality of Yeats's world as it is of that of most of the rest of us. And when Yeats writes of his supernatural experiences, this criticism, though it may be kept in the background, is nevertheless always present —his realistic sense is too strong, his intellectual integrity too high, to leave it out of the picture. Though he is much addicted to these fantastic imaginings, though he no doubt needs their support to enable him to sustain his rôle of great poet—yet when he comes to write about his spirits and their messages, he cannot help letting us in on the imposture. He believes, but—he does not believe: the impossibility of believing is the impossibility which he accepts most reluctantly, but still it is there with the other impossibilities of this world which is too full of weeping for a child to understand.

It is interesting to compare "A Vision" with that other compendious treatise on human nature and destiny by that other great writer from Dublin: Bernard Shaw's "Guide to Socialism and Capitalism." Here we can see unmistakably the differences between the kind of literature which was fashionable before the War and the kind which has been fashionable since. Shaw and Yeats, both coming as young men to London from eighteenth-century Dublin, followed diametrically opposite courses. Shaw shouldered the whole unwieldy load of contemporary sociology, politics, economics, biology, medicine and journalism, while Yeats, convinced that the world of science and politics was somehow fatal to the poet's vision, as resolutely turned away. Shaw accepted the scientific technique and set himself to master the problems of an industrial democratic society, while Yeats rejected the methods of Naturalism and applied himself to the introspective plumbing of the mysteries of the individual mind. While Yeats was editing Blake, Shaw was grappling with Marx; and Yeats was appalled by Shaw's hardness and efficiency. "I hated it," he says of "Arms and the Man"; "it seemed to me inorganic, logical straightness and not the crooked road of life and I stood aghast before its energy." And he tells us that Shaw appeared to him in a dream in the form of a sewing machine, "that clicked and shone, but the incredible thing was that the machine smiled, smiled perpetually."

In his Great Wheel of the twenty-eight phases, Yeats has situated Shaw at a phase considerably removed from his own, and where the individual is headed straight for the deformity of seeking, not the soul, but the world. And their respective literary testaments—the "Vision" and the "Guide"—published almost at the same time, mark the extreme points of their divergence: Shaw bases all human hope and happiness on an equal distribution of income, which he believes will finally make impossible even the pessimism of a Swift or a Voltaire; while Yeats, like Shaw a Protestant for whom the Catholic's mysticism was impossible, has in "A Vision" made the life of humanity contingent on the movements of the stars. "The day is far off," he concludes, "when the two halves of man can divine each its own unity in the other as in a mirror, Sun in Moon, Moon in Sun, and so escape out of the Wheel."

IV

Yet, in the meantime, the poet Yeats has passed into a sort of third phase, in which he is closer to the common world than at any previous period. He is no longer quite so haughty, so imperturbably astride his high horse, as during his middle Dantesque period. With the Dantesque mask, he has lost something of intensity and something of sharpness of outline. In "The Tower" (1928), certain words such as "bitter," "wild," and "fierce," which he was able, a few years ago, to use with such thrilling effect, have no longer quite the same force. He writes more loosely, and seems to write more easily. He has become more plain-spoken, more humorous—his mind seems to run more frankly on his ordinary human satisfactions and chagrins: he is sometimes harsh, sometimes sensual, sometimes careless, sometimes coarse.

Though he now inhabits, like Michael Robartes, a lonely tower on the outermost Irish coast, he has spent six years in the Irish senate, presiding at official receptions in a silk hat, inspecting the plumbing of the government schools and conscientiously sitting through the movies which it is one of his official duties to censor. He is much occupied with politics and society, with general reflections on human life—but with the wisdom of the experience of a lifetime, he is passionate even in age. And he writes poems which charge now with the emotion of a great lyric poet that profound and subtle criticism of life of which I have spoken in connection with his prose.

We may take, as an example of Yeats's later vein, the fine poem in "The Tower" called "Among School Children." The poet, now "a sixty year old smiling public man," has paid an official visit to a girls' school kept by nuns; and as he gazes at the children there, he remembers how the woman he had loved had told him once of some "harsh reproof or trivial event" of her girlhood which had changed "some childish day to tragedy." And for a moment the thought that she may once have looked like one of the children before him has revived the excitement of his old love. He remembers the woman in all her young beauty—and thinks of himself with his present sixty years—"a comfortable kind of old scarecrow." What use is philosophy now?—is not all beauty bound up with the body and doomed to decay with it?—is not even the divine beauty itself which is worshipped there by the nuns inseparable from the images of it they adore?

> "Labor is blossoming or dancing where
> The body is not bruised to pleasure soul,
> Nor beauty born out of its own despair,
> Nor blear-eyed wisdom out of midnight oil.
> O chestnut tree, great rooted blossomer,
> Are you the leaf, the blossom or the bole?
> O body swayed to music, O brightening glance,
> How can we know the dancer from the dance?"

Here the actual scene in the convent, the personal emotions it awakens and the general speculations which these emotions suggest, have been interwoven and made to play upon each other at the same time that they are kept separate and distinct. A complex subject has been treated in the most concentrated form, and yet without confusion. Perceptions, fancies, feelings and thoughts have all their place in the poet's record. It is a moment of human life, masterfully seized and made permanent, in all its nobility and lameness, its mystery and actuality, its direct personal contact and abstraction.

PAUL VALÉRY

PAUL VALÉRY first met Mallarmé in 1892, when Valéry was twenty-one: he became thereafter one of the most faithful and serious of Mallarmé's disciples. Valéry wrote little at this time and did not even collect his verses in a book; yet the Symbolists of what was then the younger generation seem to have acknowledged his supremacy from the beginning. What we find in these poems to-day is chiefly the chaste-celestial, the blue-and-white mood of such poems of Mallarmé's as "Apparition" in what seems a thinner diluted form. Paul Valéry, like his master, is "haunted" by the "azure"; but that azure is less a pure blue realm and more a rarefied upper air. Here and there in these early poems, however, the later Valéry is plainly recognizable: it is his characteristic interest in method apart from matter which leads him to publish two versions of the same sonnet; and in the uncompleted "Profusion du Soir," perhaps the most remarkable of these poems, by a confusion peculiar to Valéry the sunset which the poet is watching is assimilated to his state of mind until it seems sometimes only a set of images for a complex of emotions and thoughts.

Valéry has given us a curious description of his attitude toward Mallarmé at this time:

"When I began to see Mallarmé, I had almost entirely

lost my interest in literature. Reading and writing were becoming dull work for me, and I confess that they still bore me a little. The study of myself for its own sake, the comprehension of that attention itself and the desire to trace clearly for myself the nature of my own existence, almost never abandoned me. This secret disease alienates one from letters, despite the fact that it has its source in them.

"Mallarmé figured, however, in my private system as the representative of the most accomplished art, as the highest phase of the loftiest literary ambition. In a deep sense, I had his mind for a companion, and I hoped that, despite the difference in our ages, and the immense disparity of our gifts, the day would come when I should not be afraid to lay before him my difficulties and my special ideas. It was not in the least that he intimidated me, for no one was ever more kindly or more charmingly simple than he; but I felt, at that time, a sort of contrast between the practice of literature and the pursuit of a certain rigor and of a complete intellectual sincerity. The question is infinitely delicate. Should I attempt to induce Mallarmé to discuss it? I was fond of him and valued him above everybody, but I myself had renounced the adoration of that which he had adored all his life, and to which he had offered up everything, and I could not bring myself to let him know it.

"I could, however, see no more genuine homage than to lay my thought before him, and to show him how much his researches, and the very fine and precise analysis from which they proceeded, had in my eyes transformed the literary problem and had led me to give up the game. The point was that Mallarmé's efforts, which were quite opposed to the doctrines and aims of his contemporaries, were tending to order the whole domain of letters through the general consideration of forms. It is remarkable in the extreme that, through the exhaustive study of his art and with no scientific education, he should have arrived at a conception so abstract and so close to the most abstruse speculations of certain of the sciences. He never discussed his ideas except figuratively. Explaining anything explicitly was strangely repugnant to him. His profession, which he detested, counted for something in that aversion. But, in attempting to sum up to myself his tendencies, I allowed myself to formulate them in my own way. Ordinary literature seemed to me comparable to an *arithmetic,* that is to say, to an attempt to obtain particular results in which it was difficult to distinguish the principle from the example: but the kind of literature which he had conceived seemed to me analogous to an *algebra,* for it assumed the intention to emphasize, to conserve and to develop the forms of which language is capable.

"But from the moment, I said to myself, that a principle has been recognized and grasped by someone, it is quite useless to waste one's time applying it. . . .

"The day I was awaiting never came."

Mallarmé died in 1898. But Paul Valéry had already passed through a personal crisis as a result of which he had ceased to write verse. This moral and intellectual crisis was precipitated, Valéry Larbaud tells us, by an unhappy love affair. Through sleepless nights Valéry struggled with his emotions: "the will was driven back on itself, schooled itself to leap clear, to break idols, to free itself, at no matter what cost, from those falsehoods: literature and sentiment. The supreme crisis, the costly victory took place during a stormy night—one of those storms of the Ligurian coast [he was at Genoa] which are not accompanied by very much rain, but during which the lightning is so frequent and so bright that it gives the illusion of broad daylight. From that night none of the things which had hitherto made up the life of the young man mattered any longer. He left Montpellier [where he had studied at the university] and went to live in Paris, where he would be able, when he chose, to shut himself away in solitude, in order to give himself up to that 'penetration of himself,' which has now become his only concern."

During the twenty years that follow, Valéry works in the Ministry of War and in the Havas news agency, and produces no more verse. The "study of oneself for its own sake, the comprehension of that attention itself and the desire to trace clearly for oneself the nature of one's own existence" is the only thing which interests him now. During these years he writes his "Introduction to the Method of Leonardo da Vinci" and invents his mythological character, M. Teste. Both Leonardo da Vinci and M. Teste (Mr. Head, a companion creation to Rabelais's Messer Gaster, Mr. Belly) are, for Valéry, symbols of the pure intellect, of the human consciousness turned in upon itself. The mind of Leonardo in itself is something immeasurably greater than any of its manifestations in particular fields of activity—painting, writing, engineering or strategy. Action cramps and impoverishes the mind. For by itself the mind is able to deal with an infinite number of possibilities—it is not constrained by the limitations of a field. The mind by itself is omnipotent. And consequently the method, the theory, of doing anything is more interesting than the thing done. For the method may be applied so much more widely—may be universally applied. When a principle, in fact, "has been recognized and grasped, it is quite useless to waste one's time applying it."

And M. Teste, unlike Leonardo, does disdain to apply his method to anything. His whole existence is given up to the examination of his own intellectual processes. He is a symbol of the human consciousness isolated from "all the opinions and intellectual habits which spring from the common life and our external relations with other men," and disembarrassed of "all the sentiments and ideas which are engendered or excited in man by his misfortunes and his fears, his terrors and his hopes; and not freely by his sheer observations upon the world and upon himself." M. Teste is, in fact, as his creator admits, frankly a monster. And though he exerts upon us a certain fascination, we resent him—he gives us the creeps. We sympathize with Mme. Teste, who is made uneasy by M. Teste's preoccupation, by his way of entering a room as if he did not see it, by his addressing her as "Being" or "Thing."

Yet though she fears him, though she does not understand him, she has never ceased to adore him—she does not envy other women who have married ordinary men. And he, when he awakes from his meditations, sometimes seizes upon her brusquely, as if with relief, appetite and surprise. M. Teste and Mme. Teste are, after all, indispensable to each other.

In 1917, Valéry marries a lady of Mallarmé's circle. And at the end of twenty years, he begins writing again. André Gide has finally persuaded him to allow his early poems to be collected and published, and he has had the idea of adding to them a new poem of from twenty-five to fifty lines—the last, perhaps, which he will ever write. But, in the meantime, during his period of retirement, he has studied psychology, physiology, mathematics—he has become preoccupied with questions of method. "Twenty years without writing verse, without even attempting to write it, almost even without reading any! . . . Then, these problems presenting themselves again; and one's discovering that one did not know one's trade; that the little poems one had written long ago had evaded all the difficulties, suppressed what they did not know how to express; made use of an infantile language." For his new poem, he imposes upon himself "laws, constant requirements, *which constitute its true object*. It is an exercise, indeed—intended as such, and worked and reworked: a production entirely of deliberate effort; and then of a second deliberate effort, whose hard task is to mask the first. He who knows how to read me will read an autobiography, in the form. The *matter* is of small importance."

And this poem, which was to have filled but a page, occupies Valéry for more than four years and runs finally to five hundred and forty verses. At the last moment, when it is just about to be printed (1917), Valéry finds for it the title, "La Jeune Parque." But, in spite of its title, its heroic grand manner and its reverberating alexandrines, "La Jeune Parque" is no conventional French poem on a subject from Greek mythology. Valéry speaks of the "rather monstrous copulation of my system, my methods and my musical exigencies with the classical conventions." And it is certain that this mysterious poem represents a genre which has never appeared in literature before. Mallarmé's Hérodiade and his Faun are the precursors of Valéry's young Fate: they have already a certain ambiguity and seem at moments less imaginary personages than names attached to metaphysical reveries. But Valéry has carried the subtleties of conception, the complexities of presentation, of this characteristically Symbolist form much further than Mallarmé. Is "La Jeune Parque" the monologue of a young Fate, who has just been bitten by a snake? Is it the revery of the poet himself, awakening early one morning in bed and lying more or less awake till dawn? Is it the voyage of the human consciousness testing out all its limitations, exploring all its horizons: love, solitary thought, action, sleep, death?—the drama of the mind which would withdraw from the world and rise superior to it but which is inevitably pulled back into life and involved in the processes of nature? It is all of these—yet the various strata, "physical, psychological and esoteric," as Francis de Miomandre describes them, are not overlaid one upon the other as in a conventional allegory or fable. They are confused and are always melting into one another—and it is this which makes the obscurity of the poem. The things that happen in "La Jeune Parque" and in Paul Valéry's other mythological monologues—the Narcissus, the Pythoness and the Serpent of the rich period of poetic activity which followed immediately upon "La Jeune Parque"—are never, on the one hand, quite imaginable as incidents which are actually taking place and never, on the other hand, quite reducible merely to thoughts in the poet's mind. The picture never quite emerges; the idea is never formulated quite. And for all the magnificences of sound, color, and suggestion which we find in these poems stanza by stanza, it seems to me that they are unsatisfactory because they are somehow not assimilable as wholes.

Yet Paul Valéry, when we put him beside Mallarmé, whom he echoes in these poems so often, is seen to possess the more vigorous intellect and the more solid imagination. Mallarmé is always a painter, usually a water-colorist—he wrote verses for ladies' fans as he might have painted little figures and flowers on them. He has his brightness and relief, but it is only such brightness and relief as is possible to someone working in the flat—whereas Valéry's genius is sculptural rather: these mythological poems have a density of cloud-shapes heavily massed—if they were not clouds, we should call them marmoreal. He gives us figures and groups half disengaged—and he runs to effects less of color than of light: the silvery, the sombre, the sunny, the translucent, the crystalline. And his verses carry off with the emphasis of an heroic resounding diction reminiscent of Alfred de Vigny the fluid waverings, the coy ambiguities and the delicately caught nuances which he has learned from Mallarmé. If Mallarmé was to supply subjects for Debussy, Valéry, outliving Debussy's vogue, was to be inspired in "La Jeune Parque" by Gluck. Valéry is, indeed, a sort of masculine of an art of which Mallarmé is the feminine. The elements in Mallarmé which made it possible for him to edit a woman's magazine and to write with his characteristic daintiness about styles in women's clothes is complemented, in Valéry, by a genius more powerful and stout which has a natural affinity with that of the architect.

And there is more substance in Valéry than in Mallarmé. In spite of his insistence that it is only the form, only the method in his work which interests him, Valéry's poetry has a certain dramatic quality. He is preoccupied with a particular conflict—the conflict between that part of man's existence which is represented by the abstraction of M. Teste and that part which is submerged in the sensations, distracted by the accidents, of the everyday world. If one were to read only "M. Teste"—though M. Teste is presented with some humor—or if one were to read only Valéry's prose, one might take him for one of the dryest and one of the most relentlessly abstract of minds. And it is true that the point of view of M. Teste figures con-

spicuously in the poetry of Valéry, as it predominates in
his prose—that none of his characters is ever allowed to
have a life independent of the intellectual world where
at any moment he may appear as an abstraction, and
that we suspect Valéry of preferring to human subjects,
or at least of finding more satisfactory, the marble columns and stately palms which he makes the heroes of
certain of his poems. It is true that even in love he tends
to seek to suspend sensual satisfaction and keep his mis-
tress in the timeless imminence which is for him a rival
satisfaction—begging the woman in "Les Pas" not to hast-
en, for he enjoys awaiting her as much as her kiss, and
making his Serpent say to Eve, when she is on the point
of tasting the fruit of the tree:

> "Que si ta bouche fait un rêve,
> Cette soif qui songe à la sève,
> Ce délice à demi futur,
> C'est l'éternité fondante, Eve!"

He seems, in fact, to prefer women asleep, or fatigued, because he can think of them then, as in "Dormeuse," as forms
of pure abstraction, from which the personality has de-
parted, or because he can reflect, as in "La Fausse Morte,"
that the satiety of love is a kind of death; he likes to imagine them, as in "Intérieur," insubstantial transparent presences who pass before the eyes of the mind like glass
through the beams of the sun. Yet there has perhaps never
been a poet who enjoyed the sensuous world with more
gusto than Valéry or who more solidly bodied it forth. In

the reproduction, in beautiful verses, of shapes, sounds, effects of light and shadow, substances of fruit or flesh, Valéry has never been surpassed. Of the summer cicada, he writes:

"L'insecte net gratte la sécheresse" . . .

of a cemetery by the sea:

"Où tant de marbre est tremblant sur tant d'ombres" . . .

of the pool of Narcissus, when it is evening in the forest— "une tendre lueur d'heure ambiguë existe"—and the water is smooth as a mirror:

"Onde déserte, et digne
Sur son lustre, du lisse effacement d'un cygne" . . .

of a rough sea:

"Si l'âme intense souffle, et renfle furibonde
L'onde abrupte sur l'onde abbatue, et si l'onde
Au cap tonne, immolant un monstre de candeur,
Et vient des hautes mers vomir la profondeur
Sur ce roc" . . .

And his human figures are like heroic statues which have yet a vibrancy and a soft envelopment. His Serpent puts before us an Eve of Michael Angelo:

"Calme, claire, de charmes lourde,
Je dominais furtivement,
L'œil dans l'or ardent de ta laine,
Ta nuque énigmatique et pleine
Des secrets de ton mouvement!"

74

And later, when she is tempted:

> "Le marbre aspire, l'or se cambre!
> Ces blondes bases d'ombre et d'ambre
> Tremblent au bord du mouvement!"

And in one marvellous line of "Dormeuse," he reveals a whole recumbent figure:

> "Ta forme au ventre pur qu'un bras fluide drape."

Valéry's poetry is then always shifting back and forth between this palpable and visible world and a realm of intellectual abstraction. And the contrast between them, the conflict implied between the absolute laws of the mind and the limiting contingencies of life, opposites impossible to dissociate from one another, is, as I say, the real subject of his poems. Rather an unpromising subject, one might suppose—one, at any rate, entirely remote from the emotions of Romantic poetry. Yet this queer antagonism has inspired Valéry to some of the most original poetry ever written, to some of the indubitably great poetry of our time. We may take as an example of this theme treated on Valéry's full scale his most popular and perhaps most satisfactory poem, "Le Cimetière Marin," which celebrates Valéry's return to poetry after his long period of inactivity. Here the poet has stopped at noon beside a graveyard by the sea: the sun seems to stand still above him; the water looks as level as a roof on which the boats are doves walking. The external world at the moment seems to figure that absolute toward which Valéry is always turning, with which he has been for so many years obsessed. Yet, "O Noonday!" he cries, "for all your immobility, I am the secret change in you—I am the flaw in your enormous diamond!"— But the dead, there below, they have gone to join the void—they have become a part of inanimate nature. And suppose he himself, the living man, has, alive, merely the illusion of movement—like the runner or the arrow of Zeno's paradoxes?— "But no!" he exhorts himself. "Break up that brooding, that immobility, which has all but absorbed you!" The salt wind is already rising to break up the tranquil roof of the sea, and to dash it against the rocks. The world enters into movement again and the poet must go back to life!

It is quite impossible, however, in other language, to provide a scenario for one of Valéry's poems: in doing so, one must leave out almost all that is most characteristic of Valéry. In trying to clear up his meaning, one clears it up too much. The truth is that there are no real ideas, no real general reflections, in such a poem as "Le Cimetière Marin": Valéry presents, even more completely than Yeats in such a poem as "Among School Children," the emotion merged with the idea and both embedded in the scene where they have occurred. It is the aim and the triumph of the Symbolist poet to make the stabilities of the external world answer to the individual's varying apprehension of them. It is, indeed, his effect, if not his purpose, to lead us to question the traditional dualism which would make them out to be two separate things. In such a poem as "Le Cimetière Marin," there is no simple second meaning: there is a marvellously close reproduction of the very complex and continually changing relation of human consciousness to the things of which it is conscious. The noonday is inorganic Nature, but it is also the absolute in the poet's mind, it is also his twenty years of inaction—and it is also merely the noonday itself, which in a moment will no longer exist, which will be no longer either tranquil or noon. And the sea, which, during those moments of calm, forms a part of that great diamond of nature in which the poet finds himself the single blemish, because the single change, is also the image of the poet's silence, which in a moment, as the wind comes up to lash the sea, will give way to a sudden gust of utterance, the utterance of the poem itself. World and poet are always overlapping, are always interpenetrating, as they might in a Romantic poem; but the Symbolist will not even try, as the Romantic would be likely to do, to keep their relations consistent. The conventions of the poem's imagery change as quickly and as naturally as the images passing through the poet's mind.

II

Since "Charmes" (1922), Paul Valéry has published no more poetry, but a good deal of miscellaneous prose. Valéry's prose, in spite of the extravagant respect with which it is treated by his admirers, is by no means so remarkable as his verse. In the first place, it seems doubtful whether Valéry has ever really mastered a prose style. There are many admirable things in his essays, passages of a fine terseness, tightness and wit, but the prose is always liable to get snarled in a knot of words which balks the understanding at the same time that it exasperates the taste.

The opacities of Valéry's prose are usually attributed by Valéry's admirers, who in this only follow the intimations of the master himself, to the originality and profundity of his ideas. But the truth is that, when we go through Valéry's essays, we are unable to find many ideas. We find simply, as we do in his poetry, the presentation of intellectual situations, instead of the development of lines of thought. A French critic has already taxed Valéry with being a philosopher who won't philosophize; and it is true that the "rigor" of which he is always talking is rather an artistic effect of his prose, produced by certain devices of style like the artistic effects of his poems, than a quality of his logic. In spite of his passion for method, Valéry seems to have taken singularly little trouble to sort out or set in order his ideas: like M. Teste, he is occupied rather with savoring his intellectual sensations and in coining more or less mixed metaphors to convey them. And though it is possible to a certain extent to share his enjoyment of this pastime, in the long run we find it dreary and even repellent. What, we ask, has Valéry-Teste succeeded in dredging up by that abysmal self-scrutiny of his? Why, not much more than the realization, which he is hardly the first to have arrived at, that all forms of intellectual activity—even those which seem on the surface very different: poetry and mathematics, for example—are fundamentally the same sort of thing, merely arrangements or organizations of selected elements of experience. In so far as Valéry really deals in ideas, he is, in fact, a sort of super-dilettante, who, though he has many passages of pungent writing and stimulating insight, is just as likely, with groans of heavy labor, to unload a ponderous platitude. Most of Valéry's reputation for profundity comes, I believe, from the fact that he was one of the first literary men to acquire a smattering of the new mathematical and physical theory. Valéry has, it is true, made interesting use of this, but one wishes sometimes that he would either go further with it or leave philosophy alone. He never seems to have gotten over his first excitement at reading Poincaré, and he is still rather snobbish about it: he is always telling us how difficult it is going to be to make us understand this or that, and then the portentous thought, when it comes, turns out to be one of the commonplaces of modern scientific philosophy—the sort of thing which J. W. N. Sullivan, for example, has had no difficulty in explaining lucidly in the short popular essays of his "Aspects of Science."

As a literary critic, however, Valéry has both interest and importance. He is perhaps the principal exponent in France of a peculiar point of view about poetry which has gained currency with the progress of modern Symbolism. The Romantics thought of a poem as primarily a piece of self-expression—a gushing forth of emotion, a bursting into song. The conception fashionable to-day is quite different: the doctrines of Symbolism were in some ways closely analogous to the doctrines of Romanticism, but in this respect the later Symbolists are at the opposite pole from the Romantics. Paul Valéry's attitude toward poetry is both more esoteric and more scientific than that of Romantic criticism.

Valéry had already in 1894, in his "Introduction to the Method of Leonardo da Vinci," defined a work of art as "a machine intended to excite and combine the individual formations" of a particular "category of minds." And from the time of "La Jeune Parque," he has never ceased to insist that a poem is an intricate intellectual problem, a struggle with self-imposed conditions—that it is, above all, something *constructed*. Or, according to a favorite simile of Valéry's, a poem is like a heavy weight which the poet has carried to the roof bit by bit—the reader is the passer-by upon whom the weight is dropped all at once and who consequently receives from it in a moment an overwhelming impression, a complete æsthetic effect, such as the poet has never known in composing it. "Enthusiasm," says Valéry, "is not an artist's state of mind." And also: "Genius is a habit which certain people acquire." "X wants us to believe that a metaphor is a communication from Heaven. A metaphor is what occurs when one looks at things in a certain way, as getting dazzled is what occurs when one looks into a sun. When one looks at things in what way? You feel it, and some day it will perhaps be possible to explain it in the most precise terms.

Do this and that—and you have all the metaphors in the world."

This apparently cool and analytic attitude, however, is accompanied, curiously enough, by an excessively esoteric conception of poetry. This conception is most clearly stated and its weakness, it seems to be, made most clearly manifest in a preface which Valéry has just contributed to a commentary on his own "Charmes" by the French essayist Alain (this scholastic layer upon layer of commentary is itself very characteristic of the contemporary criticism of poetry). Here we find, as usual, the scientific approach—which it occurs to us, as we read, is largely a matter of scientific similes: "There are certain rather mysterious bodies which physics studies and which chemistry uses: I always think of them when I reflect upon works of art." These are the catalytic agents, which precipitate chemical changes without being affected themselves. So the work of art, says Valéry, acts upon the mind into which it is introduced. Even when chemically considered, then, the work of art remains something "mysterious." And by "works of art," it further appears that, in the department of literature, Valéry means poetry exclusively. Prose, he says, has "sense" for its sole object—but the object of poetry is something not only more mysterious, but also apparently more occult: "There is absolutely no question in poetry of one person's transmitting to another something intelligible that is going on in his mind. It is a question of creating in the latter a state whose expression is precisely and uniquely that which communicates it to him. Whatever image or emotion is formed in the amateur of poems, it is valid and sufficient if it produces in him this reciprocal relation between the word-cause and the word-effect. The result is that the reader enjoys a very great freedom in regard to ideas, a freedom analogous to that which one recognizes in the case of the hearer of music, though not so intensive."

It seems to me that a pretense to exactitude is here used to cover a number of ridiculously false assumptions, and to promote a kind of æsthetic mysticism rather than to effect a scientific analysis. In the first place, is it not absurd to assert that prose deals exclusively in "sense" as distinguished from suggestion, and that one has no right to expect from poetry, as Valéry says in another passage, "any definite notion at all"? Is verse really an intellectual product absolutely different in kind from prose? Has it really an absolutely different function? Are not both prose and verse, after all, merely techniques of human intercommunication, and techniques which have played various rôles, have been used for various purposes, in different periods and civilizations? The early Greeks used verse for their histories, their romances and their laws—the Greeks and the Elizabethans used it for their dramas. If Valéry's definitions are correct, what becomes of Homer, Virgil, Dante, Shakespeare and Goethe? They all of them deal in sense as well as suggestion and aim to convey "definite notions." These definitions have, however, obviously been framed to apply to the poetry of Valéry himself and of Mallarmé and the other Symbolists. Yet it does not really apply even to them. As we have seen, Valéry's poetry does make sense, it does deal with definite subjects, it does transmit to us "something intelligible that is going on inside his mind." Even though in calling his book of poems "Charmes," he has tried to emphasize its esoteric, magical, non-utilitarian character, we cannot admit that it is anything but an effort like another of articulate human speech. What happens when we communicate with each other, in literature as well as in curses and cries for help, and in verse as well as in prose—what part is played by "sense" and what part is played by suggestion, and whether sense and suggestion are different and separable —are questions which take us far and deep: I shall return to them in a later chapter. But Valéry has already let us see—it is even one of his favorite ideas—that he understands the basic similarity between the various forms of intellectual activity; he has taken pride in pointing out the kinship between poetry and mathematics. And if the function and methods of poetry are similar to those of mathematics, they must surely be similar to those of prose. If Valéry resembles Descartes, as he seems willingly to indulge himself in imagining, then it is impossible to make a true distinction between a philosophical or mathematical treatise and however Symbolistic a poem. Valéry betrays himself here, it seems to me, as a thinker anything but "rigorous"; and he betrays also, I believe, a desire, defensive no doubt at the same time as snobbish, to make it appear that verse, a technique now no longer much used for history, story-telling or drama and consequently not much

in popular demand, has some inherent superiority to prose.
He has not hesitated even to assure us elsewhere that
"poetry is the most difficult of the arts"!

III

With all respect for Valéry's intelligence, for his candor
and independence, it must be admitted that he is taken
too seriously—and perhaps takes himself too seriously—as
a universal sage. "Stupidity is not my forte," he says—
and though we are willing to agree, we should prefer not
to hear him say it. A great poet, we should prefer not to
have him continually explaining what superhuman labor
it has cost him to compose his poems and intimating that,
in comparison with his own work, the poetry of other
poets is mostly facile and superficial—especially when we
remember his replying to a correspondent who had complained of some awkward inversion in "La Jeune Parque"
that the reader had happened to hit upon precisely one
of those passages in the poem which Valéry had "literally
improvised in the hasty lassitude of finishing it up."

The pretentious and snobbish side of Valéry was seen at
its worst on the occasion of his election to the French
Academy, when he succeeded to Anatole France's chair
and had to deliver an address upon his predecessor—an
incident which is worth dwelling upon, however, because
it has a certain historical importance. Valéry behaved on
this occasion in a highly unconventional manner. In the
first place, it appears that at the Academy the uniforms are

passed on from generation to generation and that a new member fits himself as best he can from such old uniforms as are available—as American college graduates at commencement rent old graduation gowns. Paul Valéry, however, is reported to have astounded the Academicians by appearing in a smart brand-new uniform which he had had made for him by a fashionable tailor. The address on Anatole France which he then read is said to have been received with consternation. It has always been the custom for the newly elected member to compose an *"éloge"* on the man he is succeeding; but, instead of the usual complimentary obituary, Valéry delivered himself of a piece of criticism which can hardly be described as anything less than an attack. Anatole France had been unfriendly to Symbolism in the days when it had been new and unpopular: he had said that he could "never believe in the success of a literary school which expressed difficult thoughts in obscure language." He had made fun of Mallarmé and spoken contemptuously of Rimbaud. And in his own writing he had represented that French tradition of classical lucidity and simplicity against which the Symbolists were rebelling. Now Paul Valéry is only the second Symbolist to have been admitted to the French Academy, and his election was like a final official recognition of the literary party which had once been outlawed. His funeral sermon on Anatole France is composed in the mood of a none too generous victor, at once complaining and cocky. Valéry adopts the general tone of desiring in a patronizing way to say something kindly and appreciative about France, but everything that he says turns out to sound disparaging. He takes up *seriatim* all the charges which have been made against France since his death—such as the meaningless gossip to the effect that, if it had not been for Mme. de Caillavet, he would never have accomplished anything—and, with the air of mitigating their seriousness, somehow succeeds in giving them weight. He speaks of France's "sinuosity" and prudence in such a way as to convey the impression that he was timid and insincere (since, though France had invited popular hatred, had sacrificed his place in the Academy and had embroiled himself with his friends, in defending the innocence of Dreyfus, he had failed to understand and champion Symbolism); and he concludes that, in view of France's humble origins (he was the son of a bookseller on the quais), he had really done very well indeed. Valéry furthermore refrains throughout in a marked and insulting manner from mentioning France's name—a perfectly innocuous pseudonym derived from a family nickname for Anatole-François—and makes upon it the following comment: "He himself would not have been possible, would scarcely have been conceivable, except in France, whose name he assumed. Under that name, so difficult to carry off, and which it required so much assurance to adopt, he won the favor of the universe. He presented it, indeed, with a France possessing all those specious qualities with which, if she herself were to remain satisfied, the universe would suffer; but which were agreeable to him and to which he did not feel any objection." Valéry goes

86

on to speak at length of France, the nation (Valéry himself is half Italian, and a tendency to think in Italian is evidently at the bottom of some of the peculiarities of his style), and ends his address on a high note of patriotism.

Now one would naturally not expect Paul Valéry to go against his convictions, or even politely to conceal them with evasions, merely because he had happened to succeed to the place of a writer of whom he disapproved. Furthermore, with Valéry's criticisms of France it is partly possible to agree. It is not without reason that Anatole France has come to represent to many French literary people all that is elegantly second-rate in the writing of the previous generation. France was the last great writer of a tradition and in his work the peculiar weaknesses of the tradition became, in consequence, especially conspicuous. It is true that before he died, he had lived long enough to have produced certain books which, for their empty unctuousness and suavity, their mechanical neatness of form, do tend to discourage us rather with Renanian irony and pity and with classical symmetry and clearness. It was time that those formulas should be discarded—there was nothing more to be done along those lines. And Valéry is one of those who have abolished them. Yet, with all faith in the methods of Symbolism, with all enthusiasm for its achievements, as one reads this patronizing and feline paper one cannot help rebelling against what appears to be Valéry's assumption that it is impossible at the same time to be profound and to write as lightly and lucidly as France did. Valéry himself seems deliberately on this oc-

casion to have avoided writing attractively or clearly:
though his subject is not in the least metaphysical, though
there is nothing in the least difficult about what he is saying, this address is perhaps his masterpiece of bad writing.
Never have Valéry's viscous prose, his masses of clotted abstractions, his hindside-foremost presentations of
thought, been managed to worse advantage. To say that
the author of "Le Jardin d'Epicure" would have turned
in his grave if he could have heard Valéry's paper would
be to understate the situation: France's bitterest clerical
enemies could have wished him no more horrible punish-
ment than to have had to listen to them in Hell.

In any case, Valéry's advent to the Academy, in sug-
gesting a contrast between Valéry and France, marks even
more sharply than the divergence between Yeats and
Bernard Shaw the difference between the new methods
and attitudes of the typical literature of the period since
the War and those of the literature of the period which
the War ended. Anatole France was a popular writer: he
aimed to be persuasive and intelligible—he used frankly
to remind his secretary, Brousson, that they were "working for a bourgeois clientèle. That is the only one that
reads. Do not tear away the veil of the temple. Pluck it
off a little at a time. Riddle it with sly little holes. . . .
Leave to your reader the easy victory of seeing further
than you." His books were sold on all the bookstalls of
France and known all over the civilized world. Whereas
Paul Valéry disregards altogether the taste and intelligence of the ordinary reader: instead of allowing his

reader the easy victory, he takes pride in outstripping him completely. And he is read chiefly by other writers or by people with a special interest in literature: his poems are always out of print and his other writings are always being published in editions so expensive and limited as practically never to circulate at all. Anatole France was voluminous: he supplied his public with a whole literature of romance, history, criticism, satire, drama, poetry, philosophy, political pamphlets, newspaper articles and speeches. Paul Valéry publishes little: his whole genius has been concentrated to the production of a few magnificent poems—beyond these, he has written almost nothing but a few volumes of miscellaneous notes. Anatole France was essentially a rationalist: he did not deny the incongruities and incoherences of experience, but he attempted to write about them, at least, in a simple, logical and harmonious style. Paul Valéry has set himself, on the contrary, the task of reproducing by his very language all the complexities and confusions of our interacting sensations and ideas. The phenomena with which France usually deals are the events of life as it is lived in the world; with Valéry the object of interest is the isolated or ideal human mind, brooding on its own contradictions or admiring its own flights. When France turns away from literature, he occupies himself naturally with politics—he goes on the stump for Dreyfus, allies himself with the Socialist party, writes editorials for its paper, addresses meetings of working men and finally declares himself a Communist. But Valéry concerns himself little with politics, and then only as a detached intelligence—his extra-literary pursuits are scientific. And whereas for France, science meant exclusively a conventional nineteenth-century mechanism, with which he had become so deeply imbued that he was haunted all his life by nightmares of the dizziness of space, the extinction of the sun, the fatally automatic character of human loves and ambitions, the reversion of mankind to barbarism through a reversal of the evolutionary process—Paul Valéry has emerged into an era when the scientific point of view no longer implies this determinism. (France's attitude toward modern science was like his attitude toward Symbolism: when in his old age he met Einstein in Berlin and Einstein tried to explain to him his theories, France had no patience to listen: "When he told me that light was matter, my head began to swim and I took my leave.") For the modern scientific thought which colors Valéry's speculations has extricated itself from the conception of ineluctable laws of nature, relentless chains of cause and effect. Valéry discusses in one of his most interesting essays the oppression and panic felt by Pascal at his vision—a typically seventeenth-century vision of the scientific imagination—of the silent abysses of space. Such imaginings drove a Pascal into fanatical piety—the equivalent conceptions of two centuries later drove France to a habit of despair which came largely to counteract and invalidate his hopes for human society. To Pascal and France alike, man seemed ignominious and insignificant. But Valéry can laugh at both: he has caught already the first lights of an age in which our increasing knowledge of the universe will have come to change "not merely our ideas, but certain of our immediate reactions" and "what one might call 'Pascal's reaction' will be a rarity and a curiosity to psychologists." Man is no longer to be a tiny exile, pitting himself amidst vast space against matter: what he has been thinking of as his soul, the exclusive possession of human beings, is somehow bound up with that external nature which he has been regarding as inanimate or alien, and his mind, which has lately seemed as feeble as a spark of phosphorescence on a midnight ocean, turns out to have constructed its own universe.

It is particularly illuminating to compare Valéry's M. Teste with France's most celebrated creation, M. Bergeret of the "Histoire Contemporaine." M. Bergeret is a social being, polite, agreeable and fond of company: though sadly harassed in the community where he lives by many elements which he feels to be hostile or undesirable, the common interests of that community and of the civilization it represents are what he has chiefly at heart. He is always discussing this civilization with his neighbors, and when an important political issue arises, he is positive and prompt to take sides. But M. Teste is outside society, he has almost succeeded in dissociating himself from human relations altogether: "He neither smiled, nor said good-day nor good-bye; and seemed not to hear one's how-do-you-do"—he goes to bed and goes to sleep in the presence of a guest, and his effect on Mme. Teste is to make her feel that she is non-existent. He is ill-mannered, self-preoccupied, austere—the modern psychologists would probably diagnose him as introverted, narcissistic and manic depressive.

And in general it may be said that the strength of Anatole France's generation was the strength to be derived from a wide knowledge of human affairs, a sympathetic interest in human beings, direct contact with public opinion and participation in public life through literature. The strength of solitary labor and of earnest introspection is the strength of Valéry's.

IV

T. S. ELIOT

I HAVE noted the similarity between the English seven-teenth-century poets and the French nineteenth-century Symbolists. The poetry of T. S. Eliot has, in our own time, brought together these two traditions, as it is Eliot who, so far as I know, has for the first time called attention to their resemblance. "The form," he says, "in which I began to write, in 1908 or 1909, was directly drawn from the study of Laforgue together with the later Elizabethan drama; and I do not know anyone who started from exactly that point."

I have so far, in discussing the early Symbolists, spoken chiefly of Mallarmé. But T. S. Eliot derived, as he indicates, from a different branch of the Symbolist tradition. In 1873 there had appeared in Paris a book of poems called "Les Amours Jaunes," by a writer who signed himself Tristan Corbière. "Les Amours Jaunes" was received with complete indifference, and scarcely more than a year after it appeared, the author died of consumption. Only thirty at the time of his death, Tristan Corbière had been an eccentric and very maladjusted man: he was the son of a sea captain who had also written sea stories and he had had an excellent education, but he chose for himself the

life of an outlaw. In Paris, he slept all day and spent the
nights in the cafés or at his verses, greeting at dawn the
Paris harlots as they emerged from the station house or the
hotel with the same half-harsh, half-tender fellow-feeling
for the exile from conventional society which, when he
was at home in his native Brittany, caused him to flee
the house of his family and seek the company of the cus-
toms-men and sailors—living skeleton and invalid as he
was, performing prodigies of courage and endurance in
the navigation of a little cutter which he sailed by preference in the worst possible weather. He made a pose of his
unsociability and of what he considered his physical ugli-
ness, at the same time that he undoubtedly suffered over
them. Melancholy, with a feverishly active mind, full of
groanings and vulgar jokes, he used to amuse himself by
going about in convict's clothes and by firing guns and
revolvers out the window in protest against the singing of
the village choir; and on one occasion, on a visit to
Rome, he appeared in the streets in evening dress, with a
mitre on his head and two eyes painted on his forehead,
leading a pig decorated with ribbons. And Corbière's
poetry was a poetry of the outcast: often colloquial and
homely, yet with a rhetoric of fantastic slang; often with
the manner of slapdash doggerel, yet sure of its own morose artistic effects; full of the parade of romantic personality, yet incessantly humiliating itself with a self-mock-
ery scurrilous and savage, out of which, as Huysmans said,
would sometimes rise without warning "a cry of sharp
pain like the breaking of a 'cello string"—Corbière's verse

brought back into French poetry qualities which had been alien to its spirit since François Villon's day.

So outlandish did Corbière appear even from the point of view of the Romantics that he was dismissed, when he was noticed at all, as not merely unseemly but insane —till Paul Verlaine, in 1883, did him honor in a series of articles, "Les Poètes Maudits," which was one of the important critical events in the development of Symbolism. Verlaine himself, a more accomplished artist, but a less original and interesting personality, had been strongly influenced by "Les Amours Jaunes"—he seems, indeed, to have caught over from Corbière, not only certain artistic effects, but even something of his own poetic personality, his peculiar accent of wistful naïveté: compare Corbière's "Rondels pour Après" with Verlaine's sonnet which begins, "L'espoir luit comme un brin de paille dans l'étable"; or "Paria" with "Casper Hauser."

But another French poet, Jules Laforgue, nineteen years younger than Corbière, had independently developed a tone and technique—poignant-ironic, grandiose-slangy, scurrilous-naïve—which had much in common with Corbière's. Laforgue was the son of a schoolmaster and, for all his nonchalance in handling rudely the conventions of French poetry, much more a professional man of letters than Corbière. Laforgue even errs through preciosity in his fashion; what with Corbière seems a personal and inevitable, if eccentric, manner of speech, in Laforgue sounds self-conscious and deliberate, almost sometimes a literary exercise. He was tubercular, as Corbière was also, and dead at twenty-seven—and his gentleness and sadness are still those of a sick well-cared-for child; his asperities, his surprising images, his coquetries, his cynicism, and his impudence, are still those of a clever schoolboy. Laforgue's friends procured him a post as reader to the Empress Augusta of Germany; and, falling under the spell of German philosophy, he brought its jargon into his verse, contributing thereby to Symbolism perhaps the one element of obscurity which it had lacked.

Yet Laforgue is a very fine poet and one of the most remarkable of the Symbolists. He and Corbière had introduced a new variety of vocabulary and a new flexibility of feeling. With Mallarmé, it may be said that, on the whole, it is the imagery, not the feeling, which is variable: though sometimes playful, he is classical in the sense (as Yeats and Valéry are) that he sustains a certain grandeur of tone. But it is from the conversational-ironic, rather than from the serious-æsthetic, tradition of Symbolism that T. S. Eliot derives. Corbière and Laforgue are almost everywhere in his early work. The emphatic witty quatrains of Corbière, with their sudden lapses into tenderness or pathos, are heard again in the satiric verse of Eliot: a poem like "Mr. Eliot's Sunday Morning Service" would hardly, one imagines, have been written without Corbière's "Rapsodie Foraine." And as "Conversation Galante" derives clearly from certain poems in Laforgue's "Complaintes" and "Imitation de Notre-Dame la Lune," so the more elaborate "Portrait of a Lady" and "The Love Song of J. Alfred Prufrock" follow closely the longer poems of Laforgue. Compare the conclusion of "Mr. Prufrock" with the conclusion of the early version of Laforgue's poem "Légende":

"I grow old . . . I grow old . . .
I shall wear the bottoms of my trousers rolled.

Shall I part my hair behind? Do I dare to eat a peach!
I shall wear white flannel trousers, and walk upon the beach.
I have heard the mermaids singing, each to each.

I do not think that they will sing to me.

I have seen them riding seaward on the waves
Combing the white hair of the waves blown back
When the wind blows the water white and black.

We have lingered in the chambers of the sea
By sea-girls wreathed with seaweed red and brown
Till human voices wake us, and we drown."

. . .

"Hier l'orchestre attaqua
Sa dernière polka

Oh! L'automme, l'automme!
Les casinos
Qu'on abandonne
Remisent leurs pianos! . . .

Phrases, verroteries,
Caillots de souvenirs.
Oh! comme elle est maigrie!
Que vais-je devenir? . . .

Adieu! Les filles d'ifs dans les grisailles
Ont l'air de pleureuses de funerailles
Sous l'autan noir qui veut que tout s'en aille.

Assez, assez,
C'est toi qui as commencé.

Va, ce n'est plus l'odeur de tes fourrures.
Va, vos moindres clins d'yeux sont des parjures.
Tais-toi, avec vous autres rien ne dure.

Tais-toi, tais-toi,
On n'aime qu'une fois" . . .

Here it will be seen that Eliot has reproduced Laforgue's
irregular metrical scheme almost line for line. Furthermore, the subject of Laforgue's poem—the hesitations and
constraints of a man either too timid or too disillusioned
to make love to a woman who provokes his ironic pity at
the same time that she stirs gusts of stifled emotion—has a
strong resemblance to the subjects of "Mr. Prufrock" and
the "Portrait of a Lady." And in another poem, "La Figlia
Che Piange," Eliot has adapted a line of Laforgue's:
"Simple et sans foi comme un bonjour"—"Simple and
faithless as a smile and shake of the hand." He has even
brought over into English some of the unstressed effect of
French verse: how different, for example, is the alexandrine of Eliot's just quoted from the classical English
alexandrine "which like a wounded snake drags its slow
length along" or "with sparkless ashes loads an unla-
mented urn." (In his exhaustive "Influence du Symbo-
lisme Français sur la Poésie Américaine de 1910 à 1920,"
M. René Taupin has shown the influence of Gautier also
in Eliot's satiric poems: "The Hippopotamus," it appears,
is almost a transcript of a hippopotamus by Gautier, and

the "Grishkin is nice" passage in "Whispers of Immortality" repeats a "Carmen est maigre" of Gautier.)

It must not be supposed, however, that Eliot is not original or that he is not the equal of either of his masters. Those longer and more elaborate poems—"Derniers Vers" in the collected edition—which Laforgue was constructing at the time of his death out of more fragmentary and less mature work are certainly his most important performances: through his masterly flexibility of vocabulary and metric, he has here achieved one of the definitive expressions of the pathetic-ironic, wordly-æsthetic moods of the *fin de siècle* temperament. Yet, though Eliot has, in certain obvious respects, applied Laforgue's formula so faithfully, he cannot properly be described as an imitator because he is in some ways a superior artist. He is more mature than Laforgue ever was, and his workmanship is perfect in a way that Corbière's and Laforgue's were rarely. T. S. Eliot's peculiar distinction lies, as Clive Bell has said, in his "phrasing." Laforgue's images are often far-fetched and inappropriately grotesque: his sins in this respect are really very closely akin to those of the English metaphysical poets; but Eliot's taste is absolutely sure—his images always precisely right. And the impression that Eliot leaves, even in these earliest poems, is clear, vivid and unforgettable: we do not subordinate him to his Symbolist predecessors any more than, when we find him, as in "Gerontion," writing in the rhythms of late Elizabethan blank-verse, we associate him with Middleton or Webster.

When we come to examine Eliot's themes, we recognize

something which we have found already in Laforgue, but which appears in Eliot in a more intense form. One of the principal preoccupations of Flaubert—a great hero of Eliot's, as of Eliot's fellow-poet, Ezra Pound's—had been the inferiority of the present to the past: the Romantics had discovered the possibilities of the historical imagination; with their thirst for boldness, grandeur, and magnificence, they had located these qualities in past epochs— especially the Middle Ages and the Renaissance. And Flaubert, who shared with the Romantics this appetite for the gorgeous and the untamed, but who constrained himself, also, to confront the actual nineteenth-century world, pursued two parallel lines of fiction which lent significance and relief to each other. On the one hand, he reconstructed, in "Salammbô" and in "La Tentation de Saint-Antoine," the splendid barbarities of the pagan world and the heroic piety of the early Christian; and on the other, he caricatured, in "Madame Bovary," in "L'Education Sentimentale" and in "Bouvard et Pécuchet," the pusillanimity and mediocrity of contemporary bourgeois France. This whole point of view of Flaubert's— summed up, as it were, in "Trois Contes," where the three periods are contrasted in one book—was profoundly to affect modern literature. We shall find it later on in Joyce; but in the meantime we must note its reappearance in the poetry of Eliot. Eliot, like Flaubert, feels at every turn that human life is now ignoble, sordid or tame, and he is haunted and tormented by intimations that it has once been otherwise. In "Burbank with a Baedeker: Bleistein with a Cigar," the young American tourist in Venice, superseded in his affair with the Princess Volupine by a vulgar Austrian Jew, meditates on the clipped wings and pared claws of the Lion of St. Mark's, the symbol of the old arrogant Venice and of the world where such a city was possible. In "A Cooking Egg," the poet demands, after a call upon a very mild, dull spinster: "Where are the eagles and the trumpets?" and himself returns the saddened answer: "Buried beneath some snow-deep Alps." In "Lune de Miel," the Middle Western American travellers, stifled with the summer heat and devoured by the bed-bugs of Ravenna, are contrasted with the noble crumbling beauty of the old Byzantine church less than a league away, of which they are totally unaware and to which they have apparently no relation; and in "Mr. Eliot's Sunday Morning Service," the combined grossness and aridity of the modern clergymen is contrasted with the pure and fresh religious feeling of a picture of the baptism of Christ by "a painter of the Umbrian school." In the best and most effective of these poems, "Sweeney Among the Nightingales," the poet, during a drowsy, idiotic and mildly sinister scene in some low dive, where two of the girls are supposed to be plotting against one of the men, remembers, at the sound of nightingales singing, the murder of Agamemnon in Æschylus:

> "The host with someone indistinct
> Converses at the door apart,
> The nightingales are singing near
> The Convent of the Sacred Heart,

And sang within the bloody wood
When Agamemnon cried aloud,
And let their liquid siftings fall
To stain the stiff dishonoured shroud."

The present is more timid than the past: the bourgeois
are afraid to let themselves go. The French had been preoccupied with this idea ever since the first days of Romanticism; but Eliot was to deal with the theme from a
somewhat different point of view, a point of view characteristically American. For T. S. Eliot, though born in St.
Louis, comes from a New England family and was educated at Harvard; and he is in some ways a typical product
of our New England civilization. He is distinguished by
that combination of practical prudence with moral idealism which shows itself in its later developments as an ex-
cessive fastidiousness and scrupulousness. One of the principal subjects of Eliot's poetry is really that regret at situations unexplored, that dark rankling of passions inhibited,
which has figured so conspicuously in the work of the
American writers of New England and New York from
Hawthorne to Edith Wharton. T. S. Eliot, in this respect,
has much in common with Henry James. Mr. Prufrock
and the poet of the "Portrait of a Lady," with their helpless consciousness of having dared too little, correspond
exactly to the middle-aged heroes of "The Ambassadors"
and "The Beast in the Jungle," realizing sadly too late in
life that they have been living too cautiously and too
poorly. The fear of life, in Henry James, is closely bound
up with the fear of vulgarity. And Eliot, too, fears vul-

garity—which he embodies in the symbolic figure of "Apeneck Sweeney"—at the same time that he is fascinated by it. Yet he chafes at the limitations and pretenses of the culture represented by Boston—a society "quite uncivilized," as he says, "but refined beyond the point of civilization." He has some amusing satiric poems about old New England ladies—in one of which he reflects on his way to the house of his Cousin Harriet, how

> ". . . evening quickens faintly in the street,
> Wakening the appetites of life in some
>   And to others bringing the *Boston Evening Transcript*."

And the "Portrait of a Lady," whether the scene be laid in Boston or in London, is essentially a poem of that New England society "refined beyond the point of civilization": from the Lady, who serves tea among lighted candles—"an atmosphere of Juliet's tomb"—with her dampening efforts at flattery and flirtation through the medium of cultured conversation—her slightly stale and faded gush about Chopin and her memories of Paris in the spring—the poet is seized with an impulse to flee:

> "I take my hat: how can I make a cowardly amends
> For what she has said to me?
> You will see me any morning in the park
> Reading the comics and the sporting page.
> Particularly I remark
> An English countess goes upon the stage,
> A Greek was murdered at a Polish dance,
> Another bank defaulter has confessed.
> I keep my countenance,

I remain self-possessed
Except when a street piano, mechanical and tired,
Reiterates some worn-out common song
With the smell of hyacinths across the garden
Recalling things that other people have desired."

But he is always debating things with his conscience: his incurable moral solicitude makes him wonder:

"Are these ideas right or wrong?"

So Mr. Prufrock in the room where

". . . women come and go
Talking of Michelangelo,"

wistfully asks himself:

"Shall I say, I have gone at dusk through narrow streets
And watched the smoke that rises from the pipes
Of lonely men in shirt-sleeves, leaning out of windows?" . . .

And Mr. Prufrock wonders also whether he should not put a question to his lady—but he never gets to the point of putting it.

II

But Eliot's most complete expression of this theme of emotional starvation is to be found in the later and longer poem called "The Waste Land" (1922). The Waste Land of the poem is a symbol borrowed from the myth of the Holy Grail: it is a desolate and sterile country ruled by an impotent king, in which not only have the crops ceased to grow and the animals to reproduce, but the very human inhabitants have become incapable of having children. But this sterility we soon identify as the sterility of the Puritan temperament. On the first pages we find again the theme of the girl with the hyacinths (themselves a symbol for the rearisen god of the fertility rites who will save the rainless country from drouth) which has already figured in "La Figlia Che Piange" and "Dans le Restaurant"—a memory which apparently represents for the poet some fulfillment foregone in youth and now agonizingly desired; and in the last pages it is repeated. We recognize throughout "The Waste Land" the peculiar conflicts of the Puritan turned artist: the horror of vulgarity and the shy sympathy with the common life, the ascetic shrinking from sexual experience and the distress at the drying up of the springs of sexual emotion, with the straining after a religious emotion which may be made to take its place.

Yet though Eliot's spiritual and intellectual roots are still more firmly fixed in New England than is, I believe, ordinarily understood, there is in "The Waste Land" a good deal more than the mere gloomy moods of a New Englander regretting an emotionally undernourished youth. The colonization by the Puritans of New England was merely an incident in that rise of the middle class which has brought a commercial-industrial civilization to the European cities as well as to the American ones. T. S. Eliot now lives in London and has become an English citizen; but the desolation, the æsthetic and spiritual drouth, of Anglo-Saxon middle-class society oppresses London as well as Boston. The terrible dreariness of the great modern cities is the atmosphere in which "The Waste Land" takes place—amidst this dreariness, brief, vivid images emerge, brief pure moments of feeling are distilled; but all about us we are aware of nameless millions performing barren office routines, wearing down their souls in interminable labors of which the products never bring them profit— people whose pleasures are so sordid and so feeble that they seem almost sadder than their pains. And this Waste Land has another aspect: it is a place not merely of desolation, but of anarchy and doubt. In our post-War world of shattered institutions, strained nerves and bankrupt ideals, life no longer seems serious or coherent—we have no belief in the things we do and consequently we have no heart for them.

The poet of "The Waste Land" is living half the time in the real world of contemporary London and half the time in the haunted wilderness of the mediæval legend. The water for which he longs in the twilight desert of his dream is to quench the spiritual thirst which torments him in the London dusk; and as Gerontion, "an old man in a dry month," thought of the young men who had fought in the rain, as Prufrock fancied riding the waves with mermaids and lingering in the chambers of the sea, as Mr. Apollinax has been imagined drawing strength from the deep sea-caves of coral islands—so the poet of "The Waste Land," making water the symbol of all freedom, all fecundity and flowering of the soul, invokes in desperate need the memory of an April shower of his

youth, the song of the hermit thrush with its sound of water dripping and the vision of a drowned Phœnician sailor,
sunk beyond "the cry of gulls and the deep sea swell,"
who has at least died by water, not thirst. The poet, who
seems now to be travelling in a country cracked by drouth,
can only feverishly dream of these things. One's head may
be well stored with literature, but the heroic prelude of the
Elizabethans has ironic echoes in modern London streets
and modern London drawing-rooms: lines remembered
from Shakespeare turn to jazz or refer themselves to the
sound of phonographs. And now it is one's personal regrets again—the girl in the hyacinth-garden—"the awful
daring of a moment's surrender which an age of prudence
can never retract"—the key which turned once, and once
only, in the prison of inhibition and isolation. Now he
stands on the arid plain again, and the dry-rotted world
of London seems to be crumbling about him—the poem
ends in a medley of quotations from a medley of literatures—like Gérard de Nerval's "Desdichado," the poet is
disinherited; like the author of the "Pervigilium Veneris,"
he laments that his song is mute and asks when the spring
will come which will set it free like the swallow's; like
Arnaut Daniel, in Dante, as he disappears in the refining
fire, he begs the world to raise a prayer for his torment.
"These fragments I have shored against my ruins."

"The Waste Land," in method as well as in mood, has
left Laforgue far behind. Eliot has developed a new technique, at once laconic, quick, and precise, for representing
the transmutations of thought, the interplay of perception

and reflection. Dealing with subjects complex in the same
way as those of Yeats's poem "Among School-Children"
and Valéry's "Cimetière Marin," Eliot has found for them
a different language. As May Sinclair has said of Eliot, his
"trick of cutting his corners and his curves makes him
seem obscure when he is clear as daylight. His thoughts
move very rapidly and by astounding cuts. They move not
by logical stages and majestic roundings of the full literary
curve, but as live thoughts move in live brains." Let us
examine, as an illustration, the lovely nightingale passage
from "The Waste Land." Eliot is describing a room in
London:

> "Above the antique mantel was displayed
> As though a window gave upon the sylvan scene
> The change of Philomel, by the barbarous king
> So rudely forced; yet there the nightingale
> Filled all the desert with inviolable voice
> And still she cried, and still the world pursues,
> 'Jug Jug' to dirty ears."

That is, the poet sees, above the mantel, a picture of Philomela changed to a nightingale, and it gives his mind a moment's swift release. The picture is like a window opening
upon Milton's earthly paradise—the "sylvan scene," as
Eliot explains in a note, is a phrase from "Paradise Lost"
—and the poet associates his own plight in the modern
city, in which some "infinitely gentle, infinitely suffering
thing," to quote one of Eliot's earlier poems, is somehow
being done to death, with Philomela, raped and mutilated
by Tereus. But in the earthly paradise, there had been a
nightingale singing: Philomela had wept her woes in

song, though the barbarous king had cut out her tongue
—her sweet voice had remained inviolable. And with a
sudden change of tense, the poet flashes back from the
myth to his present situation:

> "And still she *cried*, and still the world *pursues*,
> 'Jug Jug' to dirty ears."

The song of birds was represented in old English popular
poetry by such outlandish syllables as "Jug Jug"—so
Philomela's cry sounds to the vulgar. Eliot has here, in
seven lines of extraordinary liquidity and beauty, fused the
picture, the passage from Milton and the legend from
Ovid, into a single moment of vague poignant longing.

"The Waste Land" is dedicated to Ezra Pound, to
whom Eliot elsewhere acknowledges a debt; and he has
here evidently been influenced by Pound's "Cantos." "The
Waste Land," like the "Cantos," is fragmentary in form
and packed with literary quotation and allusion. In fact,
the passage just discussed above has a resemblance to a
passage on the same subject—the Philomela-Procne myth
—at the beginning of Pound's Fourth Canto. Eliot and
Pound have, in fact, founded a school of poetry which depends on literary quotation and reference to an unprecedented degree. Jules Laforgue had sometimes parodied, in
his poems, the great lines of other poets——

> "O Nature, donne-moi la force et le courage
> De me croire en âge" . . .

And Eliot had, in his early poetry, introduced phrases

from Shakespeare and Blake for purposes of ironic effect. He has always, furthermore, been addicted to prefacing his poems with quotations and echoing passages from other poets. But now, in "The Waste Land," he carries this tendency to what one must suppose its extreme possible limit: here, in a poem of only four hundred and three lines (to which are added, however, seven pages of notes), he manages to include quotations from, allusions to, or imitations of, at least thirty-five different writers (some of them, such as Shakespeare and Dante, laid under contribution several times)—as well as several popular songs; and to introduce passages in six foreign languages, including Sanskrit. And we must also take into consideration that the idea of the literary medley itself seems to have been borrowed from still another writer, Pound. We are always being dismayed, in our general reading, to discover that lines among those which we had believed to represent Eliot's residuum of original invention had been taken over or adapted from other writers (sometimes very unexpected ones: thus, it appears now, from Eliot's essay on Bishop Andrewes, that the first five lines of "The Journey of the Magi," as well as the "word within a word, unable to speak a word" of "Gerontion," had been salvaged from Andrewes's sermons; and the "stiff dishonoured shroud" of "Sweeney Among the Nightingales" seems to be an echo of the "dim dishonoured brow" of Whittier's poem about Daniel Webster). One would be inclined *a priori* to assume that all this load of erudition and literature would be enough to sink any writer, and that such a production as "The Waste Land" must be a work of second-hand inspiration. And it is true that, in reading Eliot and Pound, we are sometimes visited by uneasy recollections of Ausonius, in the fourth century, composing Greek-and-Latin macaronics and piecing together poetic mosaics out of verses from Virgil. Yet Eliot manages to be most effective precisely—in "The Waste Land"—where he might be expected to be least original—he succeeds in conveying his meaning, in communicating his emotion, in spite of all his learned or mysterious allusions, and whether we understand them or not.

In this respect, there is a curious contrast between Eliot and Ezra Pound. Pound's work *has* been partially sunk by its cargo of erudition, whereas Eliot, in ten years' time, has left upon English poetry a mark more unmistakable than that of any other poet writing English. It is, in fact, probably true at the present time that Eliot is being praised too extravagantly and Pound, though he has deeply influenced a few, on the whole unfairly neglected. I should explain Eliot's greater popularity by the fact that, for all his fragmentary method, he possesses a complete literary personality in a way that Pound, for all his integrity, does not. Ezra Pound, fine poet though he is, does not dominate us like a master imagination—he rather delights us like a miscellaneous collection of admirably chosen works of art. It is true that Pound, in spite of his inveterate translating, is a man of genuine originality—but his heterogeneous shorter poems, and the heterogeneous passages which go to make his longer ones, never seem to come together in a whole—as his general prose writing gives scrappy expression to a variety of ideas, a variety of enthusiasms and prejudices, some ridiculous and some valid, some learned and some half-baked, which, though valuable to his generation as polemic, as propaganda and as illuminating casual criticism, do not establish and develop a distinct reasoned point of view as Eliot's prose-writings do. T. S. Eliot has thought persistently and coherently about the relations between the different phases of human experience, and his passion for proportion and order is reflected in his poems. He is, in his way, a complete man, and if it is true, as I believe, that he has accomplished what he has credited Ezra Pound with accomplishing—if he has brought a new personal rhythm into the language—so that he has been able to lend even to the borrowed rhythms, the quoted words, of his great predecessors a new music and a new meaning—it is this intellectual completeness and soundness which has given his rhythm its special prestige.

Another factor which has probably contributed to Eliot's extraordinary success is the essentially dramatic character of his imagination. We may be puzzled by his continual preoccupation with the possibilities of a modern poetic drama—that is to say, of modern drama in verse. Why, we wonder, should he worry about drama in verse—why, after Ibsen, Hauptmann, Shaw and Chekov, should he be dissatisfied with plays in prose? We may put it down to an academic assumption that English drama ended when the blank verse of the Elizabethans ran into the sands, until it occurs to us that Eliot himself is really a dramatic poet.

Mr. Prufrock and Sweeney are characters as none of the personages of Pound, Valéry or Yeats is—they have become a part of our modern mythology. And most of the best of Eliot's poems are based on unexpected dramatic contrasts: "The Waste Land" especially, I am sure, owes a large part of its power to its dramatic quality, which makes it peculiarly effective read aloud. Eliot has even tried his hand at writing a play, and the two episodes from "Wanna Go Home, Baby" which he has published in *The Criterion* seem rather promising. They are written in a sort of jazz dramatic metre which suggests certain scenes of John Howard Lawson's "Processional"; and there can be no question that the future of drama in verse, if it has any future, lies in some such direction. "We cannot reinstate," Eliot has written, "either blank verse or the heroic couplet. The next form of drama will have to be a verse drama, but in new verse forms. Perhaps the conditions of modern life (think how large a part is now played in our sensory life by the internal combustion engine!) have altered our perception of rhythms. At any rate, the recognized forms of speech-verse are not as efficient as they should be; probably a new form will be devised out of colloquial speech."

In any case, that first handful of Eliot's poems, brought out in the middle of the War (1917) and generally read, if at all, at the time, as some sort of modern *vers de société,* was soon found, as Wyndham Lewis has said, to have had the effect of a little musk that scents up a whole room. And as for "The Waste Land," it enchanted and devas-

tated a whole generation. Attempts have been made to reproduce it—by Aldington, Nancy Cunard, etc.—at least a
dozen times. And as Eliot, lately out of Harvard, assumed
the rôle of the middle-aged Prufrock and to-day, at forty,
in one of his latest poems, "The Song of Simeon," speaks
in the character of an old man "with eighty years and no
to-morrow"—so "Gerontion" and "The Waste Land" have
made the young poets old before their time. In London, as
in New York, and in the universities both here and in
England, they for a time took to inhabiting exclusively
barren beaches, cactus-grown deserts, and dusty attics over-
run with rats—the only properties they allowed themselves to work with were a few fragments of old shattered
glass or a sparse sprinkling of broken bones. They had
purged themselves of Masefield as of Shelley for dry
tongues and rheumatic joints. The dry breath of the
Waste Land now blighted the most amiable country land-
scapes; and the sound of jazz, which had formerly seemed
jolly, now inspired only horror and despair. But in this
case, we may forgive the young for growing prematurely
decrepit: where some of even the finest intelligences of the
elder generation read "The Waste Land" with blankness
or laughter, the young had recognized a poet.

III

As a critic, Eliot occupies to-day a position of distinction
and influence equal in importance to his position as a poet.
His writings have been comparatively brief and rare—he

has published only four small books of criticism—yet he has probably affected literary opinion, during the period since the War, more profoundly than any other critic writing English. Eliot's prose style has a kind of felicity different from that of his poetic style; it is almost primly precise and sober, yet with a sort of sensitive charm in its austerity —closely reasoned and making its points with the fewest possible words, yet always even, effortless and lucid. In a reaction against the impressionistic criticism which flourished at the end of the century and which has survived into our own time—the sort of criticism which, in dealing with poetry, attempts to reproduce its effect by having recourse to poetic prose—T. S. Eliot has undertaken a kind of scientific study of æsthetic values: avoiding impressionistic rhetoric and *a priori* æsthetic theories alike, he compares works of literature coolly and tries to distinguish between different orders of artistic effects and the different degrees of satisfaction to be derived from them.

And by this method, Eliot has done more than perhaps any other modern critic to effect a revaluation of English literature. We sometimes follow his literary criticism with the same sort of eagerness and excitement with which we follow a philosophical inquiry. Professor Saintsbury has played in literature much the same sort of rôle that he has played as a connoisseur of wines, that of an agreeable and entertaining guide of excellent taste and enormous experience; Edmund Gosse, often intelligent and courageous in dealing with French or Scandinavian writers, could never quite, when it came to English literature, bring himself to drop his official character of Librarian of the House of Lords—his attitude was always a little that of the Beef Eater in the Tower of London, who assumes the transcendent value of the Crown Jewels which he has been set to guard and does not presume to form a personal opinion as to their taste or their respective merits; and the moral passion of Paul Elmer More has ended by paralyzing his æsthetic appreciation. But T. S. Eliot, with an infinitely sensitive apparatus for æsthetic appreciation, approaching English literature as an American, with an American's peculiar combination of avidity and detachment and with more than the ordinary English critic's reading in the literatures, ancient and modern, of the Continent, has been able to succeed as few writers have done in the excessively delicate task of estimating English, Irish and American writers in relation to one another, and writers in English in relation to writers on the Continent. The extent of Eliot's influence is amazing: these short essays, sent out without publicity as mere scattered notes on literature, yet sped with so intense a seriousness and weighted with so wide a learning, have not only had the effect of discrediting the academic clichés of the text-books, but are even by way of establishing in the minds of the generation now in college a new set of literary clichés. With the ascendancy of T. S. Eliot, the Elizabethan dramatists have come back into fashion, and the nineteenth-century poets gone out. Milton's poetic reputation has sunk, and Dryden's and Pope's have risen. It is as much as one's life is worth nowadays, among young people, to say an approving word for Shelley or a dubious one about Donne. And as for the enthusiasm for Dante—to paraphrase the man in Hemingway's novel, there's been nothing like it since the Fratellinis!

Eliot's rôle as a literary critic has been very similar to Valéry's in France: indeed, the ideas of the two men and their ways of stating them have corresponded so closely that one guesses they must influence each other a good deal. Like Valéry, Eliot believes that a work of art is not an oracular outpouring, but an object which has been constructed deliberately with the aim of producing a certain effect. He has brought back to English criticism something of that trenchant rationalism which he admires in the eighteenth century, but with a much more catholic appreciation of different styles and points of view than the eighteenth century allowed. The Romantics, of course, fare badly before this criticism. Vague sentiment vaguely expressed, rhetorical effusion disguising bad art—these Eliot's laconic scorn has nipped. For him, Byron is "a disorderly mind, and an uninteresting one": Keats and Shelley "not nearly such great poets as they are supposed to be"; whereas the powers of Dryden are "wider, but no greater than those of Milton." Just as Valéry lately protested in a lecture that he was unable to understand the well known lines of Alfred de Musset:

> "Les plus désespérés sont les chants les plus beaux,
> Et j'en sais d'immortels qui sont de purs sanglots."

so Eliot, in an essay on Crashaw, has confessed, with a certain superciliousness, his inability to understand the following stanza from Shelley's "Skylark":

> "Keen as are the arrows
> Of that silver sphere
> Whose intense lamp narrows
> In the white dawn clear,
> Until we hardly see, who feel that it is there."

"For the first time, perhaps," says Eliot, "in verse of such eminence, sound exists without sense."

It will be seen that Eliot differs from Valéry in believing that poetry should make "sense." And he elsewhere, in his essay on Dante in "The Sacred Wood," remonstrates with Valéry for asserting that philosophy has no place in poetry. Yet Eliot's point of view, though more intelligently reasoned and expressed, comes down finally to the same sort of thing as Valéry's and seems to me open to the same sort of objection. Eliot's conclusion in respect to the relation of philosophy to poetry is that, though philosophy *has* its place in poetry, it is only as something which we "see" among the other things with which the poet presents us, a set of ideas which penetrate his world, as in the case of the "Divina Commedia": in the case of such a poet as Lucretius, the philosophy sometimes seems antagonistic to the poetry only because it happens to be a philosophy "not rich enough in feeling . . . incapable of complete expansion into pure vision." Furthermore, "the original form of philosophy cannot be poetic": the poet must use a philosophy already invented by somebody else. Now, though we may admire the justice of Eliot's judgments on the various degrees of artistic success achieved by Dante, Lucretius and others, it becomes plainer and plainer, as time goes on, that the real effect of Eliot's, as of Valéry's, literary criticism, is to impose upon us a conception of poetry as some sort of pure and rare æsthetic essence with no relation to any of the practical human uses for which, for some reason never explained, only the technique of prose is appropriate.

Now this point of view, as I have already suggested in writing about Paul Valéry, seems to me absolutely unhistorical—an impossible attempt to make æsthetic values independent of all the other values. Who will agree with Eliot, for example, that a poet cannot be an original thinker and that it is not possible for a poet to be a completely successful artist and yet persuade us to accept his ideas at the same time? There is a good deal in Dante's morality which he never got out of the Scholastics, as, for all we know, there may be a good deal in Lucretius which he never got out of Epicurus. When we read Lucretius and Dante, we are affected by them just as we are by prose writers of eloquence and imagination—we are compelled to take their opinions seriously. And as soon as we admit that prose writing may be considered on the same basis with verse, it becomes evident that we cannot, in the case of Plato, discriminate so finely as to the capacity of his philosophy for being "expanded into pure vision" that we are able to put our finger on the point where the novelist or poet stops and the scientist or metaphysician begins; nor, with Blake any more than with Nietzsche and Emerson, distinguish the poet from the aphorist. The truth is, of course, that, in Lucretius' time, verse was used for all sorts of didactic purposes for which we no longer consider it appropriate—they had agricultural poems, astronomical poems, poems of literary criticism. How can the "Georgics," the "Ars Poetica" and Manilius be dealt with from the point of view of the capacity of their material for being "expanded into pure vision"? To modern readers, the subjects of the "Georgics"—bee-keeping, stock-raising, and so forth—seem unsuitable and sometimes annoying in verse; yet for Virgil's contemporaries, the poem must have been completely successful—as, indeed, granted the subject, it is. Nor does it follow that, because we are coming to use poetry for fewer and fewer literary purposes, our critical taste is becoming more and more refined, so that we are beginning to perceive for the first time the true, pure and exalted function of poetry: that is, simply, as Valéry says, to produce a "state"—as Eliot says, to afford a "superior amusement." It is much more likely that for some reason or other, verse as a technique of literary expression is being abandoned by humanity altogether—perhaps because it is a more primitive, and hence a more barbarous technique than prose. Is it possible to believe, for example, that Eliot's hope of having verse reinstated on the stage—even verse of the new kind which he proposes—is likely ever to be realized?

The tendency to keep verse isolated from prose and to confine it to certain highly specialized functions dates in English at least from the time of Coleridge, when, in spite of the long narrative poems which were fashionable, verse was already beginning to fall into disuse. Coleridge defined a poem as "that species of composition which is opposed to works of science by proposing for its *immediate* object pleasure, not truth; and from all other species (having *this* object in common with it), it is discriminated by proposing to itself such delight from the *whole,* as is compatible with a distinct gratification from each component part." Poe, who had doubtless read Coleridge on the subject, wrote thirty years later that there was no such thing as a long poem, that "no very long poem would ever be popular again," etc. Eliot and Valéry follow Coleridge and Poe in their theory as well as in their verse, and they seem to me to confuse certain questions by talking as if the whole of literature existed simultaneously in a vacuum, as if Homer's and Shakespeare's situations had been the same as Mallarmé's and Laforgue's, as if the latter had been attempting to play the same sort of rôles as the former and could be judged on the same basis. It is inevitable, of course, that we should try to arrive at absolute values through the comparison of the work of different periods—I have just praised Eliot for his success at this—but it seems to me that in this particular matter a good many difficulties would be cleared up if certain literary discussions could be removed from the artificially restricted field of verse—in which it is assumed that nothing is possible or desirable but a quintessential distillation called "poetry," and that that distillation has nothing in common with anything possible to obtain through prose—to the field of literature in general. Has not such a great modern novel as "Madame Bovary," for example, at least as much in common with Virgil and Dante as with Balzac and Dickens? Is it not comparable from the point of view of intensity, music and perfection of the parts, with the best verse of any period? And we shall consider Joyce in this connection later.

With all gratitude, therefore, for the salutary effect of Eliot's earlier criticism in curbing the carelessness and gush of the aftermath of Romanticism, it seems plain that the anti-Romantic reaction is leading finally into pedantry and into a futile æstheticism. "Poetry," Eliot wrote in "The Sacred Wood," "is not a turning loose of emotion, but an escape from emotion; it is not the expression of personality, but an escape from personality. But, of course, only those who have personality and emotion know what it means to want to escape from them." This was valid, and even noble, in 1920 when "The Sacred Wood" was published; but to-day, after ten years of depersonalized and over-intellectualized verse, so much of it written in imitation of Eliot, the same sort of thing in the mouths of Eliot's disciples sounds like an excuse for *not* possessing emotion and personality.

Yet, in spite of the weaknesses of Eliot's position as he has sometimes been driven to state it dogmatically, he has himself largely succeeded in escaping the vices which it seems to encourage. The old nineteenth century criticism of Ruskin, Renan, Taine, Sainte-Beuve, was closely allied to history and novel writing, and was also the vehicle for all sorts of ideas about the purpose and destiny of human life in general. The criticism of our own day examines literature, art, ideas and specimens of human society in the past with a detached scientific interest or a detached æsthetic appreciation which seems in either case to lead nowhere. A critic like Herbert Read makes dull discriminations between different kinds of literature; a critic like Albert Thibaudet discovers dull resemblances between the ideas of philosophers and poets; a critic like I. A. Richards writes about poetry from the point of view of a scientist studying the psychological reactions of readers; and such a critic as Clive Bell writes about painting so exclusively and cloyingly from the point of view of the varying degrees of pleasure to be derived from the pictures of different painters that we would willingly have Ruskin and all his sermonizing back. And even Virginia Woolf and Lytton Strachey have this in common with Clive Bell that they seem to feel they have done enough when they have distinguished the kind of pleasure to be derived from one kind of book, the kind of interest to be felt in one kind of personality, from the kind to be found in another. One is supposed to have read everything and enjoyed everything and to understand exactly the reasons for one's enjoyment, but not to enjoy anything excessively nor to raise an issue of one kind of thing against another. Each of the essays of Strachey or Mrs. Woolf, so compact yet so beautifully rounded out, is completely self-contained and does not lead to anything beyond itself; and finally, for all their brilliance, we begin to find them tiresome.

Now there is a good deal in T. S. Eliot of this pedantry
and sterility of his age. He is very much given, for example, to becoming involved in literary Houses-that-Jack-
Built: "We find this quality occasionally in Wordsworth,"
he will write, "but it is a quality which Wordsworth
shares with Shenstone rather than with Collins and Gray.
And for the right sort of enjoyment of Shenstone, we
must read his prose as well as his verse. The 'Essays on
Men and Manners' are in the tradition of the great French
aphorists of the seventeenth century, and should be read
with the full sense of their relation to Vauvenargues, La
Rochefoucauld and (with his wider range) La Bruyère.
We shall do well to read enough of Theophrastus to understand the kind of effect at which La Bruyère aimed.
(Professor Somebody-or-other's book on 'Theophrastus
and the Peripatetics' gives us the clew to the intellectual
atmosphere in which Theophrastus wrote and enables
us to gauge the influences on his work—very different
from each other—of Plato and Aristotle.)" At this rate
(though I have parodied Eliot), we should have to read
the whole of literature in order to appreciate a single book,
and Eliot fails to supply us with a reason why we should
go to the trouble of doing so. Yet against the background
of the criticism of his time, Eliot has stood out unmistakably as a man passionately interested in literature. The
real intensity of his enthusiasm makes us forget the prim-
ness of his tone; and his occasional dogmatism is redeemed
by his ability to see beyond his own ideas, his willingness
to admit the relative character of his conclusions.

IV

But if Eliot, in spite of the meagreness of his production, has become for his generation a leader, it is also because his career has been a progress, because he has evidently been on his way somewhere, when many of his contemporaries, more prolific and equally gifted, have been fixed in their hedonism or despair. The poet of "The Waste Land" was too serious to continue with the same complacence as some of his contemporaries inhabiting that godforsaken desert. It was certain he would not stick at that point, and one watched him to see what he would do.

This destination has now, however, become plain. In the preface to the new 1928 edition of "The Sacred Wood," poetry is still regarded as a "superior amusement," but Eliot reports on his part "an expansion or development of interests." Poetry is now perceived to have "something to do with morals, and with religion, and even with politics perhaps, though we cannot say what." In "For Lancelot Andrewes," published in the same year, Eliot declares himself a classicist in literature, an Anglo-Catholic in religion and a royalist in politics, and announces that he has in preparation "three small books" treating of these subjects and to be called respectively "The School of Donne," "The Principles of Modern Heresy," and "The Outline of Royalism." There follows a slender selection of essays, which hint quietly at what may be expected.

We must await the further exposition of Eliot's new

body of doctrine before it will be possible to discuss it properly. In the meantime, we can only applaud his desire to formulate a consistent central position, at the same time that we may regret the unpromising character of the ideals and institutions which he invokes. One cannot but recognize in Eliot's recent writings a kind of reactionary point of view which had already been becoming fashionable among certain sorts of literary people—a point of view which has much in common with that of the neo-Thomists in France and that of the Humanists in America. "Unless by civilization," writes Eliot, "you mean material progress, cleanliness, etc. . . . if you mean a spiritual co-ordination on a high level, then it is doubtful whether civilization can endure without religion, and religion without a church." Yet you can hardly have an effective church without a cult of Christ as the son of God; and you cannot have such a cult without more willingness to accept the supernatural than most of us to-day are able to muster. We feel in contemporary writers like Eliot a desire to believe in religious revelation, a belief that it would be a good thing to believe, rather than a genuine belief. The faith of the modern convert seems to burn only with a low blue flame. "Our literature," Eliot has himself recently made a character in a dialogue say, "is a substitute for religion, and so is our religion." From such a faith, uninspired by hope, unequipped with zeal or force, what guidance for the future can we expect?

One cannot, however, doubt the reality of the experience to which Eliot testifies in his recent writings—though it seems to us less an Anglo-Catholic conversion than a reawakening of the New Englander's conscience, of the never quite exorcised conviction of the ineradicable sinfulness of man. Eliot admires Machiavelli because Machiavelli assumes the baseness of human nature as an unalterable fact; and he looks for light to the theologians who offer salvation, not through economic readjustment, political reform, education or biological and psychological study, but solely through "grace." Eliot apparently to-day regards "Evil" as some sort of ultimate reality, which it is impossible either to correct or to analyze. His moral principles seem to me stronger and more authentic than his religious mysticism—and his relation to the Anglo-Catholic Church appears largely artificial. The English seventeenth century divines whose poetry and sermons he admires so much, upon whom he seems so much to depend for nourishment, exist in a richer, a more mysterious, a more heavily saturated atmosphere, in which even monumental outlines are blurred; Eliot himself is stiffer and cooler, more intent, more relentless, more clear. He has his own sort of graciousness, but he seems, as the phrase is, a little thin-lipped. His religious tradition has reached him by way of Boston.

In any case, Eliot's new phase of piety has brought with it a new humility. He apologizes in his 1928 preface for the "assumption of pontifical solemnity" which he now detects in "The Sacred Wood," and his recent little book on Dante (a most admirable introduction) not merely surprises but almost embarrasses us by the modesty with which Eliot professes to desire nothing but to be of use to beginners and to tell us of a few of the beautiful things which he has found in the great poet. I will not say that this humility has enfeebled his poetry. The three devout little poems which he has published as Christmas cards since "The Hollow Men" announced the nadir of the phase of sterility and despair given such effective expression in "The Waste Land," seem comparatively uninspired; but the long poem or group of poems, "Ash-Wednesday" (1930), which follows a scheme somewhat similar to that of "The Waste Land," is a not unworthy successor to it.

The poet begins with the confession of his bankruptcy:

> "Because I do not hope to turn again
> Because I do not hope
> Because I do not hope to turn
> Desiring this man's gift and that man's scope
> I no longer strive to strive towards such things
> (Why should the agèd eagle stretch its wings?)
> Why should I mourn
> The vanished power of the usual reign? . . .
>
> Because these wings are no longer wings to fly
> But merely vans to beat the air
> The air which is now thoroughly small and dry
> Smaller and dryer than the will
> Teach us to care and not to care
> Teach us to sit still.
>
> Pray for us sinners now and at the hour of our death
> Pray for us now and at the hour of our death."

There follow passages in which the prayer is apparently answered: the poet's contrition and pious resignation are

128

rewarded by a series of visions which first console then lighten his heart. We find an imagery new for Eliot, a symbolism semi-ecclesiastical and not without a Pre-Raphaelite flavor: white leopards, a Lady gowned in white, junipers and yews, "The Rose" and "The Garden," and jewelled unicorns drawing a gilded hearse: these are varied by an interlude which returns to the imagery and mood of "The Waste Land," and a swirling churning anguished passage which suggests certain things of Gertrude Stein's. At last the themes of the first section recur: the impotent wings of the agèd eagle seem to revive, as,

> "From the wide window toward the granite shore
> The white sails still fly seaward, seaward flying
> Unbroken wings.
> And the lost heart stiffens and rejoices
> In the lost lilac and the lost sea voices
> And the weak spirit quickens to rebel
> For the bent golden-rod and the lost sea smell
> Quickens to recover
> The cry of quail and the whirling plover
> And the blind eye creates
> The empty forms between the ivory gates
> And smell renews the salt savour of the sandy earth . . ."

The broken prayer, at once childlike and mystically subtle, with which the poem ends seems to imply that the poet has come closer to the strength and revelation he craves: grace is about to descend.

"Blessèd sister, holy mother, spirit of the fountain, spirit of the
    garden,
Suffer us not to mock ourselves with falsehood

Teach us to care and not to care
Teach us to sit still
Even among these rocks,
Our peace in His will
And even among these rocks
Sister, mother
And spirit of the river, spirit of the sea,
Suffer me not to be separated

And let my cry come unto Thee."

The literary and conventional imagery upon which "Ash-Wednesday" so largely relies and which is less vivid because more artificial than that of Eliot's earlier poems, seems to me a definite feature of inferiority; the "devil of the stairs" and the "shape twisted on the banister," which are in Eliot's familiar and unmistakable personal vein, somehow come off better than the jewelled unicorn, which incongruously suggests Yeats. And I am made a little tired at hearing Eliot, only in his early forties, present himself as an "agèd eagle" who asks why he should make the effort to stretch his wings. Yet "Ash-Wednesday," though less brilliant and intense than Eliot at his very best, is distinguished by most of the qualities which made his other poems remarkable: the exquisite phrasing in which we feel that every word is in its place and that there is not a word too much; the metrical mastery which catches so naturally, yet with so true a modulation, the faltering accents of the supplicant, blending the cadences of the liturgy with those of perplexed brooding thought; and, above all, that "peculiar honesty" in "exhibiting the essential sickness or strength of the human soul" of which Eliot has written in connection with Blake and which, in his own case, even at the moment when his psychological plight seems most depressing and his ways of rescuing himself from it least sympathetic, still gives him a place among those upon whose words we reflect with most interest and whose tones we remember longest.

V

MARCEL PROUST

MARCEL PROUST is the first important novelist to apply the principles of Symbolism to fiction. Proust had assimilated a great variety of writers from Ruskin to Dostoevsky, and he had acquired a remarkable technical virtuosity; but, born in 1871, he had been young in the eighties and nineties, when Symbolism was in the air, and the peculiar methods and form of his great novel certainly owed much to Symbolist theory. I have said that the influence on the Symbolists of Wagner was as considerable as that of any writer of books, and it is significant of Proust's conception of his art that he should have been in the habit of speaking of his "themes." His enormous novel, "A la Recherche du Temps Perdu," is, in fact, a symphonic structure rather than a narrative in the ordinary sense. The shifting images of the Symbolist poet, with their "multiplied associations," are here characters, situations, places, vivid moments, obsessive emotions, recurrent patterns of behavior.

The book begins with an overture: we must note and remember the opening chords. *"Longtemps, je me suis couché de bonne heure,"* is the first sentence of "A la Recherche du Temps Perdu," and it is followed by a second sentence in which the word *"temps"* is twice heard. We are in the vague world of sleep: the narrator, shut away in his darkened room, has lost all sense of external reality, all consciousness even of the room itself. He fancies himself in other places where, in the course of his life, he has slept: a child at his grandfather's in the country; a visitor in a country house; at a seaside hotel in summer; in winter in a military town where the young Frenchmen serve their term in barracks; in the midst of Paris; in Venice. "Ah, I've fallen asleep at last, even though Mother never came to say good-night!" This is the first theme to be developed: we find ourselves in the grandfather's house. M. Swann is coming to dinner, and the boy's father sends him to bed without his mother's goodnight kiss. The child is sensitive and nervous: he cannot sleep till he has seen his mother. He sends her a note by the maid, but she refuses to answer it. The child is in anguish. He lies awake for hours, till he hears the doorbell ring and knows that M. Swann has left. Then he goes out into the hallway and throws himself upon his mother, as she is coming up to bed. She is angry at first: she and his grandmother, who are already aware of his tendency toward morbid sensibility, have adopted with him a policy of firmness. But the father takes pity on him and induces the mother to go in and comfort him. She reads him to sleep with a novel of George Sand's and spends the night in his room.

Thereafter we are introduced to a variety of personages associated with Combray, the small provincial town where the boy's grandfather lives: a hypochondriac aunt who refuses to stir from her bed; a provincial snob who longs to know the great people of the countryside, the Guermantes; an unhappy old music teacher, whom everybody pities because his daughter has disgraced him. M. Swann has married beneath him and comes with his wife and daughter to stay at his estate outside the town. The memories of boyhood are suddenly dropped and Proust tells us at length about Swann's marriage: though rich and in smart society, he has fallen in love, rather late in life, with a stupid *cocotte* who has begun by driving him mad with jealousy. When "Du Côté de chez Swann" first appeared, even those who recognized its genius were worried by its apparent lack of direction. To-day, we can admire the ingenuity with which Proust, in these first pages of his book, has succeeded in introducing nearly every important character. And not merely every strand of his plot, but also every philosophic theme. We are able here to note already one feature which all his characters have in common. All alike are suffering from some form of unsatisfied longing or disappointed hope: all are sick with some form of the ideal. Legrandin wants to know the Guermantes; Vinteuil is wounded in his love for his daughter; Swann, associating the beauty of Odette with that of the women of Botticelli, ridiculously and tragically identifies his passion for her with his neglected æsthetic interests. At the end of the history of Swann, we are back in the narrator's boyhood: he has himself conceived a romantic admiration for the beautiful Mme. Swann and he makes a practice of waiting to see her pass in one of the alleys of the Bois de Boulogne. This very November, he concludes—it is the end of the first movement of the symphony—he has happened to walk again in the Bois: the trees were brilliant with autumn; he describes the cold beauty of the day; but it is entirely a different beauty from the beauty which intoxicated him in youth. "The reality which I had known existed now no longer. Because Mme. Swann did not arrive at the same time as when I was young and looking as she had looked when I used to see her, the Avenue seemed quite different. The places which we have known do not belong to the world of space, where we locate them for convenience. They were only a narrow slice among the other contiguous impressions which made up our life of that time: the memory of a certain image is only the regret of a certain instant; and the houses, the roads and the avenues are fugitive, alas! like the years."

Proust had at one time had the idea of dividing his novel into three parts and calling them respectively: "The Age of Names," "The Age of Words" and "The Age of Things." We are now in the Age of Names: we see everything—love, art and the great—through the imagination of boyhood. "A l'Ombre des Jeunes Filles en Fleur" is, as it were, one long adolescent revery. It contains only one conspicuous episode. The boy makes the acquaintance of Swann's daughter, a little girl with whom he goes to play in the afternoons in the Champs-Elysées, and falls desperately in love with her. But the hysterical over-eagerness, the undisciplined need to lean excessively on other people, of the spoiled child that he has become, now that his parents have already begun to treat him like an invalid who must be humored and indulged, end by exasperating the little girl and making her indifferent to him. She snubs him one day, and he is still able to muster enough strength of will to satisfy his wounded pride by breaking off with her: he betrays his weakness, however, by carrying his policy to the extreme of refusing ever to see her again.

As I have said, we have been submerged through these volumes—and for most tastes, have been submerged far too long—in the reveries of adolescence. But people who have stuck in the "Jeunes Filles en Fleur" and thus know only the subjective Proust must acquire a false idea of what his genius is like. We are now to be violently thrown forward into the life of the world outside. The contrast between, on the one hand, the dreams, the broodings and the repinings of the neurasthenic hero, as we get them for such long stretches, and, on the other, the rich and lively social scenes, dramatized by so powerful an imagination, is one of the most curious features of the book. These latter scenes, indeed, contain so much broad humor and so much extravagant satire that, appearing in a modern French novel, they amaze us. Proust, however, was much addicted to English literature: "It is strange," he writes in a letter, "that, in the most widely different departments, from George Eliot to Hardy, from Stevenson to Emerson, there should be no other literature which exercises over me so powerful an influence as English and American." In the descriptive parts of the early volumes, we have recognized the rhythms of Ruskin; and in the social scenes which now engage us, though Proust has been compared to Henry James, who was deficient in precisely those gifts of vividness and humor which Proust, to such an astonishing degree, possessed, we shall look in vain for anything like them outside the novels of Dickens. We have already been struck, in "Du Côté de chez Swann," with the singular relief into which the characters were thrown as soon as they began to speak or act. And it seems plain that Proust must have read Dickens and that this sometimes grotesque heightening of character had been partly learned from him. Proust, like Dickens, was a remarkable mimic: as Dickens enchanted his audiences by dramatic readings from his novels, so, we are told, Proust was celebrated for impersonations of his friends; and both, in their books, carried the practice of caricaturing habits of speech and of inventing things for their personages to say which are outrageous without ever ceasing to be lifelike to a point where it becomes impossible to compare them to anybody but each other. As, furthermore, it has been said of Dickens that his villains are so amusing—in their fashion, so enthusiastically alive—that we are reluctant to see the last of them, so we acquire a curious affection for even the most objectionable characters in Proust: Morel, for example, is certainly one of the most odious characters in fiction, yet we are never really made to hate him or to wish that we did not have to hear about him, and we feel a genuine regret when Mme. Verdurin, with her false teeth and her monocle, finally van-

ishes from our sight. This generous sympathy and understanding for even the monstrosities which humanity produces, and Proust's capacity for galvanizing these monstrosities into energetic life, are at the bottom of the extraordinary success of the tragi-comic hero of Proust's
Sodom, M. de Charlus. But Charlus surpasses Dickens
and, as has been said, is almost comparable to Falstaff. In
a letter in which Proust explains that he has borrowed certain traits of Charlus from a real person, he adds that the
character in the book is, however, intended to be "much
bigger," to "contain much more of humanity"; and it is
one of the strange paradoxes of Proust's genius that he
should have been able to create in a character so special
a figure of heroic proportions.

Nor is it only in these respects that Proust reminds us
of Dickens. Proust's incidents, as well as his characters,
sometimes have a comic violence almost unprecedented
in French: Mme. Verdurin dislocating her jaw through
laughing at one of Cottard's jokes, the furious smashing
by the narrator of Charlus's hat and the latter's calm
substitution of another hat in its place, are strokes which
no one but Dickens would have dared. This heightening
in Dickens is theatrical; and we sometimes—though considerably less often—get the same impression in Proust
that we are watching a look or a gesture deliberately un-
derlined on the stage—so that Charlus's first encounter
with the narrator, when the former looks at his watch and
makes "the gesture of annoyance with which one aims to
create the impression that one is tired of waiting, but

which one never makes when one is actually waiting," and Bloch's farewell to Mme. de Villeparisis, when she attempts to snub him by closing her eyes, seem to take place in the same world as Lady Dedlock's swift second glance at the legal papers in her lover's handwriting and Mr. Merdle's profound stare into his hat "as if it were some twenty feet deep," when he has come to borrow the penknife with which he is to open his veins.—And there even seems distinguishable in the Verdurin circle an unconscious reminiscence of the Veneerings of "Our Mutual Friend": note especially the similarity between the rôles played by Twemlow in the latter and in the former by Saniette.

To return, however, the structure of the novel begins at this point to appear. Proust has made of these social episodes (often several hundred pages long) enormous solid blocks, cemented by, or rather embedded in, a dense medium of introspective revery and commentary mingled with incidents treated dramatically on a smaller scale. Proust's handling of these complex social scenes is masterly: it is only in the intermediate sections that we feel he has blurred his effects by allowing the outline of the action to become obscured by the profusion of the hero's reflections on it. We also become aware that these main scenes follow a regular progression. In the early "flashback" to the story of Swann's marriage which has been described above, we have already assisted at two social scenes on something less than the full scale. First of all, Swann has gone to dinner at the Verdurins', at whose house he first

knows Odette: the Verdurins are outside society altogether and pretend to think smart people "tiresome."
They are self-assertive and ill-bred bourgeois, who, however, have a furious appetite for entertaining and patronizing artists, and other persons whom they consider clever.
Later on, we see Swann at an evening party given by a
Mme. de Saint-Euverte: a few smart people go to Mme. de
Saint-Euverte's, but they do so with a clear consciousness
of being kind to her. In the part of the book at which we
have now arrived, the part which is predominantly social,
the narrator first attends an afternoon reception at the
house of Mme. de Villeparisis, an aunt of the Guermantes,
who, though still on good terms with her family, has
none the less become rather *déclassée* by reason of a scandalous past, but who is a rung above Mme. de Saint-
Euverte, as Mme. de Saint-Euverte is a rung above Mme.
Verdurin; then, a dinner at the house of the Duchesse de
Guermantes, who, though one of the smartest hostesses in
Paris, occupies not quite the most exalted rank; and finally
an evening reception held by the Prince and Princesse de
Guermantes, representatives of German royal families and
not merely of the purest blood, but of the most inviolable
correctitude and dignity. In the latter part of the book,
we shall assist at three more of these scenes: in the first
two, we return to the Verdurins, into whose salon the people from the upper strata have now, for one reason or
another—the bourgeoisie is absorbing the old nobility—
begun to filter down; and in the last, which occurs in the
last chapter, we return to the top again, a matinée at the

Prince de Guermantes's, where we encounter, not only Legrandin and the Saint-Euvertes, but also Odette and Morel, the son of the narrator's uncle's valet, and where the new Princesse de Guermantes turns out to be none other than Mme. Verdurin, whom the Prince, ruined by the defeat of Germany, has married for her money.

In the meantime, to return again to the section we have been discussing ("Le Côté de Guermantes" and the first part of "Sodome et Gomorrhe"), which is principally concerned with the "world" and with worldly people, we here begin also to understand for the first time the author's moral attitude. We find that each of these three major social episodes follows more or less the same formula and points the same moral. The first, the narrator's début at Mme. de Villeparisis's, is contrasted immediately with the death of the grandmother, which serves entirely to discredit the values of the snobs with whom the hero has been consorting. The grandmother, who has been ill for some time, takes the boy for a walk in the Champs-Elysées and goes to the public toilet. During her absence, the boy overhears the woman who tends the toilet talking to the keeper of the grounds: "I choose my clients," she explains, "I don't receive everybody in what I call my salons!" The grandmother returns: she too has overheard the conversation: "It sounded exactly like the Guermantes and the Verdurins," she says, as they walk away; and she quotes, as is her habit, from Mme. de Sévigné. But she keeps her head turned in order to conceal from the boy that she has just had a paralytic stroke. In a flash, by making us feel in this scene the goodness and pathos of the grandmother, for whom any sort of meanness or malice, for whom any wordliness or snobbery, is impossible, Proust has swept down the whole web of social relations which he has just been at such pains to spin. The next episode, the dinner at the Duchesse de Guermantes's, is followed by Swann's going to call on the Duc and Duchesse just as they are leaving for a costume ball. Swann, with one of those lapses of taste which we have been told are characteristic of him, clumsily discloses the fact that he has just been warned by the doctors that he is dying. But the Guermantes are made to behave with cruelty as well as tactlessness, for they are so much preoccupied with getting to the ball, they take their social activities so much more seriously than anything else, that they cannot even attempt to think of anything human to say to a man who is an old friend of both and whom the Duchesse, at least, admires. In the third episode, Swann appears at the reception of the Prince de Guermantes during the bitterest period of the Dreyfus case: Swann is a Jew and has sided with the Dreyfusards; and he is not so well received as formerly. The Prince takes him aside, and the guests murmur that he has been asked to leave. But so far from this having been the case, we learn at the end of the evening, the Prince, whom Proust, with his masterly skill at what the conjurors call "false direction," has allowed us to suppose not only stiff but stupid, is, with his aristocratic sense of responsibility and his Teutonic seriousness of mind, the only person present who has tried to form a just opinion: he has come to the conclusion that Dreyfus is probably innocent and has merely wanted to discuss it with Swann. (In the latter part of the novel, this formula is twice repeated: first, when the narrator dines with the Verdurins in the country and, returning to his hotel, hears the elevator-boy tell with pride how his sister, who is kept by a rich man, excrementally exhibits her scorn of the servant class from which she has risen; and finally when, in the midst of the second reception at the Princesse de Guermantes's—where the Princess is now the former Mme. Verdurin—we are shown the daughter and son-in-law of the great tragic actress "La Berma," who has shortened her life by returning to the stage in order to finance their social career, deserting their mother in her illness to go to the Guermantes's matinée, to which they have not even been asked.)

In each of these cases, Proust has destroyed, and destroyed with ferocity, the social hierarchy he has just been expounding. Its values, he tells us, are an imposture: pretending to honor and distinction, it accepts all that is vulgar and base; its pride is nothing nobler than the instinct which it shares with the woman who keeps the toilet and the elevator boy's sister, to spit upon the person whom we happen to have at a disadvantage. And whatever the social world may say to the contrary, it either ignores or seeks to kill those few impulses toward justice and beauty which make men admirable. It seems strange that so many critics should have found Proust's novel "unmoral"; the truth is that he was preoccupied with morality to the extent of tending to deal in melodrama. Proust was himself (on his mother's side) half-Jewish; and for all his Parisian sophistication, there remains in him much of the capacity for apocalyptic moral indignation of the classical Jewish prophet. That tone of lamentation and complaint which resounds through his whole book, which, indeed, he scarcely ever drops save for the animated humor of the social scenes, themselves in their implications so bitter, is really very un-French and rather akin to Jewish literature. The French novelist of the line of Stendhal and Flaubert and Anatole France, with whom otherwise Proust has so much in common, differs fundamentally from Proust in this: the sad or cynical view of mankind with which these former begin, which is implicit in their first page, has been arrived at by Proust only at the cost of much pain and protest, and this ordeal is one of the subjects of his book: Proust has never, like these others, been reconciled to disillusionment. This fact is clearly one of the causes of that method which we find so novel and so fascinating of making his characters undergo a succession of transformations: humanity is only gradually revealed to us in its selfishness, its weakness and its inconsistency. Anatole France would probably, for example, have put before us the whole of Odette de Crécy in a single brief description—a few facts exactly noted and two adjectives which, contradicting each other, would have pricked us with the contradiction of her stupidity and her beauty; Stendhal would have stripped her of romance in the first sentence in which he recorded the simplest of her acts. But with Proust, we are

what he calls his "demonstration." We have now become aware that the characters of "A la Recherche du Temps Perdu" all illustrate general principles and that they have been carefully selected by Proust to cover the whole of the world that he knows: Odette is all that is stupid in woman which, at the same time, arouses men's passions and enchants their dreams; Charlus, the struggle in one soul between the masculine and feminine, and beyond that, the cruel paradox of a fine mind and a sensitive nature at the mercy of instincts which humiliate them; Mme. de Guermantes, the best that a snob can hope to be without becoming a serious person, etc., etc. These colossal figures, without losing individuality—we hear the very sound of their voices—take on universal significance.

For it is only the presentation, and not the development, of Proust's characters which is discontinuous. They are designed, in Proust's own language, to illustrate certain laws; and though they appear to us in a succession of different aspects, as they are seen at different times and different places and by different observers, their behavior, their personalities, have a compelling logic. Proust's method of presenting them, however, so as to show only one aspect at a time is one of his great technical discoveries, and we must stop a moment to illustrate it. The more important characters in Proust are made to pass through so many phases that it would be impossible to trace briefly their histories. But we may note the transformations of one of the subordinate characters.

When we first meet Mme. de Villeparisis, it is at the

seaside summer resort, Balbec: the narrator's grandmother
has known her during their schooldays, but, with her
characteristic modesty and good taste, taking it for granted
that Mme. de Villeparisis belongs to a superior social
class, has never since attempted to see her. Mme. de Villeparisis, however, recognizes her old school friend at Balbec and insists upon entertaining her. The old marquise
takes the grandson out driving, and she seems to him the
perfect type of great lady; she enchants him with anec-
dotes of the famous people who had been friends of her
father's and whom as a child she had used to see at
their house. When the boy has returned to Paris, however,
she invites him to one of her receptions, and he learns now
that her social position is by no means so brilliant as he
had supposed: for some reason, she has lost caste; many
people will not come to her house. She is also a sort of blue-
stocking: she paints and publishes memoirs, and has thereby ceased to be typical of her class. She is envious, sometimes mean, a little stuffy and a little pathetic. But the
young man never ceases to wonder what dreadful sin
Mme. de Villeparisis can be guilty of to have warranted
such ostracisim: he cannot imagine anything disgraceful
enough, anything which such a woman might have done
which such women did not do every day with impunity.
He makes an attempt to find out from her nephew, Charlus, but only discovers that, so far as Charlus is concerned,
Mme. de Villeparisis is not *déclassée* at all: she is simply
his aunt and a Guermantes, and the opinion of the outside world has never penetrated to him. He explains to

the young man, however, that the late M. de Villeparisis
was a nobody, with no title of his own, and that they had
merely invented "de Villeparisis" in order that she might
still have one. But years afterwards, at Venice, the narrator sees Mme. de Villeparisis in the dining-room of the
hotel where he is stopping, and he overhears her conversation at table with the old diplomat, M. de Norpois, who
has been her lover for years. It is one of those banal and
laconic exchanges between persons who have lived long
together and who have nothing new to say to each other:
they discuss their shopping, the stock market, the menu.
Mme. de Villeparisis is disfigured by some sort of eczema
which has broken out on her face: she seems tired and
old. When an Italian prince comes over to their table, M.
de Norpois watches her relentlessly with a severe blue
eye to see that she does not commit any of the slips
,which, when they had both been younger, had amused
him. An ordinary novelist would have left it at this.
But with Proust, the point of the story is still to come—
in a final transformation which is retrospective. When the
narrator leaves the dining-room and rejoins his mother
outside, he finds also a Mme. Sazerat, an old, excellent
and rather boring neighbor from Combray. Mme. Sazerat,
ever since they have known her, has been living in very
reduced circumstances. When the narrator happens to
mention that Mme. de Villeparisis is in the dining-room,
Mme. Sazerat begs him to point her out: it was for her
sake, Mme. Sazerat explains, that her father had ruined
himself: "Now that father is dead," she adds, "my consola-

tion is that he loved the most beautiful woman of his time." The hero takes her into the dining-room and tries to show her Mme. de Villeparisis—but, "We can't be counting from the same place," Mme. Sazerat objects. "As I count, there's nobody at the second table but an old gentleman and a dreadful blowzy little hunched-up old woman." We realize with astonishment that what the young man had never been able to imagine was simply that Mme. de Villeparisis had once been beautiful, unscrupulous and cruel, had wasted lives and broken hearts, like Odette de Crécy herself. Proust's skill at producing these effects is one of the most amazing features of his art: as each successive revelation is made, we see perfectly that the previous descriptions of the character fit equally well our new conception, yet we have never foreseen the surprise. Behind the varied series of aspects, we are aware of the personality as a complete and unmistakable creation: the series, as Proust says, describes its curve.

To return, however, to the story where we left it, we now enter the inferno of the passions, of which we have previously only had glimpses. The hero's love affair with Albertine, which is balanced, near the beginning, by his childhood infatuation with Swann's daughter, is the culminating, and the most enormously elaborated, episode of the book. The narrator falls in love with a girl in almost every way the opposite of himself: she is lively, sensual, piquant. She is an orphan and has no money and is obliged to live with an aunt, who dislikes her and whom she dislikes. The aunt is a dull bourgeois, but there is

about Albertine a good deal of the Parisian gamine. While
his mother is away at Combray, the hero brings Albertine
to stay in the family apartment, where, for the time, he is
living alone. There commences between him and Albertine one of those fatal emotional see-saws which seem first
to have been described by Stendhal in the love affair between Julien Sorel and Mathilde de la Mole. So long as
Proust's hero is sure of Albertine, he finds himself indifferent to her and decides that he will not marry her; but
as soon as he suspects her of infidelity, he becomes morbidly obsessed by jealousy. In the meantime, he has grown
more self-indulgent, more lazy, more egoistic and more
hypochondriacal. He lies in bed till noon every day and
will not take Albertine out: he keeps her like a prisoner.
He leans too hard upon her, just as he leaned too hard
upon Gilberte, but with consequences far more serious,
because he has by this time lost the self-control which
might have enabled him to break off the relationship, as
he had done in the former case. He becomes at last so
exigent and so nagging that, after a jealous scene one evening, Albertine runs away the next morning before he has
gotten up. During the night, he has heard her, in her
room, violently throwing open a window—opening the
windows at night was forbidden, because the air was supposed to be bad for his asthma—as who should say: "This
life is smothering me! Asthma or no asthma, I must have
air!" And he has been shaken by an agitation more profound than any he has known since that other night in his
childhood when M. Swann had come to dinner and his

mother had failed to kiss him good-night; and as he had done on that former occasion, he goes out into the hall and stands waiting, hoping—in vain—to attract Albertine's attention.

In the morning, he finds a letter which says: "I leave you the best of myself." She goes back to her aunt in the country; and only then does it occur to her lover that she is, after all, a *jeune fille à marier* and that he has taken advantage of her situation to put her in an impossible position. He makes frantic efforts to get her back; then suddenly receives the news that she has fallen from her horse and been killed. Immediately afterwards, a letter arrives which she has written just before her death and in which she tells him she wants to come back to him. He has suspected her of Lesbian propensities, and this is one of the things which has tortured him; but he is never now to know certainly how much of what he has suspected is the product of his imagination and how much is true. Some evidence, after she is dead, leads him to believe that she is innocent; other reports, that she was even more depraved than he had ever imagined, that she had finally come to believe herself suffering from a form of "criminal insanity" and that her accident had been more or less deliberate—she had allowed herself to be killed out of remorse for a suicide she had caused. In either event, he feels that he is to blame: if she was innocent, he has wronged her; if she was guilty, he has abandoned her to the perversity which she herself dreaded: "It seemed to me that, by reason of the fact that my love had been altogether selfish, I had allowed Albertine to die, just as I had killed my grandmother." In any case, this harrowing failure undermines his own morale. At last, he completely collapses and takes refuge in a sanitarium, where he remains for a number of years.

This episode with Albertine, upon which Proust put so much labor and which he intended for the climax of his book, has not been one of the most popular sections, and it is certainly one of the most trying to read. Albertine is seen in so many varying moods, made the subject of so many ideas, dissociated into so many different images, and her lover describes at such unconscionable length the, writhings of his own sensibility, that we sometimes feel ourselves going under in the gray horizonless ocean of analysis and lose sight of the basic situation, of Proust's unwavering objective grasp of the characters of both the lovers which make the catastrophe inevitable. Furthermore, the episode of Albertine does not supply us with any of the things which we ordinarily expect from love affairs in novels: it is quite without tenderness, glamour or romance—the relation between Albertine and her lover seems to involve neither idealism nor enjoyment. But this is also its peculiar strength: it is one of the most original studies of love in fiction and, in spite of the rather highly special conditions under which it is made to take place, we recognize in it an inescapable truth. And it ends by moving us in a curious way, precisely when Proust seems indifferently to have neglected all the customary apparatus for getting effects of pathos out of themes of love and death. The tragedy of Albertine is the tragedy of the little we know and the little we are able to care about those persons whom we know best and for whom we care most; and the pages which tell how Albertine's lover forgot her after she was dead, by reason of their very departure from any other treatment of death that we remember in fiction, give us that impression of a bolder honesty, of a closer approach to reality, which we get only from deep and original genius. As in the case of Paul Valéry's "Cimetière Marin"—so characteristic of our own time and such a curious contrast to Gray's "Country Churchyard"—it is less the nostalgia for perished beauty and the pathos of wasted passions that move us than amazement at their obliteration.

This brings us, however, to Proust's central ideas, of which this episode is only the chief exemplification. We have already been shown the failure of Swann to satisfy with Odette his unrealized æsthetic longings. So the narrator's friend, Saint-Loup, has made himself miserable over a shifty little actress whom the hero has formerly known in a brothel, but who wears the aspect for Saint-Loup of all the talents and all the charms. And so the narrator has now proved for himself the fatal impossibility of finding our happiness in another individual. A woman will not, and cannot, live in the world in which we would have her—that is, the world in which we live, which we ourselves imagine; and what we love in her is merely the creation of our own imagination: we have supplied her with it ourselves. This tragic subjectivity of love is

even more striking in the case of the sexual inverts (Proust
supplements the normal love affairs of Swann and of the
narrator with, as it were, homosexual annexes, consisting
on the one hand, of Charlus and his friends, and, on the
other, of Albertine and her Lesbian companions); for
here, to the eyes of an ordinary person, there is nothing
romantic to be seen at all, and the grotesque disparity
between the ideal which is exalting or tormenting the
lover and the object in which he has located it becomes
ludicrous or disgusting. In the case of a wholly noble and
disinterested love, a devotion in which sex plays no part,
such as the grandmother's love for the boy, the discrep-
ancy is perhaps most hopeless of all: for the boy simply
takes for granted all the grandmother's solicitude and attention, is too self-centred to be aware of her sufferings
and scarcely thinks about her at all till after she is dead.
And by one of his most brilliant strokes, Proust shows us
finally that the raucous Mme. Verdurin has been a victim
of the same malady as the rest: her fierce despotism over
her "little clan," her frenzied efforts to keep them together, her nagging them to come to her house and her
persecuting them when they stay away, have been merely
the symptoms of another variety of the same passion
which has been torturing Swann, the narrator and Charlus: jealousy—but in this case transferred from an individual to a group. Nor are the lovers the only persons
who are baffled by fixing their hopes upon other human
beings, by seeking to extend their own private reality to
the external world. Legrandin, the provincial snob, lives

to abandon his snobbery; when he comes to be invited everywhere, he no longer cares to go out. And, in a gruesome final episode, Proust shows us the whole futile comedy enacted in an unexpected form: Charlus, who has been steadily degenerating, has finally arrived at a phase where all his more human impulses have decayed and he has become perverse for the sake of perversity: vice itself has become the ideal. But his efforts to degrade himself are as ill-fated as the grandmother's efforts to sacrifice herself to the welfare of others: for the persons he pays to collaborate with him care nothing about being vicious: they only want to earn an honest penny and their heart is hopelessly not in their work. Even in pursuing evil, where satisfaction depends on others, man is doomed to disappointment.

Nor does Proust's pursuit of this theme stop here. The conviction that it is impossible to know, impossible to master, the external world, permeates his whole book. It is reiterated on almost every page, in a thousand different connections: Albertine's lies; the gossip about the heir-apparent of Luxemburg; the contradictory diagnoses of the doctors who are consulted about the grandmother's illness; the attractions of Rivebelle and Balbec, mutually invisible across the water; the ticking of the watch in Saint-Loup's room, which the visitor is unable to locate; the names in the railway time-table of the towns in the neighborhood of Balbec, which first rouse romantic images in the mind of the boy and whose etymologies are explained by the curé of Combray, then become for the

young man simply the stations of the Balbec railway, and
are later explained differently and authoritatively by
Brichot, so that they take on an entirely new suggestive-
ness. And I have shown already how the characters change
their aspect, as the point of view of the observer changes.

Proust has created in this respect a sort of equivalent in
fiction for the metaphysics which certain philosophers
have based on the new physical theory. Proust had been
deeply influenced by Bergson, one of the forerunners of
the modern anti-mechanists, and this had helped him to
develop and apply on an unprecedented scale the metaphysics implicit in Symbolism. I have already suggested
in the first chapter of this book that the defense by such a
philosopher as Whitehead of the metaphysics of the Romantics should apply—and it should apply *a fortiori*—to
the metaphysics of the Symbolists. For modern physics,
all our observations of what goes on in the universe are
relative: they depend upon where we are standing when
we make them, how fast and in which direction we are
moving—and for the Symbolist, all that is perceived in
any moment of human experience is relative to the person
who perceives it, and to the surroundings, the moment,
the mood. The world becomes thus for both fourth dimen-
sional—with Time as the fourth dimension. The relativist,
in locating a point, not only finds its co-ordinates in space,
but also takes the time; and the ultimate units of his
reality are "events," each of which is unique and can never
occur again—in the flux of the universe, they can only
form similar patterns. And in Proust's world, just as the

alleys of the Bois de Boulogne which the hero had seen in his youth under the influence of the beauty of Odette have now changed into something quite different and are as irrecoverable as the moments of time in which they had had their only existence—just as his people, in spite of the logic of the processes by which they change, are always changing and will finally fade away, disintegrated by illness or old age; so love, of which we hope so much, changes and fails us, and so society, which at first seems so stable, in a few years has recombined its groups and merged and transformed its classes. And, as in the universe of Whitehead, the "events," which may be taken arbitrarily as infinitely small or infinitely comprehensive, make up an organic structure, in which all are interdependent, each involving every other and the whole; so Proust's book is a gigantic dense mesh of complicated relations: cross-references between different groups of characters and a multiplication of metaphors and similes connecting the phenomena of infinitely varied fields—biological, zoological, physical, æsthetic, social, political and financial. (These similes seemed far-fetched and silly to the first readers of Proust's novel—but Proust insisted that one of his principal concerns was to discover the real resemblances between things which superficially appeared different. And we remember that the far-fetched comparisons of the poetry of the age of Gongora and Crashaw, to which the poetry of the Symbolists seems akin, have been defended as indicating relations where none had previously been perceived.)

Proust has further, in a larger way, varied the color, tone and pace of his narrative to correspond to the various periods of the hero's life. To the shimmering reveries of boyhood succeed the chatter, the sociability and the vivacity of young manhood; and to these, with that extraordinary sunrise which brings to the hero, not the splendor of the morning, but the dawning of the realization of human corruption and cruelty, succeeds a nightmare of the passions, which at its climax, in the almost demoniacal scene where the Verdurins set Morel against Charlus, seems blasted with the dry breath of Hell. It is characteristic of Proust that, though the vices he here deals with fascinated him and though he extracts from them a good deal of comedy, he should have given to this part of his novel the Scriptural title "Sodom and Gomorrah," and that he should make us feel that all the characters are damned. The grandmother and Swann are now dead. Bergotte dies; and at his death it is intimated, as it has already been intimated in connection with the composer Vinteuil, that only in artistic creation may we hope to find our compensation for the anarchy, the perversity, the sterility and the frustrations of the world.

There is, however, yet another phase. After the death of Albertine, the fumes begin to clear away. When the narrator, after the War, finally emerges from his sanitarium, the world seems more sober, more level, less colorful, less troubling. He accepts—for the first time in years—an invitation to a reception at the Princesse de Guermantes's. Just as he is arriving, he is crowded off the roadway

by one of the carriages going to the party, and as he steps
up on to the kerb, he is visited by a strange sensation—the
moment of stepping up seems to be charged with some
mysterious significance. He has known such puzzling
moments before: in the early part of the story he has told
us of the inexplicable impression made upon him by the
combination of certain church steeples which he had seen
on a drive in his childhood and again, at a later age, by
a clump of trees near Balbec. Why had these sights seemed
to mean something special? Why had he derived from
them a special satisfaction? To-day he resolves to get to
the bottom of his feeling in connection with the kerb: he
fixes his mind upon it and presently finds himself experi-
encing a whole series of similar sensations. In every case,
he now comes to realize, some accident of the physical
world—some odor, touch, taste or sound—has served to
revive in his consciousness what he had felt at some moment of the past when a similar sense-impression had occurred—as the uneven steps of the kerb, by reminding
his body of the water-steps of Venice, has brought back
for an instant into his mind, divorced from the rest of
Venice, the bright Venetian light and water. And these
memories which move him so deeply, which spring back
into his consciousness so promptly at the most irrelevant
provocation, must possess some peculiar value. Are they
not symbols for the fundamental truths of that internal
world of our consciousness which is all we know of
reality? Are they not alone among our experiences in having an existence outside Time?—in yielding us a kind of

truth independent of Time's flux, independent of the in-
coherent and ever-changing succession of our other impressions? He must apply himself to deciphering their
hieroglyphics.

When he finally goes in among the guests and after
his long absence meets the people he has known, he feels
acutely the passage of time, which has profoundly affected
them all. Still haunted by the image of Albertine, as he
had first seen her at the seaside at Balbec, he begs Gilberte
Swann (who has since been married) to introduce him to
some young girls. Gilberte brings her daughter over, and
when he sees her, he knows fully at last that he himself
is old. He has a vision of the time which he has lived and
which he is still dragging with him in memory. While
waiting in the library, he has happened to take down the
same novel of George Sand with which his mother had
read him to sleep that night, so many years ago, when he
had lain awake so long because she had not come up to
kiss him. And now, across all the years, he hears again the
ringing of the bell which had announced M. Swann's
departure, and is terrified suddenly to know that it must
ring in his mind forever. From that night when his
parents had first indulged him had dated the decline of
his will. The slope on which he had started then has
brought him to the debacle with Albertine and has left
him, already old, with his wasted life, "le temps perdu"—
a hypochondriac like his aunt Léonie, who had seemed to
him so eccentric in his youth and whom he had never
dreamed of coming to resemble. For Proust, in spite of

his æstheticism and malingering, was, on one of his sides,
as I have said, a merciless moralist—indeed, by the time
we have finished his book, we have ceased to be surprised
at his admiration for George Eliot, have come to see how
much he has in common with her.

Proust's hero, at any rate, must now retrieve the defeat
of his will—this sorry past which he now carries along
with him, with no power to change it, to better it. He
will turn, he vows, away from the world; but he is too
selfish to live for others as his grandmother had done. Too
selfish and too skeptical—for what had his grandmother
ever found in those to whom she sacrificed herself but im-
pervious egoism? and what had she ever earned but suffering? It is hopeless to seek happiness in others—in society or in love. One must turn in upon oneself—one finds
the true reality only there: in those enduring extra-tem-
poral symbols—incidents and personalities as well as land-
scapes—which have been precipitated out by the interac-
tion of one's continually changing consciousness with the
continual change of the world. He will make of his life a
book, and he will base it upon these symbols. So he may
assert his will at last and retrieve his moral surrender—so
he may turn at last to swim against the current of the
undammed, unchannelled sensibility with which he has
been drifting all his life—and at the same time master the
world, rejoin the reality which has always seemed to elude
him, and, opposing the flow of Time, establish something
outside it: a work of art.

For Proust, though all his observations seem relative,

does, like Einstein, build an absolute structure for his world of appearances. His characters may change from bad to good, from beautiful to ugly, as Einstein's measuring-rods shrink and elongate, his clocks become accelerated or retarded; yet as Einstein's mathematical apparatus enables us to establish certain relations between the different parts of the universe, in spite of the fact that we do not know how the heavenly bodies are moving in respect to one another and no matter from what point of view our measurements have been made—so Proust constructs a moral scheme out of phenomena whose moral values are always shifting. (Perhaps the narrator's grandmother may be taken as playing for Proust the same rôle that the speed of light does for Einstein: the single constant value which makes the rest of the system possible!)

These last pages of Proust's novel, like the death and forgetting of Albertine, make no appeal to any of the emotions in which novelists usually deal. They are occupied simply with the genesis of the book which we have just read. Yet they have a strange dramatic power, and they move us—as Proust is always able to do—just when there seems to be nothing more to be said. Through this queer exaltation of an artistic and intellectual passion divorced from every other source of human joy is heard the door-bell still ringing from Combray, more distinct because isolated now and with a new and sombre significance—as Edith Wharton says, like the knock of Fate at the door. And in the long last sentence of the book the word "Time" begins to sound, and it closes the symphony as it began it.

II

The fascination of Proust's novel is so great that, while we are reading it, we tend to accept it *in toto*. In convincing us of the reality of his creations, Proust infects us with his point of view, even where this point of view has falsified his picture of life. It is only in the latter part of his narrative that we begin seriously to question what he is telling us. Is it really true, we begin to ask ourselves, that one's relations with other people can never provide a lasting satisfaction? Is it true that literature and art are the only forms of creative activity which can enable us to meet and master reality? Would not such an able doctor as Proust represents his Cottard as being enjoy, in supervising his cases, the satisfaction of knowing that he has imposed a little of his own private reality upon the world outside? Would not a diplomat like M. de Norpois in arranging his alliances?—or a hostess like Mme. de Guermantes in creating her social circle? Might not a more sympathetic and attentive lover than Proust's hero have even succeeded in recreating Albertine at least partly in his own image? We begin to be willing to agree with Ortega y Gasset that Proust is guilty of the mediæval sin of *accidia,* that combination of slothfulness and gloom which Dante represented as an eternal submergence in mud.

For "A la Recherche du Temps Perdu," in spite of all its humor and beauty, is one of the gloomiest books ever written. Proust tells us that the idea of death has "kept him company as incessantly as the idea of his own iden-

tity"; and even the water-lilies of the little river at Combray, continually straining to follow the current and continually jerked back by their stems, are likened to the
futile attempts of the neurasthenic to break the habits
which are eating his life. Proust's lovers are always suffering: we scarcely ever see them in any of those moments
of ecstasy or contentment which, after all, not seldom
occur even in the case of an unfortunate love affair—and
on the rare occasions when they *are* supposed to be en-
joying themselves, the whole atmosphere is shadowed by
the sadness and corrupted by the odor of the putrescence
which are immediately to set in. And Proust's artists are
unhappy, too: they have only the consolations of art.
Proust's interminable, relentlessly repetitious and finally
almost intolerable disquisitions on these themes end by
goading us to the same sort of rebellion that we make
against those dialogues of Leopardi in which, in a similar
insistent way, Leopardi rings the changes on a similar
theme: that man is never happy, that there is no such
thing as satisfaction in the present. We have finally to
accept with dismay the fact that Leopardi is a sick man
and that, in spite of the strength of his intellect, in spite
of his exact, close, sober classical style, all his thinking is
sick. And so with Proust we are forced to recognize that
his ideas and imagination are more seriously affected by
his physical and psychological ailments than we had at
first been willing to suppose. His characters, we begin to
observe, are always becoming ill like the hero—an immense number of them turn out homosexual, and homo-

sexuality is "an incurable disease." Finally, they all suddenly grow old in a thunderclap—more hideously and humiliatingly old than we have ever known any real group of people to be. And we find that we are made more and more uncomfortable by Proust's incessant rubbing in of all these ignominies and disabilities. We begin to feel less the pathos of the characters than the author's appetite for making them miserable. And we realize that the atrocious cruelty which dominates Proust's world, in the behavior of the people in the social scenes no less than in the relations of the lovers, is the hysterical sadistic complement to the hero's hysterical masochistic passivity. What, we ask, is the matter with Proust?—and what is it that has happened to his novel? The hero of "A la Recherche du Temps Perdu" is not the same person as the author—the man who is supposed to be telling the story represents only specially selected aspects of the man who is actually composing the novel, and he is kept strictly within certain limits. For further light on Proust's career and personality, we must go to his other writings and his letters, and to the memoirs of his friends.

We learn from these that Proust's chronic asthma developed, like that of his hero, very early; and that Proust himself was aware from the beginning of the neurotic character of his ailment. One specialist, to whom his friends, the Bibescos, had insisted upon his going, told him that his asthma had "become a nervous habit," and that the only way for him to be cured was to go to a sanitarium in Germany, where they would break him of

the asthma habit ("because I shall certainly not go," says
Proust, to explain his use of the conditional) "as morphine
addicts are cured of the morphine habit"; and another
doctor (perhaps the same) told Proust that he would prefer not to attempt to cure him, as even if he should be
successful, Proust would simply develop a different set of
symptoms. Proust had evidently come to use his illness as
a pretext for escaping the ordinary contacts with the
world, for being relieved from the obligations of punctu-
ality and from embarrassing encounters. His super-normal
sensitiveness must have made the social life which so fascinated him inordinately difficult for him; and his illness
gave him a sort of counter-advantage over people whom,
with the deep-rooted snobbery which coexisted with a
bold and searching intelligence, he imagined to possess
some advantage over him. His illness enabled him to come
late and, by doing so, to attract attention; to attract attention and provoke compassion by sitting at dinner in his
overcoat; or not to come at all and, by stimulating people's interest, to make them all the more eager to entertain him. He had already, apparently, reached the point at
an early stage of his career of compelling Prince Antoine
Bibesco and his brother to come in late at night and describe to him what had been going on at parties from
which he had stayed away. And when the Bibescos arranged to have him meet their cousin, the Princess Marthe
Bibesco, who had written a clever book and whom he
had expressed a great desire to know, he appeared at the
ball where she was to be present "livid and bearded" and

constantly shivering, "his collar turned up over his white tie" and "his body encased in a pelisse which was too big for him," so that "he had the appearance of having come with his coffin," and sat staring at her, as she danced, "with great sad eyes"—until he had made her so self-conscious and nervous, that, when she was finally introduced to him, she snubbed him.

In 1896, when Proust was twenty-five, some men friends of his own age put on a little amateur revue. Proust had then just brought out his first book, "Les Plaisirs et les Jours," rather a gaudy de luxe affair, for which, with his passion for smartness, for combining fashion with art, he had succeeded in obtaining a preface by Anatole France, pictures by Madeleine Lemaire and musical settings for some of his poems by Reynaldo Hahn; and one of the characters in the revue was made to protest to a character made up as Proust about the high price of "Les Plaisirs et les Jours"—to which Proust was made to reply with hyperbolic politeness and abysmal self-depreciation. When Proust saw this scene at a rehearsal, he went away mortally wounded and would not come to any of the performances. And at the time when he was much in love with a young lady—the present Jeanne Pouquet and apparently one of the originals of Gilberte—and was in the habit of going out to Neuilly to talk to the girls and bring them refreshments while the young men were playing tennis, he would be troubled by dark suspicions—probably not, says Mme. Pouquet, unjustified—when a tennis ball would be suddenly landed in the midst of the conversation and lunch. The girl married Proust's friend, Gaston de Caillavet, and Proust ceased for many years to see them. Late one evening, however, at a time when Proust had long been living as a recluse, he called at the Caillavets's without warning and, pouring forth a thousand apologies, insisting that they were not to disturb themselves, asked the butler whether he could see them. When Mme. de Caillavet and her husband appeared, he begged to be presented to their daughter, who had grown up without his having known her (as the narrator in his novel asks to meet the daughter of Gilberte). The young girl had gone to bed, but Proust implored them to make her come down. Mlle. de Caillavet was accordingly summoned and appeared in a very bad humor—but ended by finding Proust charming and talking to him for more than an hour.

One has heard much of Proust's exquisite politeness, but as we read his letters, we come gradually to sympathize with those inconsiderate friends of his youth who had kidded him about it in their revue. The interminable and finespun solicitude with which Proust caresses his friends in his letters all too often only serves to emphasize the fundamental lack of consideration which allows him to use his asthma as an excuse for holding them at his disposition without making definite appointments with them or for compelling them to wait upon him at inconvenient hours. Such a letter as the following to Mme. Scheikevitch is not merely polite to excess: it exhibits a peculiar kind of overcultivated and fundamentally uncon-

vincing sensibility to which it would be hard to find anything equal even in the eighteenth century: "How distress-
ing to learn that you have been ill, what an additional
source of distress to learn it only now—not to have been
able to be sad when you were suffering, because I knew
nothing about it. How was it that I did not know? Probably because I have seen the Princess Soutzo so rarely and
with so many people about—it is she who has just told me.
It is in a retrospective manner, now that you are well
again, that I must return in my imagination and mount
your Calvary—sleep through, or rather, not sleep through,
your nights of fever. So treacherously malignant is our
human fate that, as if it were not painful enough for me
to have to grieve about you with my friendship of to-day,
the past of your suffering restores to me for a moment my
more lively friendship of a year ago. It is with that friendship that I commiserate with you for all the distress that
you have had and it makes me accord a maximum force
of compassion at a time when the compassion which
would be dictated by the present leaf of the calendar of
my friendship would be already sorrowful enough." Later,
when Mme. Scheikevitch had lost her money as a result of
the Bolshevik revolution, Proust wrote—mentioning at the
beginning of his letter that he was "very tired to write to
you to-night"—to offer to share with her the proceeds
from the sale of a part of his furniture which he was con-
templating at the time—though "in my cardiac condition
to-night I shan't be able to get up safely for two days."
Mme. Scheikevitch declined this suggestion "with some

vivacity," and Proust was infinitely grieved. He now advanced the even more inacceptable proposal that she should engage to supply *Le Temps* with a daily article and that Proust should write it for her.

"It is impossible," writes Jacques-Emile Blanche, "to understand his correspondence (his mania), letters of six or eight or ten pages to anybody at all, unless one divines the difficulty of establishing peaceful and normal interchanges with a person so remote and inaccessible, who, from politeness, *'gentillesse,'* smothered you with flowers."

Here we are still, however, dealing merely with the superficial aspects of Proust's life. For further insight into his personality, we must go to that early collection of stories and sketches which—remarkable as they are—because they are immature, expose as Proust's great novel does not do, his special fantasies and preoccupations. "Les Plaisirs et les Jours," written when Proust was between twenty and twenty-three, contains already all the characteristic motifs of "A la Recherche du Temps Perdu." We discover here, not without surprise and uneasiness, that the disillusionment and the valetudinarianism which we had supposed at least painfully earned by an arduous progress of the soul to maturity, had in reality already been present in a completely developed form in the gifted and well-to-do young man scarcely out of his teens. The hero of the first of these stories, "La Mort de Baldassare Silvande, Vicomte de Sylvanie," is a sensitive and accomplished nobleman who composes music and plays the violin, who is always accompanied when at home on his estate by two pet peacocks and a pet kid, and who values, with jealous vanity, the friendship and attentions of the Duke of Parma. But though the Vicomte is rich, brilliant, smart and usually successful in love, he is dying of general paralysis at the age of thirty-five: he will never see thirty-six. And in the knowledge that he is surely dying, Baldassare Silvande is truly happy for the first time in his life—he loves to lie in bed savoring the last moments of his life, foretasting the sad sweetness of last partings. The women whom he has easily possessed have meant comparatively little to the Vicomte, but he is madly in love with and furiously jealous of a little Syracusan princess who loves another and cares nothing about him. Now, however, that Baldassare is on the point of death, the little princess often comes to see him and treats him with tenderness.

But, after a time, to Baldassare's surprise, and to the surprise of the doctors who are attending him, he finds himself taking a turn for the better: he begins to walk again and is evidently on the point of getting well. But, faced with unexpected recovery, Baldassare is brought to the realization that he would much prefer to die: he had prepared to take leave of life and he no longer cares to bother with living—what he really enjoys is a dying condition. And, after a month of steady recovery, he begins to relapse into his invalid state and is soon unable to walk again. He summons the perverse Syracusan princess and begs her, as his dying request, for his sake to stay away from a ball where he knows that she is to lead the cotillion with her lover. "I cannot promise you that," she replies. "It is two months now since I have seen him, and I may never see him again." "Then remember me for a moment," he pleads—"for the little time that, if I were there, you might be obliged to spend with me in order to avoid the appearance of being too much with him." "I hardly dare promise you that," she answers, "the ball will last so short a time. Even if I am with him all the time, I shall hardly have time to see him. I will give you a moment every day afterwards." "That won't be possible, you will forget me, but if, in a year's time—or perhaps even longer, alas!—something sad that you might happen to be reading, a death or a rainy night, should make you think of me, what a kindness you would be doing me!" Baldassare arranges himself to die. In his last pathetic and exquisite moments, he watches from the window a ship setting sail for India and listens to the chime of a distant village "imperceptible and profound as a heartbeat." He remembers how his mother had used to kiss him good-night in bed, how she had chafed his bare feet in her hands and sat beside him when he could not sleep— and how, when his engagement to be married had been broken, only his mother had been able to console him. And amidst a sorrowing family, he expires—just as the Duke of Parma arrives.

It is easy to recognize in the hero of this preposterous story both the narrator of Proust's novel and Swann— especially as we first see Baldassare precisely, as we do Swann, through the eyes of a small boy, his nephew, who does not thereafter play any rôle in the story and whose sole office in it seems to be to swell the grandeur of the *grand seigneur* by showing him in the perspective of a child's imagination. It is, in fact, almost as if the half-romantic Vicomte were a projection of the child's imagination.

In another story, "La Confession d'une Jeune Fille," a young girl—who tells the story herself—has spent the sweetest hours of her life with her mother on a family estate; but at the age of fourteen, an "already very vicious" little cousin had taught her "things which made her thrill at once with voluptuousness and remorse." She had finally torn herself away, feeling a desperate need for her mother, whom she supposed to be still in Paris. Suddenly, however, as she was wandering through the grounds, she had found her mother sitting on a bench, smiling and holding out her arms. The young girl had thrown herself upon her and confessed, weeping, all that had happened. But at sixteen the girl was further corrupted by a "perverse and wicked" young man; and from that time on, "once the habit had been acquired, there was no lack of immoral young men to exploit it." By the time the girl has reached twenty, the mother's health has begun to fail and she wishes to see her daughter married. The girl, in order "to prove to her mother how much she loves her," agrees to marry "precisely the young man who was likely to have upon her the happiest influence." He had also the special qualification of being willing to come and live with the family so that the girl and her mother need not be separated. But almost on the very eve of the wedding, while the young girl's fiancé is out of town, her family entertain at dinner the man who has first led her astray. At the insistence of a convivial uncle and against her better inclination she permits herself to drink three glasses of champagne, whereupon, going into another room and locking the door, she and her evil genius fall into each other's arms. When they are about to join the company again, the girl looks at herself in the mirror and sees her "shining eyes, her flushed cheeks, her offered mouth—a sensual, stupid and brutal joy," with, beside them, "the mouth of Jacques, avid beneath its mustaches." Then, from the mirror, she becomes aware that her mother is standing behind them watching them from the balcony outside the window. The mother's heart is weak: she falls backwards and is instantly killed. The young girl, at the beginning of her confession, has declared that she is about to commit suicide.

The first thing that strikes us about this story is its similarity to that curious incident at the beginning of "A la Recherche du Temps Perdu," in which Mlle. Vinteuil is made to derive a sadistic satisfaction from allowing her Lesbian companion to spit on her father's picture. To what extent this improbable scene was the creation of Proust's imagination we learn from Mme. de Gramont, who, in her book of memoirs of Montesquiou and Proust, prints a letter in which Proust explains to her that the situation had been based on a real incident. Mme. de Gramont, however, tells us that she herself had heard the anecdote, and that, as a matter of fact, it was perfectly harmless and merely amusing: Proust had actually, either misunderstanding it or remembering it wrongly—distorting it at any rate in his own mind along the lines of his peculiar obsessions—substituted for the original story a sinister invention of his own. But, beyond this, we are able to identify in the incident of Mlle. Vinteuil and in its prototype, "La Confession d'une Jeune Fille," the embryo of which the long novel is only the growth into a larger organism. Not that the behavior itself of the narrator of "A la Recherche du Temps Perdu" is presented as corresponding entirely with the behavior of these two wayward young girls; but in the large design of the novel, the pattern is unmistakably repeated. In order to recognize it, however, we must first consider how the book is constructed and by what methods its meanings are conveyed.

The real elements, of course, of any work of fiction, are the elements of the author's personality: his imagination embodies in the images of characters, situations and scenes the fundamental conflicts of his nature or the cycle of phases through which it habitually passes. His personages are personifications of the author's various impulses and emotions: and the relations between them in his stories are really the relations between these. One of the causes, in fact, of our feeling that certain works are more satisfactory than others is to be found in the superior thoroughness and candor with which the author has represented these relations. We feel his world to be real and complete, not merely in proportion to the variety of elements it includes, but also in proportion as we recognize these elements as making up an organic whole. From this point of view, Dostoevsky is one of the most satisfactory of novelists; Myshkin and Rogozhin thrill us because they are the opposite poles of one nature; the three brothers Karamazov move us because they are the spirit, mind and body of one man. And if we ask ourselves why even so great a novelist as Dickens does not make upon us so profound an impression as Dostoevsky, we realize that it is because in the case of Dickens, wide and varied as the world of his novels is, the novelist himself is not sufficiently conscious of the significance of what happens there, so that, except in the very best of them, he has admitted a larger conventional element than the greatest novelists ordinarily allow and has been content to press into service melodramatic "good" characters and villains into whom he has scarcely projected himself at all. Now if Dickens falls short of Dostoevsky in this respect, Proust has passed a good deal beyond him. In Dostoevsky, as in Dickens, though the characters are as much the embodiment of the novelist's impulses and emotions as the images of a dream, there is always the framework of the story to account for and carry them. But there is hardly any such framework in Proust. I have said that Proust's novel was a symphony, and I have indicated its relation to Symbolism—and I have explained Proust's special idea of the kind of symbols which were valid for literature, the kind of symbols of which his own novel was to be made. Like all the graduates of the Symbolist school, Proust was a determined opponent of

Naturalism: in the last part of "A la Recherche du Temps Perdu," when he explains the plan of his novel, he expresses himself emphatically and at great length on the futility of trying to represent reality by collecting and organizing the data of the external world, and he handles with what is evidently deliberate carelessness all those facts which a Naturalistic novelist would have been scrupulous to have consistent and precise. What is more, there is no explicit logical connection between the different elements of "A la Recherche du Temps Perdu." There is a story, the story of the narrator, his illusions and disillusions in connection with the world of snobbery and his attachments for Gilberte and Albertine; yet what must have been, what would by any other novelist be presented as having been, some of the most important relations and experiences of his life are scarcely touched upon at all. We hear much about the narrator's grandmother, but almost nothing about his father and are never told precisely what his father does; we hear much about his holidays at the seashore, but nothing about his education; we are told at length about his visit to Saint-Loup when the latter is doing his year of military service, but nothing save through casual allusion about his own term in barracks. On the other hand, certain of the characters that figure most prominently in the novel have almost no relation to the hero at all—at least no relation which the story accounts for: Swann is merely a friend of the family whom the narrator has occasionally seen in his youth, Charlus a person he sometimes meets later on. Yet these two characters almost dominate, respectively, the earlier and the later parts of the book—and as we read, we never question their significance: it is only when we think to examine Proust's novel from the point of view of ordinary fiction that we become aware of their irrelevance to the main narrative. Then we perceive that "A la Recherche du Temps Perdu," which begins in the darkened room of sleep, stands alone as a true dream-novel among works of social observation. It has its harmony, development and logic, but they are the harmony, development and logic of the unconscious.

I do not mean, however, to suggest that Proust accomplished this result unconsciously. In retelling the stories from "Les Plaisirs et les Jours," which must inevitably sound rather absurd, I have perhaps made them seem more naïve than, as Proust writes them, they actually are. Proust is already, in his early twenties, not by any means unaware of the neurotic psychology of his characters—this is, in fact, in spite of his clothing their history in much lyric elegiac prose of the *fin de siècle* sensibility, one of the chief sources of his interest in them. We ask ourselves in surprise, as we finish one of these curious tales, whether Proust has not intended, after all, for all his apparent deliquescent Romanticism, to present us with a realistic case history. And so the more we meditate on his novel, the more clearly we come to realize that the shifting proportions and juxtapositions of its elements, the order in which they are introduced, tell a fuller and somewhat different story than the rather meagre and uneventful one of the narrator, whose own innocuous enough case is so soon extinguished in a sanitarium (to which, one remembers, Proust himself would not go). We recognize, on a prodigious scale, the pattern of the Vinteuil episode in "Swann" and of the "Confession d'une Jeune Fille."

The rôle of Mlle. Vinteuil's father in the first of these, of the young girl's mother in the second, is played in the novel to some extent by the mother of the hero, but chiefly by the hero's grandmother. We know what place Proust's own mother had held in his life: he had lived with her up to the time of her death, when Proust was thirty-four, and in the same room he had had as a child. "The death of his mother," says Mme. Pouquet, "was for Marcel the greatest grief of his life, a veritable rending asunder. He had always remained for her a little child. She surrounded him with every attention, every vigilance. She knew how to look after him without ever imposing herself on him or importuning him. She cushioned his life. She accepted all Marcel's caprices as perfectly natural things." And we know from the "Sentiments Filiaux d'un Parricide" in the miscellany "Pastiches et Mélanges" that he bitterly and morbidly blamed himself for having saddened and perhaps shortened her life. Now the hero of the novel is represented as causing his grandmother and mother much anxiety and as reproaching himself extravagantly for doing so, but he is not made to sin against them —their simplicity, piety, rigor, their too protective affection—in the same perverse way in which the *jeune fille* and Mlle. Vinteuil do. Yet the impression we get is the same. About the middle of "A la Recherche du Temps

Perdu," in a series of touching, wonderfully written, but exceedingly cruel scenes, the hero's grandmother is made to die; and immediately afterwards, the figure of Charlus begins to swell to enormous proportions: to the salute of a sulphurous overture, the most formidable set-piece in the book, the demon of homosexuality rises.

This subject does take on, in Proust, a truly demoniacal character: Proust does not try to sell us homosexuality by making it appear attractive and respectable, as André Gide, for example, does. The tone of the overture to "Sodome et Gomorrhe," which so sepulchrally groans and wails over the hard lot of the homosexuals, is gruesome rather than tragic; and as we read on, we become aware of something special and rather suspect about Proust's attitude toward this subject. It seems to me plain, in spite of all the rumors as to the ambiguity of Albertine's sex, that both Proust's hero and himself were exceedingly susceptible to women: we are certainly made to feel the feminine attraction of both Albertine and Odette, and the spell of their lovers' infatuation, whereas, on the other hand, none of the male homosexual characters is ever made to appear anything but horrible or comic. Proust had apparently, in his youth, been in love at different times with several women—Mme. Pouquet was evidently one of these —had fared rather badly with them and had never forgiven them to the end of his days. And he shows in "A la Recherche du Temps Perdu" more resentment against the opposite sex than enthusiasm for his own. Homosexuality figures in Proust almost exclusively under the aspect of perversity, and it is in general unmistakably associated, as in the incident of Mlle. Vinteuil, with another kind of perversity, sadism. The cruel and nasty side of Proust is the inevitable reaction against, the inevitable compensation for, the good-little-boy side which—see the letters quoted above to Mme. Scheikevitch—was a great deal too good to be human—or, more precisely, which remained rather puerile. Proust himself has given the key to the situation in his comment on Mlle. Vinteuil: "It was not that she derived pleasure from the idea of doing evil, that evil seemed agreeable to her. It was that pleasure seemed to her wicked. And since, whenever she gave herself up to it, it was accompanied for her by evil thoughts which were otherwise foreign to her virtuous nature, she ended by finding in pleasure something diabolical, by identifying it with Evil."

The grandmother, in the novel, dies in agony; and the demon Charlus pops up. The narrator, still in his mother's house, tortures himself over his inability to hold Albertine, whom he has brought there in his mother's absence, at the same time that he is never able to make up his mind whether he has ever really wanted her. When Albertine finally leaves him, the emotional life of the book becomes progressively asphyxiated by the infernal fumes which Charlus has brought with him—until such a large percentage of the characters have tragically, gruesomely, irrevocably, turned out to be homosexual that we begin for the first time to find the story a little incredible. Charlus is obviously a projection of the later Proust, an extension of the history of the narrator, as Swann has been of the earlier and as Baldassare Silvande seemed to be of the young nephew who magnified him. We assist at Charlus's moral debacle and we leave him finally in a state of semi-idiocy. And the ultimate degradation of Charlus is followed immediately, with an effect of recovery and contrast, by the narrator's heroic resolve to retrieve the waste of his self-indulgent life by shutting himself away from the world and giving himself up to writing his novel—a retirement by which, he strangely explains, he will also punish himself for the anxiety he had caused his grandmother, for the suffering and illness which she had been forced to endure in solitude.

The elements here of Proust's dependence on his mother; his unsatisfactory relations with women; and his impulses toward a sterile and infantile perversity, would, no doubt, be explained in somewhat different ways by the different schools of modern psychology: Proust is a perfect case for psychoanalysis. But that there is a relation between these elements is plain. Proust was never able to find any other woman to care for him as his mother did. His friends have testified to the fact that it was impossible for any friend or inamorata to meet the all-absorbing demands for sympathy and attention which he was accustomed to having satisfied at home; and he was unwilling or unable to make the effort to adjust himself to any non-filial relation. The ultimate result was that strange state of mind which often disconcerts us in his novel: a state of mind which combines a complacent egoism with a plain-tive malaise at feeling itself shut off from the world, a dismay at the apparent impossibility of making connections with other human beings. We end by feeling that, after all, he enjoys the situation of which he is always complaining. Did he not prefer, after all, his invalid's cell, with his mother ministering to him, to the give and take of human intercourse? The death of his mother upset this situation and we probably owe his novel to it. Proust, with his narcotics, his fumigations, his cork-lined chamber, his faithful servants and his practice of sleeping all day, arranged for himself an existence as well protected as it had been during his mother's lifetime; but lacking that one human relationship which had sustained him, he was obliged to supply something to take its place and for the first time he set himself seriously to work. His need now to rejoin that world of humanity from which he had allowed himself to be exiled became much more pressing, and his book was a last desperate effort to satisfy it. But the book itself had been undertaken, if not quite, as he says, "on the eve of death, knowing nothing of my trade," at least late in life and with no experience of writing to be read, of putting himself into communication with his readers; and the penalties for this were the unassimilably long sentences and the tiresome repetitious analyses—self-indulgences on Proust's part even here—which sometimes make him so exasperating to read.

And it is further true that Proust's novel as a whole, superb as are the qualities of objective dramatic imagination which have gone into it, was never quite disengaged from his sick-room. "That work which I was bearing inside me," he calls it in "Le Temps Retrouvé"—he never entirely got it out. Is he telling us his own case-history with symbols? Is he presenting the world as he believes it to be? He is never perhaps quite sure himself. That he could doubt what seem to be the book's basic assumptions is indicated by one of his letters in which he confesses to having cut out a long passage of "A la Recherche du Temps Perdu" in which he had asserted that reciprocal love was not merely difficult and rare, but universally impossible— leaving only an expression of skepticism as to whether anyone was any better off than he. And I believe that those aspects of his novel which seem ambiguous or distorted are due to Proust's own uncertainty as to whether he is exemplifying universal principles of human conduct or projecting by images sometimes monstrous the elements of a personality which he knew to be morbid and special.

Proust's novel kept him up till he had finished it; but when he had finished it, he died. His mother died in 1905; and between 1906 and 1912, Proust had written the whole of a first version of "A la Recherche du Temps Perdu" (without the chapter about the War, which was added afterwards). The first volume was brought out in 1913; and thereafter, though his illness grew worse, though he seemed on the point of succumbing at last to that death which since his early twenties when he had written "La Mort de Baldassare Silvande" he had indulged himself continually in anticipating, he survived long enough to revise and supervise the publication of almost the whole.

But he did not quite see it through. The last sections
which he sent to the press were the volumes called "La
Prisonnière"—the climax of the narrator's story, his struggle and failure with Albertine. After that, in the novel itself, there is nothing but demoralization and decay until
the end, when the narrator makes a stand, in the only way
which now seems possible, against the universal disintegration: by setting himself to reintegrate experience in a
work of literature—the point, therefore, at which Proust
himself had sixteen years earlier begun. He did not live to
finish correcting the proofs of "La Prisonnière"—who will
wonder that so neurotic a man was unable to remain alive
to put in order the final chapters of so dispiriting a story?
Early in the October of 1922 he caught a chill and ran up
a high fever, but stubbornly refused to see a doctor. He
worked at his novel harder than ever, as if he had been
racing with the death which at the same time he was
frankly inviting. As his fever grew continually worse, he
ceased to take any nourishment except a little iced beer
which he had brought in, in a pail, from the Ritz. When
his brother, a doctor, came to see him, Proust, fearing to
be dislodged from his apartment, threatened to jump out
of the window if he were not let alone, but promised to
allow medical treatment as soon as he had finished his
work. The day of his death, in mid-November, he summoned his maid at three in the morning and dictated to
her some supplementary notes on the death of the novelist,
Bergotte—remarking when he had finished that he
thought what he had added was good. It is at the death of

Bergotte that Proust's narrator, in what is perhaps the noblest passage of the book, affirms the reality of those obligations, culminating in the obligation of the writer to do his work as it ought to be done, which seem to be derived from some other world, "based on goodness, scrupulousness, sacrifice," so little sanction can we recognize them as having in the uncertain and selfish world of humanity—those "laws which we have obeyed because we have carried their precepts within us without knowing who inscribed them there—those laws to which we are brought by every profound exercise of the intelligence, and which are invisible only—and are they really?—to fools." But at about this time, and perhaps as a result of the effort of dictating these revisions, an abscess burst in Proust's lung and the next day he was dead.

III

In spite of all the less reassuring or less agreeable aspects of Proust which appear more plainly in his letters and the memoirs of him than in "A la Recherche du Temps Perdu"—his self-coddling, his chronic complaining, his perversity, his overcultivated sensibility—we get the impression from them, as we do in his novel, of an intellect and imagination vigorous, comprehensive and deep. One of the things which strikes us most is his capacity for keeping in intimate touch with various circles of friends, as with various fields of activity, sympathizing with the emotions, understanding the interests, and following the affairs of each, though of the several groups already represented by the memoirs which have so far been published, all seem pretty well independent of each other and some scarcely at any point to overlap. And in spite of all his parade of weakness, in spite of all his masks and indirections, we remember him as a personality of singular magnanimity, integrity and strength. That he was capable of showing considerable spirit was shown by his behavior at the time of the Dreyfus case and by his fighting a duel with a journalist over a review of "Les Plaisirs et Les Jours." "There were in Marcel Proust," says Lucien Daudet, "all the elements of a spoiled child: he never actually became one, because his genius had the corrective effect of dissociating these elements—his genius, his personal dignity and also his sense of humor."

And so though we may regret the spoiled child in Proust, the spoiled child of rich parents who has never had to meet the world on equal terms and who has never felt the necessity of relating his art and ideas to the general problems of human society; though the tragedy of the Guermantes' light reception of Swann's announcement of his mortal illness may come to seem to us somewhat less tragic in retrospect—though we may come to feel a little impatient at having our pity so continually solicited for valetudinarian neurotics who are at least always provided with enough money to be neurotic in peace and comfort; though Proust's dramatic progressive revelation of the anomalies and miseries of the world may come to appear to us less profound when we begin to realize the extreme

naïveté of some of the assumptions upon which he proceeds—snobbish naïveté in regard to the importance of social differences and naïveté in regard to sex and to human
relations in general; none the less, we must recognize in
Proust, it seems to me, one of the great minds and imaginations of our day, absolutely comparable in our own
time, by reason both of his powers and of his influence, to
the Nietzsches, the Tolstois, the Wagners and the Ibsens
of a previous generation. He has recreated the world of the
novel from the point of view of relativity: he has supplied
for the first time in literature an equivalent on the full scale
for the new theory of modern physics.

Imaginatively and intellectually, Proust is prodigiously
strong; and if we feel an element of decadence in his
work, it may be primarily due to the decay of the society
in which he lived and with which his novel exclusively
deals—the society of the dispossessed nobility and the fashionable and cultivated bourgeoisie, with their physicians
and their artists, their servants and their parasites. We are
always feeling with Proust as if we were reading about the
end of something—this seems, in fact, to be what he
means us to feel: witness the implications of the bombard-
ment of Paris during the War when Charlus is in the last
stages of his disintegration. Not only do his hero and most
of his other characters pass into mortal declines, but their
world itself seems to be coming to an end. And it may be
that Proust's strange poetry and brilliance are the last fires
of a setting sun—the last flare of the æsthetic idealism of
the educated classes of the nineteenth century. If Proust is

more dramatic, more complete and more intense than Thackeray or Chekov or Edith Wharton or Anatole France, it may be because he comes at the close of an era and sums up the whole situation. Surely the lament over the impossibility of ideal romantic love which Proust is always chanting on a note which wavers between the tragic and the maudlin announces by its very falling into absurdity the break-up of a whole emotional idealism and its ultimate analysis and readjustment along lines which Proust's own researches, running curiously close to Freud, have been among the first to suggest. "A la Recherche du Temps Perdu" subsumes, in this respect, "The Great Gatsby," "The Sun Also Rises," "The Bridge of San Luis Rey," the sketches of Dorothy Parker, and how many contemporary European novels! Proust is perhaps the last great historian of the loves, the society, the intelligence, the diplomacy, the literature and the art of the Heartbreak House of capitalist culture; and the little man with the sad appealing voice, the metaphysician's mind, the Saracen's beak, the ill-fitting dress-shirt and the great eyes that seem to see all about him like the many-faceted eyes of a fly, dominates the scene and plays host in the mansion where he is not long to be master.

VI

JAMES JOYCE

JAMES JOYCE'S first work of fiction, the volume of short stories called "Dubliners," was finished in 1904 and was to have been brought out by a Dublin publisher; but for a combination of reasons, including the supposed impropriety of certain of the stories, the introduction by name of the Dublin shops, restaurants and pubs, and some disrespectful references to Queen Victoria and Edward VII on the part of one of the characters, the Irish publishers could never bring themselves to publish the book until it had first been brought out in England in 1914, ten years after it had been written. "A Portrait of the Artist as a Young Man" was published first in New York in 1916. Neither of these books had much in common with the English fiction then being written: the typical novelists of that time were H. G. Wells and Arnold Bennett, and Joyce was not in the least like either. In their recent literary renaissance the Irish had been closer to the Continent than to London; and James Joyce, like George Moore, was working in the tradition, not of English, but of French fiction. "Dubliners" was French in its objectivity, its sobriety and its irony, at the same time that its paragraphs ran with a music and a grace quite distinct from the taut metallic quality of Maupassant and Flaubert. And "A Portrait of the Artist as a Young Man," coming at a time when the public was already surfeited with the early histories of sensitive young men—the Edward Ponderevos, the Clayhangers, the Jacob Stahls, the Michael Fanes—not only was able to attract attention, but had the effect of making most of these books look psychologically superficial and artistically shoddy.

"Ulysses" was published in Paris in 1922. It had originally been conceived as a short story for "Dubliners," and was to have been called "Mr. Bloom's Day in Dublin" or something of the sort. But this idea was afterwards combined with the further history of Stephen Dedalus, the hero of the autobiographical "Portrait of the Artist as a Young Man." "Ulysses," however, in its final form as a volume of seven hundred-odd large pages, took shape as something entirely different from either of Joyce's earlier books, and it must be approached from a different point of view than as if it were merely, like the others, a straight work of Naturalistic fiction.

The key to "Ulysses" is in the title—and this key is indispensable if we are to appreciate the book's real depth and scope. Ulysses, as he figures in the "Odyssey," is a sort of type of the average intelligent Greek: among the heroes, he is distinguished for cunning rather than for exalted wisdom, and for common sense, quickness and nerve rather than for, say, the passionate bravery of an Achilles or the steadfastness and stoutness of a Hector. The "Odyssey" exhibits such a man in practically every situation and relation of an ordinary human life—Ulysses, in the course of his wanderings, runs the whole gauntlet or temptations and ordeals and through his wits he survives them all to return at last to his home and family and to reassert himself there as master. The "Odyssey" thus provides a classical model for a writer attempting a modern epic of the ordinary man—and a model particularly attractive to a modern writer by reason of the apparently calculated effectiveness, the apparent sophistication, of its form. By a device suggestive of some of the novels of Conrad, Homer has framed the wanderings of Ulysses between an introductory group of books in which our interest is aroused in the hero before we meet him by Telemachus's search for his lost father, and a culminating group of books which present dramatically and on a larger scale the wanderer's return home.

Now the "Ulysses" of Joyce is a modern "Odyssey," which follows closely the classical "Odyssey" in both subject and form; and the significance of the characters and incidents of its ostensibly Naturalistic narrative cannot properly be understood without reference to the Homeric original. Joyce's Telemachus of the opening books is Stephen Dedalus—that is, Joyce himself. The Dedaluses, as we have already learned from "A Portrait of the Artist as a Young Man," are a shabby-genteel family of Dubliners. Stephen's father, Simon Dedalus, has run through a great variety of employments to end up as nothing in particular, a drinker, a decayed sport, an amateur tenor, a well-known character of the bars. But Stephen has been given a good education at a Jesuit college, and we have seen him, at the end of the earlier novel, on the point of

leaving for France to study and write. At the beginning
of "Ulysses," he has been back in Dublin a year: he had
been summoned home from Paris by a telegram that his
mother was dying. And now, a year after her death, the
Dedalus family, already reduced to poverty, has become
completely demoralized and disintegrated. While Stephen's young sisters and brothers have hardly enough to
eat, Simon Dedalus makes the rounds of the pubs. Stephen, who has always resented his father, feels now that
in effect he has none. He is more isolated in Dublin than
ever. He is Telemachus in search of a Ulysses. His friend,
the medical student, Buck Mulligan, with whom he is living in an old tower on the coast and who believes himself
to share Stephen's artistic tastes and intellectual interests,
really humiliates him by patronizing him and turns to
ridicule his abilities and ambitions. He is Antinous, that
boldest of Penelope's suitors, who, while Ulysses is away,
tries to make himself master of his house and mocks at
Telemachus. Stephen has announced at the end of the
earlier book that he is going forth "to forge in the smithy
of my soul the uncreated conscience of my race"; and now
he has returned to Dublin baffled and disinherited—his
life with Mulligan is dissolute and unproductive. Yet as
Telemachus finds friends and helpers, so Stephen is reminded by the old woman who brings the milk for breakfast in the tower of that Ireland whose uncreated conscience it is still his destiny to forge: "Old and secret . . .
maybe a messenger." She is Athene in the guise of Mentor
who provides Telemachus with his ship; and the memory

of Kevin Egan, an Irish exile in Paris, is the Menelaus
who speeds him on his way.

The scene now shifts, as it does in the "Odyssey," to the
lost Ulysses himself. Joyce's Ulysses is a Dublin Jew, an
advertisement canvasser named Bloom. Like Stephen, he
dwells among aliens: a Jew and the son of a Hungarian
father, he is still more or less of a foreigner among the
Irish; and a man of something less than mediocre abilities, but of real sensibility and intelligence, he has little in
common with the other inhabitants of the lower middle-
class world in which he lives. He has been married for
sixteen years to the buxom daughter of an Irish army
officer, a professional singer, of prodigious sexual appetite, who has been continually and indiscriminately un-
faithful to him. They have had one daughter, who is
already growing up and apparently going the way of her
mother; and one son, of whom Bloom had hoped that he
might resemble, that he might refine upon, himself, but
who died eleven days after he was born. Things have
never been the same between the Blooms since the death
of this son; it is now more than ten years since Bloom has
attempted complete intercourse with his wife—it is as if
the birth of the sickly Rudy had discouraged him and
made him doubt his virility. He is aware that his wife has
lovers; but he does not complain or try to interfere—he is
even resigned to her accepting money from them. He is
a Ulysses with no Telemachus and cut off from his Penelope.

We now follow Bloom's adventures on the day of June

16, 1904 (the whole of "Ulysses" takes place within less than twenty-four hours). Lotus-eaters allure him; he is affrighted by Laestrygonians. He assists at the burial of an Elpenor and descends with him in imagination to the underworld; he suffers from the varying favor of an Æolus. He escapes by ruse from the ferocity of a Cyclops and he disengages himself through prudence from the maiden charms of a Nausicaa. And he emerges finally a man again from the brothel of a Circe who had transformed him into a swine.

The comings and goings of Stephen during the day are woven in and out among the wanderings of Bloom: the two encounter each other twice but do not recognize each other. Both men, we become aware, are constantly accompanied and oppressed by ideas which they have tried to dismiss from their minds: the family situation of each really lies back of and explains all that he does that day. In Stephen's case, it is only a few days from the anniversary of his mother's death, and he is haunted by the memory of it: she had begged him on her deathbed to kneel down and pray for her soul and, in rebellion against the Catholic education which had disciplined and maimed his spirit, jealous of the independence he had won and in fear of the past to which he had returned, he had cruelly refused and had allowed her to die without the comfort of believing that he had repented of his apostasy. But now that she is dead, this incident tortures him. He has in the early morning reproached Mulligan—accusing really himself—for something the latter had said about Ste-

phen's mother at the time of her death which Stephen
had overheard and resented; and, as he has looked out
upon the bright morning sea, the pathos and horror of
her life have become suddenly vivid to him—he has been
dragged back to relive all that she had suffered. Then,
"No, mother!" he has cried out within himself as he
thrust her memory down out of his mind, "let me be and
let me live!" But through his whole bitter and baffled day,
it is his helpless feeling of guilt toward his mother, his
hopeless discouragement and disgust with his father,
which govern all his thoughts and movements. When he
teaches school, he brings the class to a close by a hysterical joke about "the fox burying his grandmother under a
hollybush," and in a stupid boy who cannot do his sums
he can see now only his own graceless youth which his
mother had shielded from the world. After school, he has
gone to walk on the beach and has contemplated paying
a visit to the family of a maternal uncle whom he de-
spises, as if he could do penance in this fashion for his
hardness to his mother and somehow make it up to her
now by kindness to her wretched relatives; but again
the counter-impulse which had proved too strong on the
former occasion comes into play to block his intention:
his mind drifts off to other things and he walks beyond
where he should have turned. The artist still conflicts with
the son—the two are irreconcilable: he sets out to compose a poem, but the poem itself breaks down and he is
left gazing at a silent homing ship.—Visiting the library
later in the day, he improvises a long, pretentious lecture

on the relation of Shakespeare to his father—a lecture which has little to do with Shakespeare, but a good deal to do with Stephen himself.

And as Stephen is ridden by thoughts of his parents, so Bloom is ridden by thoughts of his wife. He has seen Molly at breakfast get a letter which he suspects—and suspects rightly—to be from Blazes Boylan, a flashy buck about town who is managing a concert tour for her and with whom she is having a love affair. All day he has to change the subject when Boylan's name is mentioned— all day he avoids meeting him in the street. In the afternoon, while Bloom is eating at the Ormond Hotel, Boylan comes into the bar, gets a drink and sets off to call on Mrs. Bloom, and when he has gone, Bloom hears the men in the bar talking and laughing about Molly's easy favors. And the conversation, later on in the pub, about Boylan's having won money in a boxing-match—in spite of Bloom's gently insistent efforts to induce the company to talk about tennis—is one of the incidents which give rise to an antagonism between Bloom and the rest of the company and eventually to the quarrel between the Cyclops-Citizen and Bloom. At the end of the Nausicaa episode, the voice of the cuckoo-clock from the priest's house tells Bloom that he is now a cuckold.

In the evening, Bloom goes to a maternity hospital to inquire after the wife of a friend who has been having a hard delivery: there he meets and recognizes Stephen, who is drinking with the medical students. In the "Odyssey," the final shipwreck of Ulysses and his subsequent

misfortunes are the result of the impiety of his companions, who in defiance of all his warnings have killed and
eaten the Oxen of the Sun. So Bloom is pained by the impiety of the medical students as they joke obscenely about
childbirth and maternity. On the part of Stephen, whose
mother died only a year ago, this levity seems especially
shocking, but Stephen's very feeling of guilt about her
makes him particularly blasphemous and brutal. Yet
Bloom has himself in his own way offended against the
principle of fertility by his recent prolonged neglect of
Molly: the Calypso who has detained him since his shipwreck is the nymph who hangs in his bedroom and whom
he makes the object of amorous fantasies. It is this sin
against fertility which—at the hour when Mrs. Bloom is
entertaining Boylan—has landed Bloom on the Phæacian
strand indulging in further erotic daydreams in connection with little Gerty MacDowell, the Nausicaa of the
Dublin beach.

When Mrs. Purefoy's child has finally been born, the
party rushes out to a public house; and, later on—after a
drunken altercation between Dedalus and Buck Mulligan
at the tram station, in which Antinous and Telemachus
apparently dispute over the key to the tower and Telemachus goes away homeless—Stephen, with one of his
companions and with Bloom following some distance behind, proceed to a brothel. Both, by this time, are pretty
drunk—though Bloom, with his invincible prudence, is
not so drunk as Stephen. And in their drunkenness, in
the sordid gaslight and to the tune of the mechanical

piano of the brothel, their respective preoccupations emerge fully for the first time since the morning into their conscious minds: Bloom beholds himself, in a hideous vision, looking on at Blazes Boylan and Molly, an abject cuckold, the laughing-stock of the world; and there rises suddenly in Stephen's imagination the figure of his dead mother come back from the grave to remind him of her bleak disheartened love and to implore him to pray for her soul. But again he will not, cannot, acquiesce; in a desperate drunken gesture, intolerably torn by his conflict of impulses, by his emotions which deadlock each other, he lifts his stick and smashes the chandelier—then rushes out into the street, where he gets embroiled with two English Tommies and knocked down. Bloom has followed and, as he bends over Stephen, beholds an apparition of his own dead son, little Rudy, as Bloom would have had him live to be—learned, cultivated, sensitive, refined: such a youth, in short, as Stephen Dedalus. Ulysses and Telemachus are united.

Bloom picks Stephen up and takes him first to a coffee-stand, then home to his own house. He tries to talk to him of the arts and sciences, of the general ideas which interest him; but Stephen is morose and exhausted and makes little response. Bloom begs him to spend the night—to come and live with them, but Stephen declines and presently takes his leave. Bloom goes up, goes to bed with Molly, describes to her his adventures of the day, and soon drops off to sleep.

But Bloom's encounter with Stephen is to affect both

Stephen's life and the relations between the Blooms. To have rescued and talked with Stephen has somehow restored Bloom's self-confidence. He has gotten into the habit in the past of cooking breakfast for Molly in the morning and bringing it to her in bed—it is the first thing we have seen him doing at the beginning of the day; but to-night, before he goes to sleep, he gives her to understand that he expects her to get breakfast next morning herself and to bring it up to him. This amazes and disconcerts Mrs. Bloom, and the rest of the book is the record of her meditations as she lies awake thinking over Bloom's homecoming. She has been mystified by his recent behavior, and her attitude toward him now is at first a mixture of jealousy and resentment. She congratulates herself upon the fact that, if Bloom neglects her nowadays, her needs are ably supplied by Blazes Boylan. But as she begins to ruminate on the possibility of Stephen Dedalus's coming to live with them, the idea of Blazes Boylan's coarseness becomes intolerable to her: the thought of Stephen has made her fastidious, and, rapidly becoming very tender about him, she prefigures a relation between them of an ambiguous but intimate character, half-amorous, half-maternal. Yet it is Bloom himself who has primarily been the cause of this revolution in Molly's mind: in telling her about Stephen, he has imposed upon her again his own values; in staying away from the house all day and coming back very late at night, and in asking for his breakfast in bed, he has reasserted his own will. And she goes back in her mind over her experience of Bloom—

their courtship, their married life. She remembers how, when she had promised to marry him, it had been his intelligence and his sympathetic nature, that touch of imagination which distinguished him from other men, which had influenced her in his favor—"because he understood or felt what a woman is and I knew I could always get around him"; and on the day when he had first kissed her, he had called her "a flower of the mountain." It is in the mind of his Penelope that this Ulysses has slain the suitors who have been disputing his place.

As for Stephen, unresponsive as he has seemed to Bloom's interest and cordiality, he has at last, none the less, found in Dublin someone sufficiently sympathetic to himself to give him the clew, to supply him with the subject, which will enable him to enter imaginatively—as an artist—into the common life of his race. It is possible that Molly and Bloom, as a result of Bloom's meeting with Stephen, will resume normal marital relations; but it is certain that Stephen, as a result of this meeting, will go away and write "Ulysses." Buck Mulligan has told us that the young poet says he is going "to write something in ten years": that was in 1904—"Ulysses" is dated at the end as having been begun in 1914.

II

This is the story of "Ulysses" in the light of its Homeric parallel; but to describe the book in such a way gives no idea of what it is really like—of its psychological and technical discoveries or of its magnificent poetry.

"Ulysses" is, I suppose, the most completely "written" novel since Flaubert. The example of the great prose poet of Naturalism has profoundly influenced Joyce—in his attitude toward the modern bourgeois world and in the contrast implied by the Homeric parallel of "Ulysses" between our own and the ancient world, as well as in an ideal of rigorous objectivity and of adaptation of style to subject—as the influence of that other great Naturalistic poet, Ibsen, is obvious in Joyce's single play, "Exiles." But Flaubert had, in general, confined himself to fitting the cadence and the phrase precisely to the mood or object described; and even then it was the phrase rather than the cadence, and the object rather than the mood, with which he was occupied—for mood and cadence in Flaubert do not really vary much: he never embodies himself in his characters nor identifies his voice with theirs, and as a result, Flaubert's own characteristic tone of the sombre-pompous-ironic becomes, in the long run, a little monotonous. But Joyce has undertaken in "Ulysses" not merely to render, with the last accuracy and beauty, the actual sights and sounds among which his people move, but, showing us the world as his characters perceive it, to find the unique vocabulary and rhythm which will represent the thoughts of each. If Flaubert taught Maupassant to look for the definitive adjectives which would distinguish a given cab-driver from every other cab-driver at the Rouen station, so Joyce has set himself the task of finding the precise dialect which will distinguish the thoughts of a given Dubliner from those of every other Dubliner. Thus the mind of Stephen Dedalus is represented by a weaving of bright poetic images and fragmentary abstractions, of things remembered from books, on a rhythm sober, melancholy and proud; that of Bloom by a rapid staccato notation, prosaic but vivid and alert, jetting out in all directions in little ideas growing out of ideas; the thoughts of Father Conmee, the Rector of the Jesuit college, by a precise prose, perfectly colorless and orderly; those of Gerty-Nausicaa by a combination of school-girl colloquialisms with the jargon of cheap romance; and the ruminations of Mrs. Bloom by a long, unbroken rhythm of brogue, like the swell of some profound sea.

Joyce takes us thus directly into the consciousness of his characters, and in order to do so, he has availed himself of methods of which Flaubert never dreamed—of the methods of Symbolism. He has, in "Ulysses," exploited together, as no writer had thought to do before, the resources both of Symbolism and of Naturalism. Proust's novel, masterly as it is, does perhaps represent a falling over into decadence of psychological fiction: the subjective element is finally allowed to invade and to deteriorate even those aspects of the story which really ought to be kept strictly objective if one is to believe that it is actually happening. But Joyce's grasp on his objective world never slips: his work is unshakably established on Naturalistic foundations. Where "A la Recherche du Temps Perdu" leaves many things vague—the ages of the characters and sometimes the actual circumstances of their lives, and—what is worse—whether they may not be merely bad dreams that the hero has had; "Ulysses" has been logically thought out and accurately documented to the last detail: everything that happens is perfectly consistent, and we know precisely what the characters wore, how much they paid for things, where they were at different times of the day, what popular songs they sang and what events they read of in the papers, on June 16, 1904. Yet when we are admitted to the mind of any one of them, we are in a world as complex and special, a world sometimes as fantastic or obscure, as that of a Symbolist poet—and a world rendered by similar devices of language. We are more at home in the minds of Joyce's characters than we are likely to be, except after some study, in the mind of a Mallarmé or an Eliot, because we know more about the circumstances in which they find themselves; but we are confronted with the same sort of confusion between emotions, perceptions and reasonings, and we are likely to be disconcerted by the same sort of hiatuses of thought, when certain links in the association of ideas are dropped down into the unconscious mind so that we are obliged to divine them for ourselves.

But Joyce has carried the methods of Symbolism further than merely to set a Naturalistic scene and then, in that frame, to represent directly the minds of his different characters in Symbolistic monologues like "Mr. Prufrock" or "L'Après-midi d'un Faune." And it is the fact that he has not always stopped here which makes parts of "Ulysses" so puzzling when we read them for the first time. So long as we are dealing with internal monologues in realistic settings, we are dealing with familiar elements merely combined in a novel way—that is, instead of reading, "Bloom said to himself, 'I might manage to write a story to illustrate some proverb or other. I could sign it, Mr. and Mrs. L. M. Bloom,'" we read, "Might manage a sketch. By Mr. and Mrs. L. M. Bloom. Invent a story for some proverb which?" But as we get further along in "Ulysses," we find the realistic setting oddly distorting itself and deliquescing, and we are astonished at the introduction of voices which seem to belong neither to the characters nor to the author.

The point is that of each of his episodes Joyce has tried to make an independent unit which shall blend the different sets of elements of each—the minds of the characters, the place where they are, the atmosphere about them, the feeling of the time of day. Joyce had already, in "A Portrait of the Artist," experimented, as Proust had done, in varying the form and style of the different sections to fit the different ages and phases of his hero—from the infantile fragments of childhood impressions, through the ecstatic revelations and the terrifying nightmares of adolescence, to the self-possessed notations of young manhood. But in "A Portrait of the Artist," Joyce was presenting everything from the point of view of a single particular character, Dedalus; whereas in "Ulysses" he is occupied with a number of different personalities, of whom Dedalus is no longer the centre, and his method, furthermore,

of enabling us to live in their world is not always merely
a matter of making us shift from the point of view of one
to the point of view of another. In order to understand
what Joyce is doing here, one must conceive a set of Symbolistic poems, themselves involving characters whose
minds are represented Symbolistically, depending not
from the sensibility of the poet speaking in his own person, but from the poet's imagination playing a rôle absolutely impersonal and always imposing upon itself all the
Naturalistic restrictions in regard to the story it is telling
at the same time that it allows itself to exercise all the
Symbolistic privileges in regard to the way it tells it. We
are not likely to be prepared for this by the early episodes
of "Ulysses": they are as sober and as clear as the morning
light of the Irish coast in which they take place: the characters' perceptions of the external world are usually distinct
from their thoughts and feelings about them. But in the
newspaper office, for the first time, a general atmosphere
begins to be created, beyond the specific minds of the characters, by a punctuation of the text with newspaper heads
which announce the incidents in the narrative. And in the
library scene, which takes place in the early afternoon, the
setting and people external to Stephen begin to dissolve
in his apprehension of them, heightened and blurred by
some drinks at lunch-time and by the intellectual excitement of the conversation amid the dimness and tameness
of the library—"Eglintoneyes, quick with pleasure, looked
up shybrightly. Gladly glancing, a merry puritan, through
the twisted eglantine." Here, however, we still see all

through Stephen's eyes—through the eyes of a single character; but in the scene in the Ormond Hotel, which takes
place a couple of hours later—our reveries absorb the
world about us progressively as daylight fades and as the
impressions of the day accumulate—the sights and sounds
and the emotional vibrations and the appetites for food
and drink of the late afternoon, the laughter, the gold-
and-bronze hair of the barmaids, the jingling of Blazes
Boylan's car on his way to visit Molly Bloom, the ringing
of the hoofs of the horses of the viceregal cavalcade clang-
ing in through the open window, the ballad sung by Simon Dedalus, the sound of the piano accompaniment and
the comfortable supper of Bloom—though they are not all,
from beginning to end, perceived by Bloom himself—all
mingle quite un-Naturalistically in a harmony of bright
sound, ringing color, poignant indistinct feeling and de-
clining light. The scene in the brothel, where it is night
and where Dedalus and Bloom are drunk, is like a slowed-
up moving-picture, in which the intensified vision of reality is continually lapsing into phantasmagoric visions;
and the let-down after the excitement of this, the lassitude
and staleness of the cabmen's shelter where Bloom takes
Stephen to get him some coffee, is rendered by a prose as
flavorless, as weary and as banal as the incidents which it
reports. Joyce has achieved here, by different methods, a
relativism like that of Proust: he is reproducing in literature the different aspects, the different proportions and
textures, which things and people take on at different
times and under different circumstances.

III

I do not think that Joyce has been equally successful with all these technical devices in "Ulysses"; but before it will be possible to discuss them further, we must approach the book from another point of view.

It has always been characteristic of Joyce to neglect action, narrative, drama, of the usual kind, even the direct impact on one another of the characters as we get it in the ordinary novel, for a sort of psychological portraiture. There is tremendous vitality in Joyce, but very little movement. Like Proust, he is symphonic rather than narrative. His fiction has its progressions, its developments, but they are musical rather than dramatic. The most elaborate and interesting piece in "Dubliners"—the story called "The Dead"—is simply a record of the modification brought about during a single evening in the relations of a husband and wife by the man's becoming aware, from the effect produced on the woman by a song which she has heard at a family party, that she has once been loved by another man; "A Portrait of the Artist as a Young Man" is simply a series of pictures of the author at successive stages of his development; the theme of "Exiles" is, like that of "The Dead," the modification in the relations of a husband and wife which follows the reappearance of a man who has been the wife's lover. And "Ulysses," again, for all its vast scale, is simply the story of another small but significant change in the relations of yet another married couple as a result of the impingement on their household of the personality of an only slightly known young man. Most of these stories cover a period of only a few hours, and they are never carried any further. When Joyce has explored one of these situations, when he has established the small gradual readjustment, he has done all that interests him.

All, that is, from the point of view of ordinary incident. But though Joyce almost entirely lacks appetite for violent conflict or vigorous action, his work is prodigiously rich and alive. His force, instead of following a line, expands itself in every dimension (including that of Time) about a single point. The world of "Ulysses" is animated by a complex inexhaustible life: we revisit it as we do a city, where we come more and more to recognize faces, to understand personalities, to grasp relations, currents and interests. Joyce has exercised considerable technical ingenuity in introducing us to the elements of his story in an order which will enable us to find our bearings: yet I doubt whether any human memory is capable, on a first reading, of meeting the demands of "Ulysses." And when we reread it, we start in at any point, as if it were indeed something solid like a city which actually existed in space, and which could be entered from any direction—as Joyce is said, in composing his books, to work on the different parts simultaneously. More than any other work of fiction, unless perhaps the "Comédie Humaine," "Ulysses" creates the illusion of a living social organism. We see it only for twenty hours, yet we know its past as well as its present.

We possess Dublin, seen, heard, smelt and felt, brooded over, imagined, remembered.

Joyce's handling of this immense material, his method of giving his book a shape, resembles nothing else in modern fiction. The first critics of "Ulysses" mistook the novel for a "slice of life" and objected that it was too fluid or too chaotic. They did not recognize a plot because they could not recognize a progression; and the title told them nothing. They could not even discover a pattern. It is now apparent, however, that "Ulysses" suffers from an excess of design rather than from a lack of it. Joyce has drawn up an outline of his novel, of which he has allowed certain of his commentators to avail themselves, but which he has not allowed them to publish in its entirety (though it is to be presumed that the book on "Ulysses" which Mr. Stuart Gilbert has announced will include all the information contained in it); and from this outline it appears that Joyce has set himself the task of fulfilling the requirements of a most complicated scheme—a scheme which we could scarcely have divined except in its more obvious features. For even if we had known about the Homeric parallel and had identified certain of the correspondences—if we had had no difficulty in recognizing the Cyclops in the ferocious professional Fenian or Circe in the brothel-keeper or Hades in the cemetery—we should never have suspected how closely and how subtly the parallel had been followed—we should never have guessed, for example, that when Bloom passes through the National Library while Stephen is having his discussion with the literary men, he is escaping, on the one hand, a Scylla—that is, Aristotle, the rock of Dogma; and, on the other, a Charybdis—Plato, the whirlpool of Mysticism; nor that, when Stephen walks on the seashore, he is reënacting the combat with Proteus —in this case, primal matter, of whose continual transformations Stephen is reminded by the objects absorbed or washed up by the sea, but whose forms he is able to hold and fix, as the Homeric Proteus was held and vanquished, by power of the words which give him images for them. Nor should we have known that the series of phrases and onomatopoetic syllables placed at the beginning of the Sirens episode—the singing in the Ormond Hotel—and selected from the narrative which follows, are supposed to be musical themes and that the episode itself is a fugue; and though we may have felt the ironic effect of the specimens of inflated Irish journalism introduced at regular intervals in the conversation with the patriot in the pub—we should hardly have understood that these had been produced by a deliberate technique of "gigantism"—for, since the Citizen represents the Cyclops, and since the Cyclops was a giant, he must be rendered formidable by a parade of all the banalities of his patriotic claptrap swollen to gigantic proportions. We should probably never have guessed all this, and we should certainly never have guessed at the ingenuity which Joyce has expended in other ways. Not only, we learn from the outline, is there an elaborate Homeric parallel in "Ulysses," but there is also an organ of the human body and a human science or art featured in every episode. We look these up, a little incredulously, but there, we find, they all actually are—buried and disguised beneath the realistic surface, but carefully planted, unmistakably dwelt upon. And if we are tipped off, we are able further to discover all sorts of concealed ornaments and emblems: in the chapter of the Lotos-Eaters, for example, countless references to flowers; in the Laestrygonians, to eating; in the Sirens, puns on musical terms; and in Æolus, the newspaper office, not merely many references to wind but, according to Mr. Gilbert— the art featured in this episode being Rhetoric—some hundred different figures of speech.

Now the Homeric parallel in "Ulysses" is in general pointedly and charmingly carried out and justifies itself: it does help to give the story a universal significance and it enables Joyce to show us in the actions and the relations of his characters meanings which he perhaps could not easily have indicated in any other way—since the characters themselves must be largely unaware of these meanings and since Joyce has adopted the strict objective method, in which the author must not comment on the action. And we may even accept the arts and sciences and the organs of the human body as making the book complete and comprehensive, if a little laboriously systematic —the whole of man's experience in a day. But when we get all these things together and further complicated by the virtuosity of the technical devices, the result is sometimes baffling or confusing. We become aware, as we examine the outline, that when we went through "Ulysses" for the first time, it was these organs and arts and sciences and Homeric correspondences which sometimes so discouraged our interest. We had been climbing over these obstacles without knowing it, in our attempts to follow Dedalus and Bloom. The trouble was that, beyond the ostensible subject and, as it were, beneath the surface of the narrative, too many other subjects and too many different orders of subjects were being proposed to our attention.

It seems to me difficult, then, not to conclude that Joyce elaborated "Ulysses" too much—that he tried to put too many things into it. What is the value of all the references to flowers in the Lotos-Eaters chapter, for example? They do not create in the Dublin streets an atmosphere of lotus-eating—we are merely puzzled, if we have not been told to look for them, as to why Joyce has chosen to have Bloom think and see certain things, of which the final explanation is that they are pretexts for mentioning flowers. And do not the gigantic interpolations of the Cyclops episode defeat their object by making it impossible for us to follow the narrative? The interpolations are funny in themselves, the incident related is a masterpiece of language and humor, the idea of combining them seems happy, yet the effect is mechanical and annoying: in the end we have to read the whole thing through, skipping the interpolations, in order to find out what has happened. The worst example of the capacities for failure of this too synthetic, too systematic, method seems to me the scene in the maternity hospital. I have described above what actually takes place there as I have worked it out, after several readings and in the light of Joyce's outline. The Oxen of the Sun are "Fertility"—the crime committed against them is "Fraud." But, not content with this, Joyce has been at pains to fill the episode with references to real cattle and to include a long conversation about bulls. As for the special technique, it seems to me in this case not to have any real appropriateness to the situation, but to have been dictated by sheer fantastic pedantry: Joyce describes his method here as "embryonic," in conformity to the subject, maternity, and the chapter is written as a series of parodies of English literary styles from the bad Latin of the early chronicles up through Huxley and Carlyle, the development of the language corresponding to the growth of the child in the womb. Now something important takes place in this episode—the meeting between Dedalus and Bloom—and an important point is being made about it. But we miss the point because it is all we can do to follow what is happening at the drinking-party, itself rather a confused affair, through the medium of the language of the Morte d'Arthur, the seventeenth-century diaries, the eighteenth-century novels, and a great many other kinds of literature in which we are not prepared at the moment to be interested. If we pay attention to the parodies, we miss the story; and if we try to follow the story, we are unable to appreciate the parodies. The parodies have spoiled the story; and the necessity of telling the story through them has taken most of the life out of the parodies.

Joyce has as little respect as Proust for the capacities of

the reader's attention; and one feels, in Joyce's case as in Proust's, that the *longueurs* which break our backs, the mechanical combinations of elements which fail to coalesce, are partly a result of the effort of a supernormally energetic mind to compensate by piling things up for an inability to make them move.

We have now arrived, in the maternity hospital, at the climactic scenes of the story, and Joyce has bogged us as he has never bogged us before. We shall forget the Oxen of the Sun in the wonderful night-town scene which follows it—but we shall be bogged afterwards worse than ever in the interminable let-down of the cabman's shelter and in the scientific question-and-answer chapter which undertakes to communicate to us through the most opaque and uninviting medium possible Dedalus's conversation with Bloom. The night-town episode itself and Mrs. Bloom's soliloquy, which closes the book, are, of course, among the best things in it—but the relative proportions of the other three latter chapters and the jarring effect of the pastiche style sandwiched in with the straight Naturalistic seem to me artistically absolutely indefensible. One can understand that Joyce may have intended the colorless and tiresome episodes to set off the rich and vivid ones, and also that it is of the essence of his point of view to represent the profoundest changes of our lives as beginning naturally between night and morning without the parties' appreciating their importance at the time; but a hundred and sixty-one more or less deliberately tedious pages are too heavy a dead weight for even the brilliant flights of the other hundred and ninety-nine pages to carry. Furthermore, Joyce has here half-buried his story under the virtuosity of his technical devices. It is almost as if he had elaborated it so much and worked over it so long that he had forgotten, in the amusement of writing parodies, the drama which he had originally intended to stage; or as if he were trying to divert and overwhelm us by irrelevant entertainments and feats in order that we might not be dissatisfied with the flatness—except for the drunken scene—of Dedalus's final meeting with Bloom; or even perhaps as if he did not, after all, quite want us to understand his story, as if he had, not quite conscious of what he was doing, ended by throwing up between us and it a fortification of solemn burlesque prose—as if he were shy and solicitous about it, and wanted to protect it from us.

IV

Yet even these episodes to which I have objected contribute something valuable to "Ulysses." In the chapter of parodies, for example, Joyce seems to be saying to us: "Here are specimens of the sort of thing that man has written about himself in the past—how naïve or pretentious they seem! I have broken through these assumptions and pretences and shown you how he must recognize himself to-day." And in the question-and-answer chapter, which is written entirely from the conventional point of view of science and where we are supplied with every possible physical, statistical, biographical and astronomical fact about Stephen's visit to Bloom: "This is all that the twentieth-century man thinks he knows about himself and his universe. Yet how mechanical and rigid this reasoning seems when we apply it to Molly and Bloom—how inadequate to explain them!"

For one of the most remarkable features of "Ulysses" is its interest as an investigation into the nature of human consciousness and behavior. Its importance from the point of view of psychology has never, it seems to me, been properly appreciated—though its influence on other books and, in consequence, upon our ideas about ourselves, has already been profound. Joyce has attempted in "Ulysses" to render as exhaustively, as precisely and as directly as it is possible in words to do, what our participation in life is like—or rather, what it seems to us like as from moment to moment we live. In order to make this record complete, he has been obliged to disregard a number of conventions of taste which, especially in English-speaking countries, have in modern times been pretty strictly observed, even by the writers who have aimed to be most scrupulously truthful. Joyce has studied what we are accustomed to consider the dirty, the trivial and the base elements in our lives with the relentlessness of a modern psychologist; and he has also—what the contemporary Naturalist has seldom been poet enough for—done justice to all those elements in our lives which we have been in the habit of describing by such names as love, nobility, truth and beauty. It is curious to reflect that a number of critics—including, curiously enough, Arnold Bennett—

should have found Joyce misanthropic. Flaubert is misanthropic, if you like—and in reproducing his technique, Joyce sometimes suggests his acrid tone. But Stephen, Bloom and Mrs. Bloom are certainly not either unamiable or unattractive—and for all their misfortunes and shortcomings, they inspire us with considerable respect. Stephen and Bloom are played off a little against the duller and meaner people about them; but even these people can scarcely be said to be treated with bitterness, even when, as in the case of Buck Mulligan or the elder Dedalus, Stephen's feeling about them is bitter. Joyce is remarkable, rather, for equanimity: in spite of the nervous intensity of "Ulysses," there is a real serenity and detachment behind it—we are in the presence of a mind which has much in common with that of a certain type of philosopher, who in his effort to understand the causes of things, to interrelate the different elements of the universe, has reached a point where the ordinary values of good and bad, beautiful and ugly, have been lost in the excellence and beauty of transcendent understanding itself.

I believe that the first readers of "Ulysses" were shocked, not merely by Joyce's use of certain words ordinarily excluded to-day from English literature, but by his way of representing those aspects of human nature which we tend to consider incongruous as intimately, inextricably mingled. Yet the more we read "Ulysses," the more we are convinced of its psychological truth, and the more we are amazed at Joyce's genius in mastering and in presenting, not through analysis or generalization, but by the complete recreation of life in the process of being lived, the relations of human beings to their environment and to each other; the nature of their perception of what goes on about them and of what goes on within themselves; and the interdependence of their intellectual, their physical, their professional and their emotional lives. To have traced all these interdependences, to have given each of these elements its value, yet never to have lost sight of the moral through preoccupation with the physical, nor to have forgotten the general in the particular; to have exhibited ordinary humanity without either satirizing it or sentimentalizing it—this would already have been sufficiently remarkable; but to have subdued all this material to the uses of a supremely finished and disciplined work of art is a feat which has hardly been equalled in the literature of our time.

In Stephen's diary in "A Portrait of the Artist," we find this significant entry apropos of a poem by Yeats: "Michael Robartes remembers forgotten beauty and, when his arms wrap her round, he presses in his arms the loveliness which has long faded from the world. Not this. Not at all. I desire to press in my arms the loveliness which has not yet come into the world."

And with "Ulysses," Joyce has brought into literature a new and unknown beauty. Some readers have regretted the extinction in the later Joyce of the charming lyric poet of his two little books of poems and the *fin de siècle* prose writer of the *fin de siècle* phases of "A Portrait of the Artist as a Young Man" (both the prose and verse of the early Joyce showed the influence of Yeats). This poet is still present in "Ulysses": "Kind air defined the coigns of houses in Kildare Street. No birds. Frail from the housetops two plumes of smoke ascended, pluming, and in a flaw of softness softly were blown." But the conventions of the romantic lyric, of "æsthetic" *fin de siècle* prose, even of the æsthetic Naturalism of Flaubert, can no longer, for Joyce, be made to accommodate the reality of experience. The diverse elements of experience are perceived in different relations and they must be differently represented. Joyce has found for this new vision a new language, but a language which, instead of diluting or doing violence to his poetic genius, enables it to assimilate more materials, to readjust itself more completely and successfully than that of perhaps any other poet of our age to the new self-consciousness of the modern world. But in achieving this, Joyce has ceased to write verse. I have suggested, in connection with Valéry and Eliot, that verse itself as a literary medium is coming to be used for fewer and fewer and for more and more special purposes, and that it may be destined to fall into disuse. And it seems to me that Joyce's literary development is a striking corroboration of this view. His prose works have an artistic intensity, a definitive beauty of surface and of form, which make him comparable to the great poets rather than to most of the great novelists.

Joyce is indeed really the great poet of a new phase of the human consciousness. Like Proust's or Whitehead's or Einstein's world, Joyce's world is always changing as it is perceived by different observers and by them at different times. It is an organism made up of "events," which may be taken as infinitely inclusive or infinitely small and each of which involves all the others; and each of these events is unique. Such a world cannot be presented in terms of such artificial abstractions as have been conventional in the past: solid institutions, groups, individuals, which play the parts of distinct durable entities—or even of solid psychological factors: dualisms of good and evil, mind and matter, flesh and spirit, instinct and reason; clear conflicts between passion and duty, between conscience and interest. Not that these conceptions are left out of Joyce's world: they are all there in the minds of the characters; and the realities they represent are there, too. But everything is reduced to terms of "events" like those of modern physics and philosophy—events which make up a "continuum," but which may be taken as infinitely small. Joyce has built out of these events a picture, amazingly lifelike and living, of the everyday world we know— and a picture which seems to allow us to see into it, to follow its variations and intricacies, as we have never been able to do before.

Nor are Joyce's characters merely the sum of the particles into which their experience has been dissociated: we come to imagine them as solidly, to feel their personalities as unmistakably, as we do with any characters in fiction; and we realize finally that they are also symbols. Bloom himself is in one of his aspects the typical modern man: Joyce has made him a Jew, one supposes, partly in order that he may be conceived equally well as an inhabitant of any provincial city of the European or Europeanized world. He makes a living by petty business, he leads the ordinary middle-class life—and he holds the conventional enlightened opinions of the time: he believes in science, social reform and internationalism. But Bloom is surpassed and illuminated from above by Stephen, who represents the intellect, the creative imagination; and he is upheld by Mrs. Bloom, who represents the body, the earth. Bloom leaves with us in the long run the impression that he is something both better and worse than either of them; for Stephen sins through pride, the sin of the intellect; and Molly is at the mercy of the flesh; but Bloom, though a less powerful personality than either, has the strength of humility. It is difficult to describe the character of Bloom as Joyce finally makes us feel it: it takes precisely the whole of "Ulysses" to put him before us. It is not merely that Bloom is mediocre, that he is clever, that he is commonplace—that he is comic, that he is pathetic—that he is, as Rebecca West says, a figure of abject "squatting" vulgarity, that he is at moments, as Foster Damon says, the Christ—he is all of these, he is all the possibilities of that ordinary humanity which is somehow not so ordinary after all; and it is the proof of Joyce's greatness that, though we recognize Bloom's perfect truth and typical character, we cannot pigeonhole him in any familiar category, racial, social, moral, literary or even—because he does really have, after all, a good deal in common with the Greek Ulysses—historical.

Both Stephen and Molly are more easily describable because they represent extremes. Both are capable of rising to heights which Bloom can never reach. In Stephen's rhapsody on the seashore, when he first realizes his artist's vocation, in "A Portrait of the Artist as a Young Man," we have had the ecstasy of the creative mind. In the soliloquy of Mrs. Bloom, Joyce has given us another ecstasy of creation, the rhapsody of the flesh. Stephen's dream was conceived in loneliness, by a drawing apart from his fellows. But Mrs. Bloom is like the earth, which gives the same life to all: she feels a maternal kinship with all living creatures. She pities the "poor donkeys slipping half asleep" in the steep street of Gibraltar, as she does "the sentry in front of the governor's house . . . half roasted" in the sun; and she gives herself to the bootblack at the General Post Office as readily as to Professor Goodwin. But, none the less, she will tend to breed from the highest type of life she knows: she turns to Bloom, and, beyond him, toward Stephen. This gross body, the body of humanity, upon which the whole structure of "Ulysses" rests—still throbbing with so strong a rhythm amid obscenity, commonness and squalor—is laboring to throw up some knowledge and beauty by which it may transcend itself.

These two great flights of the mind carry off all the ignominies and trivialities through which Joyce has made us pass: they seem to me—the soaring silver prose of the one, the deep embedded pulse of the other—among the supreme expressions in literature of the creative powers of humanity: they are, respectively, the justifications of the woman and the man.

V

Since finishing "Ulysses," Joyce has been engaged upon another work, about half of which has been published in the transatlantic monthly, *Transition*. It is not possible to judge this book properly in the imperfect form in which it has appeared. It is intended as a sort of complement to "Ulysses"; Joyce has explained that, as "Ulysses" deals with the day and with the conscious mind, so his new work is to deal with the night and with the subconscious. The whole book is apparently to occupy itself with the single night's sleep of a single character. Joyce has already exhibited in "Ulysses" a unique genius for the representation of special psychological states: I know of nothing else in literature, for example, like the drunken night-town scene, with its astounding recreation of all the deliriums, dazes, gibberings, exaltations and hallucinations of drunkenness. And Joyce's method of rendering the phases of sleep is similar to his methods in the Circe episode. But he is here attempting something even more difficult, and his way of doing it raises an important question in regard to all Joyce's later work. Joyce, as I have said, always nowadays represents the consciousness of his characters directly: but his method of representing consciousness is to let you overhear his characters talking to themselves. Joyce's people think and feel exclusively in terms of words, for Joyce himself thinks in terms of words. This is partly due, no doubt, to his defective eyesight, which of late years has become so serious as to make it difficult for him to work. There is an interesting passage in "A Portrait of the Artist" in which Joyce himself discusses this aspect of his writing:

"He drew forth a phrase from his treasure and spoke it softly to himself:

"—A day of dappled seaborne clouds.——

"The phrase and the day and the scene harmonized in a chord. Words. Was it their colors? He allowed them to glow and fade, hue after hue: sunrise gold, the russet and green of apple orchards, azure of waves, the greyfringed fleece of clouds. No, it was not their colors: it was the poise and balance of the period itself. Did he then love the rhythmic rise and fall of words better than their associations of legend and color? Or was it that, being as weak of sight as he was shy of mind, he drew less pleasure from the reflection of the glowing sensible world through the prism of a language many colored and richly storied than from the contemplation of an inner world of individual emotions mirrored perfectly in a lucid supple periodic prose."

And in "Ulysses" we hear the characters far more plainly than we see them: Joyce supplies us with descriptions of them in sparse, scrupulous phrases, one trait here, another there. But the Dublin of "Ulysses" is a city of voices. Who has a clear idea of how Bloom or Molly Bloom looks?—and should we have a clear idea of Stephen if we had never seen photographs of Joyce? But their eternally soliloquizing voices become our intimate companions and haunt us long afterwards.

Joyce already seems sometimes, in "Ulysses," to go a little beyond the probabilities in the vocabulary which he allows Bloom to command. When Bloom, in the drunken scene, for example, imagines himself giving birth to "eight male yellow and white children," all "with valuable metallic faces" and each with "his name printed in legible letters on his shirt-front: Nasodoro, Goldfinger, Chrysostomos, Maindorée, Silversmile, Silberselber, Vi-fargent, Panargyros"—we have difficulty in believing that he would have been learned enough for this. Yet I do not suppose that Joyce means us to think of Bloom as actually formulating these words in his mind: it is the author's way of conveying in words a vision which on the part of Bloom must have been a good deal less distinct, or at least a good deal less literary, than this. Now, in his new book, Joyce has tried to make his hero express directly in words, again, states of mind which do not usually in reality make use of words at all—for the subconscious has no language —the dreaming mind does not usually speak—and when it does, it is more likely to express itself in the looking-glass language of "Jabberwocky" than in anything resembling ordinary speech. Joyce's attempts to write the language of dreams have a good deal in common with those of Lewis Carroll; but the difference between his new novel and the Alice books is that, whereas in the Alice books it is the author who is supposed to be telling in

straight English the adventures which his heroine thinks
she is having and the literary language peculiar to dreams
appears only in a poem which she reads, in Joyce's book
he is plunging us directly into the consciousness of the
dreamer itself, which is presented, without explanations
by the author, entirely in the Jabberwocky language. The
book is thus more easily comprehensible to literary people
than to people who are not "word-minded," whose minds
do not habitually breed words in response to sensations,
emotions and thoughts. Yet it is worth making the effort
to understand, because what Joyce is trying to do is both
artistically and psychologically extremely interesting, and
it may be that he will turn out to have written the most
remarkable piece of dream-literature in existence.

The best way to understand Joyce's method is to note
what goes on in one's own mind when one is just drop-
ping off to sleep. Images—or words, if one thinks in words
like Joyce—which were already in the conscious mind will
suddenly acquire an ominous significance which has nothing to do with their ordinary functions; some vivid incident which may have taken place just before one went to
bed will begin to swell with a meaning, an emotion,
which at first we do not recognize because it has come up
from the submerged part of the mind and is attempting
to pass itself off in the clothes of an immediate experience
—because it is dissociated from the situation out of which
it originally arose. Or conversely, one may rid oneself of a
troublesome abstract idea with which one has been preoccupied by allowing it to transform itself into some in-

nocuous concrete image more easily dismissed from the attention: the page of a philosophical book, for example, where one had been continually stumbling over phrases and terms may vanish on the threshold of sleep in the guise of a spotted man, the spots having substituted themselves for the impenetrable words and phrases. And so the images which our waking mind would keep distinct from one another incongruously mix in our sleep with an effect of perfect congruity. A single one of Joyce's sentences, therefore, will combine two or three different meanings—two or three different sets of symbols; a single word may combine two or three. Joyce has profited, in inventing his dream-language, by Freud's researches into the principles which govern the language actually spoken in dreams: certain people, it appears, do make up "portmanteau-words" in their sleep; but we are not, I take it, to suppose that Joyce's hero necessarily frames all these sentences to himself. Except when he dreams he is reading something or carrying on a conversation, the language is merely a literary equivalent for sleeping states not even articulate in fancy. Nor are we to assume that Joyce's sleeper is actually master of all the languages or understands all the allusions of which Joyce makes him avail himself in his dream. We are now at a level below particularized languages—we are in the region whence all languages arise and where the impulses to all acts have their origin.

The hero of the night's sleep in question is, we gather, a man named H. C. Earwicker, a Norwegian or descen-

dant of Norwegians, living in Dublin. He seems to have
attempted a number of occupations—to have been a post-
man, to have worked in Guiness's Brewery, to have kept
a hotel and a shop. He is married and has children, but
has apparently been carrying on a flirtation with a girl
named Anna Livia. This, along with other lapses from
respectability associated with it in his mind, troubles his
conscience and his repose. We are introduced, at the very
beginning, into Earwicker's drowsing consciousness, and
we have to make what we can of the names, the shapes,
and above all, of the voices, which fill that dim and shifting world—they combine and recombine, they are always
changing into one another—but as we go on, we find
the same themes recurring and we begin to be able to
understand them in relation to one another—we become
familiar with the character of Earwicker—we begin to
guess at his condition and history. We identify Maggie
and the children, the house in which they live, the four
old men with the donkey, Earwicker's drunken misdemeanors and his fear of being caught by the police, the
washerwomen gathering up their washing, Anna Livia
on the bank of the Liffey, the Hill of Howth, the tree and
the stone. But none of these elements is seen clearly or
objectively—they are all aspects, the dramatic projection of
aspects, of Earwicker himself: men and women, old and
young, stronger and weaker, river and mountain, tree and
stone—it is the dreamer who speaks or is spoken to, who
sees or is seen, in all of them. The old men come to admire
him as he is sleeping on the mountainside, but in a mo-

ment it is Earwicker himself who is talking about himself; or he splits up into two personalities, one of whom bullies or accuses the other. He is coming out of a pub into the street with a party of drunken companions, many people are standing about but the revellers do not care how much attention they attract: they egg on one of their number to sing but the song turns out to be a recital of all Earwicker's failures and sins—he has proved himself a fool and a swindler to the derision of all Dublin, his wife is going to read him the Riot Act. Or he sets out very sweetly to explain something by a fable of "the Mookse and the Gripes": the Mookse comes swaggering up to the Gripes, who is hanging on a tree—a sort of altercation takes place, and it turns into rather a painful reënactment of one of Earwicker's encounters with the police—but dusk falls and the washerwomen come out and carry off the Mookse and the Gripes, who are now merely two pieces of laundry.

One of the most remarkable parts which have so far appeared is the *allegro* conclusion to the first of the four long sections which are to make up the completed work. (Joyce has allowed it to be published separately in a little book called "Anna Livia Plurabelle.") Here the washerwomen have become identified with the stone and elm on the riverbank—we hear them gossiping about Anna Livia, who is both the girl with whom the hero is in love and the river Liffey; and their gossip is the voice of the river itself, light, rapid, incessant, almost metrical, now monotonously running on one note, now impeded and syncopated, but vivaciously, interminably babbling its indistinct rigmarole story, half-unearthly, half-vulgarly human, of a heroine half-legendary, half-real:

"Oh tell me all about Anna Livia! I want to hear all about Anna Livia. Well, you know Anna Livia? Yes, of course, we all know Anna Livia. Tell me all. Tell me now, You'll die when you hear. . . . Tell me, tell me, how cam she camlin through all her fellows, the neckar she was, the diveline? Linking one and knocking the next, tapting a flank and tipting a jutty and palling in and pietaring out and clyding by on her eastway. Waiwhou was the first thurever burst? . . . She says herself she hardly knows whuon the annals her graveller was, a dynast of Leinster, a wolf of the sea, or what he did or how blyth she played or how, when, why, where and who offon he jumnpad her. She was just a young thin pale soft shy slim slip of a thing then, sauntering, by silvamoonlake, and he was a heavy trudging lurching lieabroad of a Curraghman, making his hay for whose sun to shine on, as tough as the oaktrees (peats be with them!) used to rustle that time down by the dykes of killing Kildare, that forstfellfoss with a plash across her. She thought she's sankh neathe the ground with nymphant shame when he gave her the tigris eye!"

As darkness falls between stone and elm, the voices grow husky and vague:

"And ho! Hey? What all men. Hot? His tittering daughters of Whawk?

"Can't hear with the waters of. The chittering waters

of. Flittering bats, fieldmice, bawk talk. Ho! Are you not gone ahome? What Tom Malone? Can't hear with bawk of bats, all the liffeying waters of. Ho, talk save us. My foos won't moos. I feel as old as yonder elm. A tale told of Shaun or Shem? All Livia's daughtersons. Dark hawks hear us. Night! Night! My ho head halls. I feel as heavy as yonder stone. Tell me of John or Shaun? Who were Shem and Shaun the living sons or daughters of? Night now! Tell me, tell me, tell me, elm! Night night! Tell me tale of stem or stone. Beside the rivering waters of, hitherandthithering waters of. Night!"

Night is just falling in this first section of the book, and the shadow of the past, the memory presumably of the day before, darkens the hero's sleep—the vulgarities of his waking life oppress him and pursue him; but after midnight, as dawn approaches, as he becomes dimly aware of the first light, the dream begins to brighten and to rise unencumbered. If I am not mistaken, the middle-aged Earwicker reverts to the period of his youth, once again he is carefree, attractive, well-liked—his spirit turns refreshed to the new day. Are we to leave him on the verge of waking or are we finally to see the fantasies of the dream closed down into the commonplace fate which we have already been able to divine?

This new production of Joyce's exaggerates the qualities we have noted in "Ulysses." There is even less action than in "Ulysses." Joyce has set out with certain definite themes and the themes are evidently all to have their developments, but these developments take a long time. We

make progress—we pass from night to morning—and no
doubt, when the whole book is before us, we shall see that
some sort of psychological drama has been played out in
Earwicker's mind—but, as we progress, we go round and
round. And whereas in "Ulysses" there is only one parallel, in this new book there are a whole set: Adam and
Eve, Tristan and Isolde, Swift and Vanessa, Cain and
Abel, Michael and Lucifer, Wellington and Napoleon.
The multiplication of references does, to be sure, deepen
and extend the significance of Earwicker: he and Anna
Livia are the eternal woman and the eternal man, and
during the early hours of heaviness and horror of Earwicker's dream, he is an Adam fallen from grace—to be
redeemed, Joyce is said to have announced, with the renewal of the morning light. And it would seem that
Joyce has provided plausible reasons for the appearance of
all these personages in his hero's dream: Napoleon and
Wellington have gotten in by way of the Wellington
monument in the Phœnix Park, near which one of Earwicker's misdemeanors has been committed; and Michael
and Lucifer—it appears from the last instalment published, in which Earwicker is partly waked up toward
morning by the crying of one of his children—by a picture
on the bedroom wall. Yet the effect of the superposition,
one upon the other, of such a variety of parallels seems
sometimes less to enrich the book than to give it a mere
synthetic complication. Joyce is again, we come to the
conclusion, trying to do too many things at once. The
style he has invented for his purpose works on the prin-

ciple of a palimpsest: one meaning, one set of images, is written over another. Now we can grasp a certain number of such suggestions simultaneously, but Joyce, with his characteristic disregard for the reader, apparently works over and over his pages, packing in allusions and puns. This appears clearly from the different versions which have been published in various places of the Anna Livia Pluribelle section (I have given in an appendix three stages of the same passage from this). Joyce has improved it in making the texture denser, but this enrichment also obscures the main outlines and somewhat oversolidifies and impedes the dim ambiguous fluidity of the dream—especially when it takes the form of introducing in the final version puns on the names of some five hundred rivers. And as soon as we are aware of Joyce himself systematically embroidering on his text, deliberately inventing puzzles, the illusion of the dream is lost.

Yet, on the whole, this illusion is created and kept up with extraordinary success. There is a curious fascination about becoming gradually acquainted with a character whom we know only from the inside and from his dreams. And without the complications of his vocabulary, Joyce would no doubt never be able to paint for us with so sensitive and sure a hand the turbid life of that mental half-world where the unconscious is merged with the conscious—as without his machinery of history and myth, he would not be able to give his subject any poetic freedom of significance beyond the realistic framework which holds it firm. We are to see in H. C. Earwicker Everyman (he imagines his initials standing for Here Comes Everybody). We are to find in his dream all human possibilities—for out of that human nature, that psychological plasm, which swims dark and deep beneath the surface of the meagre words, the limited acts, the special mask, of one man's actual daytime career, all history and myth have arisen—victim and conqueror, lover and beloved, childhood and old age—all the forms of human experience. And what humor, what imagination, what poetry, what psychological wisdom, Joyce has put into Earwicker's dream! I have offered the criticisms above only tentatively and without assurance: when we come to think about what we take at first to be the defects in Joyce's work, we find them so closely involved with the depth of his thought and the originality of his conception that we are obliged to grant them a certain necessity. And whatever difficulties we may have with this book in its present fragmentary and incomplete state, I feel confident that, when we read it as a whole, we shall find, not only that it is not unworthy—as the snappers at the heels of genius have been so eager and prompt to assert—of the great master of letters who wrote it, but that he is still at the height of his power.

VII

GERTRUDE STEIN

GERTRUDE STEIN, born in Allegheny, Pennsylvania, a student of psychology and medicine who is said to have been considered by William James the most brilliant woman pupil he had ever had, published in 1909 a book of fiction called "Three Lives." It was brought out by a small and obscure publisher and at that time attracted little attention, but, loaned from hand to hand, it acquired a certain reputation. "Three Lives," which bore on its title-page a quotation from Jules Laforgue, was a work of what would at that time have been called realism, but it was realism of rather a novel kind. The book consisted of three long short stories—the histories of three women, two of them German servant-girls, the other a mulatto girl. What is most remarkable in these stories—especially if we compare them with such a typically Naturalistic production as Flaubert's "Un Cœur Simple," in which we feel that the old family servant has been seen from a great distance and documented with effort—is the closeness with which the author has been able to identify herself with her characters. In a style which appears to owe nothing to that of any other novelist, she seems to have caught the very rhythms and accents of the minds of her heroines: we find ourselves sharing the lives of the Good Anna and Gentle Lena so intimately that we forget about their position and see the world limited to their range, just as in Melanctha's case—and this is what makes her story one of the best as well as one of the earliest attempts of a white American novelist to understand the mind of the modern Americanized negro—we become so immersed in Melanctha's world that we quite forget its inhabitants are black. And we discover that these histories have a significance different from that of ordinary realistic fiction: Miss Stein is interested in her subjects, not from the point of view of the social conditions of which they might be taken as representative, but as three fundamental types of women: the self-sacrificing Anna, who combines devotion with domination; the dreamy and passive Lena, for whom it is natural to allow herself to be used and effaced from life by other lives; and the passionate and complex Melanctha, who "was always losing what she had in wanting all the things she saw." Behind the limpid and slightly monotonous simplicity of Gertrude Stein's sentences, one becomes aware of her masterly grasp of the organisms, contradictory and indissoluble, which human personalities are.

"Three Lives," though not widely circulated, exercised a considerable influence. Carl Van Vechten wrote about it; Eugene O'Neill and Sherwood Anderson read it with admiration. It is interesting to note that all three of these writers were to occupy themselves later with negro life, in regard to which Miss Stein had given an example of an attitude not complicated by race-consciousness. And Sherwood Anderson seems to have learned from her, in his own even less Naturalistic, even more dreamlike, fiction, both his recurrent repetitions with their effect of ballad refrains and his method of telling a story in a series of simple declarative sentences of almost primer-like baldness.

Gertrude Stein's next book was a long novel, "The Making of Americans," written between 1906 and 1908, but not published till 1925. I confess that I have not read this book all through, and I do not know whether it is possible to do so. "The Making of Americans" runs to almost a thousand large pages of small closely-printed type. The first chapters show the same remarkable qualities as "Three Lives," though in a somewhat diluted form. Miss Stein sets before us the men and women of her German-Jewish families with all the strong sense we have already admired for the various and irreducible entities of human character; and we are made, as we are in "Three Lives," to feel life as her people feel it, to take for granted just as they do the whole complex of conditions of which they are part. But already some ruminative self-hypnosis, some progressive slowing-up of the mind, has begun to show itself in Miss Stein's work as a sort of fatty degeneration of her imagination and style. In "Three Lives," the rhythmic repetitions were successful in conveying the recurrences, the gradual unwinding of life, and in the dialogue they produced the effect of the speech of slow-minded people: "I never did use to think I was so much on being real modest, Melanctha, but now I know really I am, when I hear you talking. I see all the time there are many people living just as good as I am, though they are a little different to me. Now with you, Melanctha, if I understand you right what you are talking, you don't think that way of no other one that you are ever knowing." But, though in "The Making of Americans" this sort of thing is appropriate to the patient and brooding repetitiousness of the German-Jewish Americans of the first and second generations, it is here carried to such immoderate lengths as finally to suggest some technique of mesmerism. With sentences so regularly rhythmical, so needlessly prolix, so many times repeated and ending so often in present participles, the reader is all too soon in a state, not to follow the slow becoming of life, but simply to fall asleep. And the further we get, the more difficult we find it to keep our mind on what we are reading: Miss Stein abandons altogether for long stretches any attempt to tell her story by reporting what her characters do and say, and resorts to a curious abstract vein of generalization: "Some are needing themselves being a young one, an older one, a middle aged one, an older one, an old one to be ones realizing what any one telling about different ways of feeling anything, of thinking about anything, of doing anything is meaning by what that one is telling. Some are needing themselves being a young one, an older one, a middle aged one, an older one, an old one to be one being certain that it is a different thing inside in one being a young one, from being an older one, from being a middle aged one, from being an older one, from being an old one," etc., etc. The psychological truth is still there, no doubt, but it is in a solution of about one percent to the total volume of the dose, and the volume of the dose is enormous.

This repetitious and abstract vein of the last pages of "The Making of Americans" persists still in the psychological portraits of Picasso and Matisse published in 1912: "One was quite certain that for a long part of his being one being living he had been trying to be certain that he was wrong in doing what he was doing and then when he could not come to be certain that he had been wrong in doing what he had been doing, when he had completely convinced himself that he would not come to be certain that he had been wrong in doing what he had been doing he was really certain then that he was a great one and he certainly was a great one. Certainly every one could be certain of this thing that this one is a great one."

This is queer and very boring, like a good deal of "The Making of Americans," but it is still intelligible. A little later, however, Miss Stein published privately another "portrait" which represented something of a new departure. In the "Portrait of Mabel Dodge," she seems to be groping for the instinctive movements of the mind which underlie the factitious conventional logic of ordinary intercourse, and to be trying to convey their rhythms and reflexes through a language divested of its ordinary meaning.

"Tender Buttons," which appeared in 1914 and was the first of Miss Stein's books to attract attention, went even further than the "Portrait of Mabel Dodge" in the direction of dislocating words from their meanings. The pieces in "Tender Buttons" are in a different vein from anything she had published before: she has here given up her long rhythms and writes pungently, impressionistically, concisely. Miss Stein had by this time gone to live in Paris (where she has remained ever since) and had become interested in the modern French painting of the generation of Picasso and Matisse, which she was one of the first to appreciate and collect; and the pieces in "Tender Buttons"—the title was supposed to describe the contents—are said to have been intended as prose still-lifes to correspond to those of such painters as Picasso and Braque. A pattern of assorted words, though they might make nonsense from the traditional point of view, would be analogous to a Cubist canvas composed of unidentifiable fragments.

"*Red Roses*. A cool red rose and a pink cut pink, a collapse and a sold hole, a little less hot.

"*A Sound*. Elephant beaten with candy and little pops and chews all bolts and reckless rats, this is this.

"*Custard*. Custard is this. It has aches, aches when. Not to be. Not to be narrowly. This makes a whole little hill.

"It is better than a little thing that has mellow real mellow. It is better than lakes whole lakes, it is better than seeing.

"*Chicken*. Alas a dirty word, alas a dirty third, alas a dirty bird."

Gertrude Stein is said, at this period, to have made a practice of shutting herself up at night and trying utterly to banish from her mind all the words ordinarily associated with the ideas she had fixed upon. She had come to believe that words had other values than those inherent in their actual meanings, and she was attempting to produce a kind of literature which should work with these values exclusively.

In "Have They Attacked Mary He Giggled—A Political Satire" (1917), she developed, however, still another genre, which at least partially left to language its common meanings—a sort of splintered stenographic commentary made up of scraps of conversation as they reverberate in the mind and awaken unspoken responses. The volumes of miscellaneous pieces which have followed—"Geography and Plays" (1922) and "Useful Knowledge" (1928)—contain examples of all her previous styles as well as several variations, including a curious kind of "play" which consists simply of long lists of phrases divided into acts. Among these, some of the satires are funny, some of the portraits rather interesting and bits of the "abstract" impressionism charming, and there are one or two really excellent short stories such as "Miss Furr and Miss Skeene," in which the repetitive rigmarole manner is admirably suited to render the monotony and insipidity of the feminine lives which are being narrated. But most of what Miss Stein publishes nowadays must apparently remain absolutely unintelligible even to a sympathetic reader. She has outdistanced any of the Symbolists in using words for pure purposes of suggestion—she has gone so far that she no longer even suggests. We see the ripples expanding in her consciousness, but we are no longer supplied with any clew as to what kind of object has sunk there.

II

Sometimes these writings of Gertrude Stein make us laugh: her humor is perhaps the one of her qualities which comes through in her recent books most clearly; and I should describe them as amusing nonsense, if "nonsense" were not a word which had so often been used in derogation both of the original Symbolists and of the contemporary writers dealt with in this book. If I should say that Miss Stein wrote nonsense, I might be thought to be implying that she was not serious or that she was not artistically successful. As a matter of fact, one should not talk about "nonsense" until one has decided what "sense" consists of—and one cannot investigate this without becoming involved in questions which go to the bottom of the whole Symbolist theory and throw further light on the issues it raises.

The original Symbolists supposed themselves to be defending the value of suggestion in literature as against the documentation of Naturalism and the logic of rationalism—and both they and their opponents seemed to tend to take it for granted that the suggestion was all on one side and the sense all on the other. We have already noted this tendency in Valéry, in Eliot and in Yeats, and we have stumbled over the difficulties it leads to. Now, as a matter of fact, all literature, all writing, all speech, depends equally upon suggestion; the "meaning" of words is what they suggest. Speaking accurately, it is impossible to say that one kind of writing suggests, whereas another kind proves or states. Any literary work, if it accomplishes its purpose, must superinduce in the reader a whole complex of what we are accustomed to call thoughts, emotions and sensations—a state of consciousness, a state of mind; it depends for its effectiveness upon a web of associations as intricate and in the last analysis as mysterious as our minds and bodies themselves. Our words themselves are the prime symbols, and the only originality of the Symbolists consisted in reminding people of the true nature and function of words. It is of course possible to think of words abstractly so that they shall seem to have pure definite meanings, but the fact remains that as soon as we begin to use them, we cannot help pouring them full of suggestion by our inflections, our pauses, our tones or by their order and collocation on the page, and in any case by selecting them in such a way as to bring out certain previous associations.

Let us examine passages from various books, ranging from what we should call the most nonsensical to what we should call the most rational. Most people, I suppose, would grant to-day that it is the business of poetry to suggest and that it is possible to write very fine poetry which is neither logical in the ordinary sense nor true; and most people, I suppose, could be persuaded, after a moment or two of reflection, that there is really no difference in kind between poems like "Kubla Khan" and "Ulalume" and poems like "Jabberwocky," "The Jumblies" and "The Owl and the Pussycat" (unless it constitutes a difference in kind that Lear and Carroll intend to be amusing whereas Coleridge and Poe do not)—and even to admit that this realization should have the effect of making one think more highly of Lear and Carroll rather than less highly of Coleridge and Poe. But *prose* the ordinary reader might claim, as we have seen that Paul Valéry does, ought to convey a "sense." Yet there is a prose which, as anyone will recognize, is extremely close to poetry. Take one of the passages I have already quoted from Yeats:

"We make out of the quarrel with others, rhetoric, but of the quarrel with ourselves, poetry. Unlike the rhetoricians, who get a confident voice from remembering the crowd they have won or may win, we sing amid our uncertainty, and, smitten even in the presence of the most high beauty by the knowledge of our solitude, our rhythm shudders."

This appears a fairly reasonable statement, yet must we not confess, when we come to examine it, that we are being moved by beautiful words rather than convinced of a psychological fact? And in Yeats's own mind there is a line unmistakably drawn between this kind of prose and certain other kinds. In "A Vision," he writes as follows of that phase of human personality in his Great Wheel to which he assigns Bernard Shaw: "Style exists now but as a sign of work well done, a certain energy and precision of movement; in the artistic sense it is no longer possible, for the tension of the will is too great to allow of suggestion."

From Yeats's point of view, then, the prose of Shaw is devoid of suggestion, and, consequently, even of style. Yet let us look at a typical passage from "The Intelligent Woman's Guide to Socialism and Capitalism," a masterpiece of prose exposition:

"Naturally the squires were not disposed to take this defeat lying down. They revenged themselves by taking up Lord Shaftesbury's agitation for the Factory Acts, and showing that the employer's little finger was thicker than the country gentleman's loins; that the condition of the factory employees was worse than that of the slaves on the American and West Indian plantations; that the worst cottages of the worst landlords had at least fresher air than the overcrowded slums of the manufacturing towns; that if the employers did not care whether their 'hands' were Church of England or Methodist, neither did they care whether they were Methodists or Atheists, because they had no God but Mammon; that if they did not persecute politically it was only because the hands had no votes; they persecuted industrially as hard as they could by imprisoning Trade Unionists; and that the personal and often kindly relations between the peasantry and the landlords, the training in good manners and decent housekeeping traditions learnt by the women in domestic service in the country houses, the kindnesses shown to the old and sick on the great estates, were all lost in the squalor and misery, the brutality and blasphemy, the incestuous overcrowding, and the terrible dirt epidemics in the mining and factory populations where English life was what the employer's greed had made it."

If we scrutinize this paragraph on industrial conditions, we see at once that it depends as much on suggestion as the passage on rhetoric and poetry which has just been quoted from Yeats. Yeats suggests a state of mind where we are preoccupied with solitude and introspection, whereas Shaw suggests a state of mind where we are preoccupied with our relation to society; but that is the only difference. Shaw wants to turn our attention out, whereas Yeats wants to turn it in; but both use words not merely to reason but to put a spell on us and excite our emotions. What makes the passage by Shaw effective is the belligerent sound of such homely figures as "showing that the employer's little finger was thicker than the country gentleman's loins" and "because they had no God but Mammon"; it is the rousing rhythm of the piled-up indictment. The whole passage is loaded with suggestion from beginning to end: the suggestion produced by calling harsh names, by violent antithesis, by shifting quickly from a picture of horrible conditions to a picture of attractive ones and then abruptly shifting back to another picture more horrible still.

Let us, however, take another passage from a work which makes no claim to be literature, in which in fact the utmost effort has been exerted to keep as far away from poetry and to make sense as plainly as possible—let us take a passage from the United States Courts-Martial Manual:

"The Army is an emergent arm of the public service which the Nation holds ready for a time of great peril. Military service is an obligation which every citizen owes to the government. It is settled law that such service may be compelled, if necessary, by draft. Nor is the obligation of the soldier who volunteers for a fixed period different from that of the drafted soldier. By his act of volunteering he consecrates himself to the military service. His engagement, supported by an oath of allegiance, is that the nation may depend upon him for such service during the fixed period, whatever may be the emergency. When this engagement is breached a high obligation to the nation is disregarded, a solemn oath of allegiance is violated, and the government is defrauded in the amount of its outlay incident to inducting the soldier into the military service, training, clothing and caring for him while he remains in that service, and transporting him to the station from which he deserts. Desertion is thus seen to be, not simply a breach of contract for personal service, but a grave crime against the Government; in time of war perhaps the gravest that a soldier can commit, and at such times punishable with death."

It will be seen that the Courts-Martial Manual also deals in metaphors: "The Army is an emergent arm of the public service"; and its cumulative rhythms: "When this engagement is breached a high obligation to the nation is disregarded, a solemn oath of allegiance is violated, and the government is defrauded," etc. And the word "death" is made to dominate the paragraph by being placed at the end of the sentence. The author of the Courts-Martial Manual is trying like Bernard Shaw, but even more single-mindedly, to suggest a state of mind in which we shall be conscious of ourselves only in our relation to society.

Now let us turn to a recent piece of Gertrude Stein's:

A PATRIOTIC LEADING

Verse I

    Indeed indeed
    Can you see.
    The stars
    And regularly the precious treasure.
    What do we love without measure.
    We know.

Verse II

    We suspect the second man.

Verse III

    We are worthy of everything that happens.
    You mean weddings.
    Naturally I mean weddings.

Verse IV

    And then we are,
    Hail to the nation.

Verse V

    Do you think we believe it.

Verse VI

    It is that or bust.

Verse VII

    We cannot bust.

Verse VIII
Thank you.

Verse IX
Thank you so much.

Gertrude Stein is here attempting to convey an impression exactly the opposite of the impression which the author of the Courts-Martial Manual is aiming at: she and he diverge in the same directions as Yeats and Bernard Shaw, but they are even farther apart. Miss Stein is trying to superinduce a state of mind in which the idea of the nation will seem silly, in which we shall be conscious of ourselves as creatures who do not lend themselves to that conception. Yet the methods by which she accomplishes her ends are very similar to those of the author of the Manual. Like him, she proceeds by incantation. And "The Army is an emergent arm of the public service which the Nation holds ready," etc. is actually as metaphorical as Miss Stein's statement, in another recent piece of writing, that "toasted Susie is my ice-cream." The Army is not an emergent arm of anything: it is a collection of human beings. The difference between Gertrude Stein and the author of the Courts-Martial Manual is entirely a technical one: it is a difference simply of syntax and of the order in which each evokes his or her selected group of images.

This discussion would, of course, lead us, if we pursued it, to the nature of language itself and hence to the mysteries of human psychology and what we mean when we talk about such things as "reason," "emotion," "sensation" and "imagination." And this must be left to the philosophers, who are largely in the dark about it themselves. But it is well to remember the mysteriousness of the states with which we respond to the stimulus of works of literature and the primarily suggestive character of the language in which these works are written, on any occasion when we may be tempted to characterize as "nonsense," "balderdash" or "gibberish" some new and outlandish-looking piece of writing to which we do not happen to respond. If other persons say they do respond, and derive from doing so pleasure or profit, we must take them at their word.

Gertrude Stein is a singular case in this respect. Widely ridiculed and seldom enjoyed, she has yet played an important rôle in connection with other writers who have become popular. I have spoken of her influence on Sherwood Anderson—and Ernest Hemingway, not only in such short stories as "Mr. and Mrs. Elliot" (who recall Miss Furr and Miss Skeene), but also in certain passages of "The Sun Also Rises" and "A Farewell to Arms," where he wants to catch the slow rhythm of time or the ominous banality of human behavior in situations of emotional strain, owes her a similar debt. Most of us balk at her soporific rigmaroles, her echolaliac incantations, her half-witted-sounding catalogues of numbers; most of us read her less and less. Yet, remembering especially her early work, we are still always aware of her presence in the background of contemporary literature—and we picture her as the great pyramidal Buddha of Jo Davidson's statue of her, eternally and placidly ruminating the gradual developments of the processes of being, registering the vibrations of a psychological country like some august human seismograph whose charts we haven't the training to read. And whenever we pick up her writings, however unintelligible we may find them, we are aware of a literary personality of unmistakable originality and distinction. Sherwood Anderson, who is so sensitive to her quality, has written of it admirably as follows:

"In the great kitchen of my fanciful world in which I [see] Miss Stein standing, there is a most sweet and gracious aroma. Along the walls are many shining pots and pans, and there are innumerable jars of fruits, jellies, and preserves. Something is going on in the great room, for Miss Stein is a worker in words with the same loving touch in her strong fingers that was characteristic of the women of the kitchens of the brick houses in the town of my boyhood. She is an American woman of the old sort, one who cares for the handmade goodies and who scorns the factory-made foods, and in her own great kitchen she is making something with her materials, something sweet to the tongue and fragrant to the nostrils."

III

This may be an appropriate place to mention the systematic comic nonsense called Dadaism. There is no need to describe it at length—I have given in an appendix an entertaining history of the Dadaist Movement written in

1922 by Tristan Tzara, a Rumanian poet, who was perhaps its chief promoter. Many of the jokes of the Dadaists were pretty bad: a piece of silliness, obscenity or bad taste should have spontaneity to carry it off, whereas the antics of the Dadaists seem too often deliberately and mechanically perpetrated by essentially rather humorless young men. But it was natural in the Paris of the years immediately after the War for the youngest writers to produce a literature—they intended it as a campaign against literature—which should aim to set people's teeth on edge. The Dadaists were both cynical and hysterical, and their work was one of the symptoms of the social, intellectual and moral chaos of Europe after the Armistice. The exhaustion of the resources of life had had the result of rendering desperate and sterile even the youngest generation of Frenchmen who had scarcely taken part in the fighting, but who had grown up in the atmosphere of the War.

Dadaism was a queer special development of Symbolism. The writings of the Dadaists grew directly out of the Symbolist tradition, as their hoaxes and practical jokes recall the perverse *non sequitur* capers of Jules Laforgue's "Pierrot Fumiste" and Tristan Corbière's stroll in Rome with a mitre, a dress-suit and a pig. The writer, however, of the first Symbolist generation whom the Dadaists seem most to have admired was a man named Isidore Ducasse, the author of the "Chants de Maldoror," who signed himself "Comte de Lautréamont." Ducasse was a Frenchman born in Uruguay, who came to Paris in 1867 when he was twenty-one and, full of the literature of the Romantics from Byron to Baudelaire, composed an immature but not unpromising book in which the expression of what had become by that time the conventional attitudes of Romanticism was given a slightly new accent and handled in a slightly new way. "Les Chants de Maldoror" is full of the familiar ferocities and blasphemies, the familiar sombre confessions of uncommon and magnificent sins, carried, however, to unprecedented lengths by a young writer who evidently felt that his predecessors had set him a high standard to surpass; but the images of his nightmares and tirades have that peculiar phantasmagoric quality which was to be characteristic of Symbolism. Very little is known about Ducasse, but he has been identified with considerable plausibility with a man of the same surname, a particularly violent social-revolutionary orator who attracted a certain amount of notice at the popular meetings authorized by Napoleon III on the eve of the Franco-Prussian War. Ducasse was found dead in his room one morning, three years after he had come to Paris, and there are reasons for believing that he was murdered by Napoleon's secret police. At any rate, a legendary Ducasse, thin, catlike, small and dry, with a shrill grating voice and a "tête de décapité," half-buffoon but with a demon's energy, hushing crowds with his bloodthirsty speeches and dashing down at top speed during his solitary nights a book of sadistic and scandalous visions, became the patron saint of Dadaism.

The Dadaists were themselves, as time went on, to turn social-revolutionary: their savage spirit of opposition found a new field in political journalism. And, discarding the name of Dadaists though still intent on the destruction of conventional literature, they took to automatic writing, which they called "Surréalisme."

VIII

AXEL AND RIMBAUD

THE six writers with whom I have here been concerned represent then a further development of the
methods and ideals of the Symbolists. These æsthetic
ideals of Symbolism implied, however, a general point of
view which was also given a further development by this
second set of writers.

"One's great objection to the Symbolist school," writes
André Gide, "is its lack of curiosity about life. With perhaps the single exception of Vielé-Griffin (and it is this
that gives his verse so special a savor), all were pessimists,
renunciants, resignationists, 'tired of the sad hospital'
which the earth seemed to them—our 'monotonous and
unmerited fatherland,' as Laforgue called it. Poetry had
become for them a refuge, the only escape from the hideous realities; they threw themselves into it with a desperate fervor.

"Divesting life as they did of everything which they
considered mere vain delusion, doubting whether it were
'worth living,' it was not astonishing that they should
have supplied no new ethic—contenting themselves with
that of Vigny, which at most they dressed up in irony---
but only an æsthetic."

This ideal of renunciation of the experience of the out-

side world for the experience of the imagination alone,
this withdrawal of the individual from society, did, however, give rise to an attitude quite distinct from the stoi-
cism of Vigny. It had already been indicated in England
by Walter Pater:

"Those childish days of revery," he writes of "Marius
the Epicurean" (1885), "when he played at priests, played
in many another day dream, working his way from the
actual present, as far as he might, with a delightful sense
of escape in replacing the outer world of other people
by an inward world as himself really cared to have it, had
made him a kind of 'idealist.' He was become aware of
the possibility of a large dissidence between an inward
and somewhat exclusive world of vivid personal apprehension, and the unimproved, unheightened reality of the
life of those about him. As a consequence, he was ready
now to concede, somewhat more easily than others, the
first point of his new lesson, that the individual is to himself the measure of all things, and to rely on the exclusive
certainty to himself of his own impressions. To move afterwards in that outer world of other people, as though
taking it at their estimate, would be possible henceforth
only as a kind of irony."

But this doctrine had been preached to that generation
perhaps most uncompromisingly and emphatically by a
work of which Yeats has told us that he read it in his
early manhood "slowly and laboriously as one reads a
sacred book" and which Lalou, the author of the "Histoire de la Littérature Française Contemporaine," has de-

scribed as "the 'Faust' of the later nineteenth century."

Villiers de l'Isle-Adam's "Axel," which was published in 1890, is a sort of long dramatic poem in prose, which, as it was the last thing Villiers wrote, sums up and gives final expression to his peculiar idealism. Count Axel of Auersburg is a young man "of an admirable virile beauty," with "a paleness almost radiant" and "an expression mysterious from thought." He inhabits, in an atmosphere half-Wagnerian, half-romantic-Gothic, an ancient and isolated castle in the depths of the Black Forest, where he has given himself up to the study of the hermetic philosophy of the alchemists and is being prepared by a Rosicrucian adept for the revelation of the ultimate mysteries. And this castle entombs its own secret: when Napoleon's armies had menaced Frankfort, the people from miles around had brought in gold, jewels and other valuables to be deposited in the Frankfort National Bank, and it had been decided to send the gigantic treasure, amounting to three hundred and fifty million thalers, under an escort headed by Axel's father to a secret place of safe-keeping. But certain villainous government officials had plotted to murder the Count and possess themselves of the treasure, making it appear that he had allowed himself to fall into the hands of the French. The Count, however, before succumbing to this treachery, has had the time to hide the treasure underground somewhere in his vast estate, imparting the secret to no one but his wife, who has died without divulging it.

Now, during the winter when the drama opens, a

cousin of Axel's, the Commander Kaspar, has come to the castle and got wind of the treasure. The Commander, who declares "I am *real life!*," is represented as an insufferable vulgarian. Axel's life of pure reflection and imagination seems to him morbid, unprofitable and empty, and he tries to tempt his young cousin away by telling him of the glories of the court and the pleasures of amorous conquest; but the fastidious and fiercely proud young Count brushes these suggestions politely aside. When, however, the Commander comes to touch upon the treasure, which he urges Axel to take steps to recover, the young man instantly summons a servant and orders two swords to be brought. He reveals now, in resounding language, his contempt for the Commander's conceptions of honor and pleasure; explains his defiance of and voluntary exile from a society which has betrayed and murdered his father; asserts his supremacy and his haughty independence in the forest fastnesses where he has chosen to dwell; reviews at overpowering length the loyal forces he can call to his defence; describes impressively the enormous masked trenches in which he could cause the mightiest armies to be engulfed—and in a duel runs the Commander through.

In the meantime, however, the secret of the whereabouts of the treasure has been discovered in a Book of Hours formerly belonging to Axel's mother, by a young French noblewoman, who has been put in the convent to which the book has passed. This young girl makes a daring escape just as the nuns have almost compelled her to take the veil, and finds her way to Axel's castle, where he offers her a lodging for the night. Sara waits till she thinks everybody is asleep, then descends secretly to the family tombs in the crypt below the castle. Seeking out a certain heraldic death's-head, she presses with the point of a dagger a button between its eyes, and from behind a sliding panel the treasure comes pouring forth in cataracts of burning gold-pieces, cloud-bursts of pearls and diamonds. But in a moment she has become aware that Axel has been watching her unnoticed, and whipping out two fine pistols of steel, fires them at him one after the other—only wounding him, however, slightly in the chest. Axel seizes her and wrests away her dagger, with which she had been preparing to attack him, but she is as beautiful as Axel is handsome, and in a moment they have fallen in love.

Sara turns out to be a Rosicrucian, too: her escape from the convent has been signalized by the blooming of the mystic rose. She and Axel embrace in an ecstasy: for the first time, these two chaste and haughty spirits have found objects worthy of their passion. "Say, beloved," breathes Sara to Axel, speaking as if in a dream, "wouldst thou travel to those lands where the caravans pass in the shade of the palm-trees of Cashmir or Mysore? Wouldst to Bengal to choose in the bazaars roses, stuffs and Armenian maidens as white as the ermine's skin? Wouldst raise armies and, like a young Cyaxares, foment rebellion in northern Iran?—or shall we rather set sail for Ceylon, with its white elephants carrying vermilion towers, with its fiery macaws in the trees and with its dwellings all drenched in sun, where the rain of the fountains falls in the marble courts? . . . How delightful to fasten on our skates on the roads of pale Sweden! or in the region of Christiania, among the dazzling fjords and passes of the mountains of Norway!"—and so on for four solid pages. They are holding the whole world in their hands—they have love, youth, social position, power, the supernatural backing of the Rosicrucian spirits and three hundred and fifty million thalers' worth of treasure—"all the dreams to realize," says Sara.

But here Axel, "grave and impenetrable," strikes an unexpected note. "Why realize them?" he asks. "They are so beautiful!" And to her plea of "come and live!" he replies: "Live? No. Our existence is full—and its cup is running over! What hour-glass can count the hours of this night! The future? . . . Sara, believe me when I say it: we have just exhausted the future. All the realities, what will they be to-morrow in comparison with the mirages we have just lived? . . . The quality of our hope no longer allows us the earth. What can we ask from this miserable star where our melancholy lingers on save the pale reflections of such moments? The Earth, dost thou say? What has the Earth ever realized, that drop of frozen mud, whose Time is only a lie in the heavens? It is the Earth, dost thou not see? which has now become the illusion! Admit, Sara: we have destroyed, in our strange hearts, the love of life—and it is in REALITY indeed that ourselves have become our souls. To consent, after this, to live would be but sacrilege against ourselves. Live? our servants will do that for us. . . . Oh, the external world! Let us not be made dupes by the old slave, chained to our feet in broad daylight, who promises us the keys to a palace of enchantments when it clutches only a handful of ashes in its clenched black fist! Just now, thou wast speaking of Bagdad, of Palmyra, of—what was it?— Jerusalem? If thou didst but know what a heap of uninhabitable stones, what a sterile and burning soil, what dens of loathsome creatures, those wretched places in *reality* are—though they appear to thee all glamorous with memories far away in that imaginary Orient which thou carriest within thyself! And what sad weariness the mere sight of them would cause thee!"

He proposes that they shall kill themselves at once. Sara demurs: she suggests one night of love. But Axel begs her not to be trivial. "Oh, my beloved," he tries to explain to her, "to-morrow I should be the prisoner of thy wondrous body! Its delights would have enchained the chaste energy which animates me now!"—and then, their love could never endure: some cursed day they would find it burnt out. She pleads still: "But remember the human race!" "The example I leave it," he answers, "is well worth those it has given me." "Those who fight for Justice say that to kill oneself is to desert." "The verdict of beggars," he declares, "for whom God is but a way to earn their bread." "It might be nobler to think of the general good!" "The universe devours itself: at that price is the good of all." And he finally succeeds in persuading her:

they drink a goblet of poison together and perish in a rapture.

It will easily be seen that this super-dreamer of Villiers's is the type of all the heroes of the Symbolists, of our day as well as of his: Pater's contemplative, inactive Marius, the exquisitely sensitive young men of his "Imaginary Portraits"; Laforgue's Lohengrin, who, the night of his wedding, shrinking from union with his Elsa, turns his back on her and embraces his pillow begging it to carry him away—his Salome, "the victim of having tried, like all of us, to live in the factitious instead of in the honest everyday"; the Hamlet of Mallarmé's posthumous drama, "Igitur," who is the only character in the play and does nothing but soliloquize. And above all, Huysmans's Des Esseintes, who set the fashion for so many other personalities, fictitious and real, of the end of the century: the neurotic nobleman who arranges for himself an existence which will completely insulate him from the world and facilitate the cultivation of refined and bizarre sensations; who sleeps by day and stays up at night and whose favorite reading is Silver Latin and the Symbolists. Des Esseintes is living up to the ideal of Axel and Sara when, having set out to visit London—excited by the novels of Dickens—he turns back at the railroad station: he has already driven in a cab through a foggy day in Paris, visited Galignani's English book-store, dined at an English restaurant on oxtail soup, haddock, beefsteak and ale —and as he remembers that he has left his tooth-brush, it occurs to him that on a former occasion he had been

sadly disappointed by a visit to Holland and that the real
London cannot possibly come up to the one he has just
been imagining. It is difficult to agree with M. Lalou as
to the literary merits of "Axel," but it is certainly true
that it is in a sense a *fin de siècle* "Faust." And if we compare Villiers's point of view with the point of view of the
Romantics, we see plainly the fundamental difference between Symbolism and Romanticism.

The later movement, as I have already said, was an antidote to nineteenth-century Naturalism, as the earlier had
been an antidote to the neo-classicism of the seventeenth
and eighteenth centuries: Symbolism corresponds to Romanticism, and is in fact an outgrowth from it. But
whereas it was characteristic of the Romantics to seek experience for its own sake—love, travel, politics—to try the
possibilities of life; the Symbolists, though they also hate
formulas, though they also discard conventions, carry on
their experimentation in the field of literature alone; and
though they, too, are essentially explorers, explore only
the possibilities of imagination and thought. And whereas the Romantic, in his individualism, had usually re-
volted against or defied that society with which he felt
himself at odds, the Symbolist has detached himself from
society and schools himself in indifference to it: he will
cultivate his unique personal sensibility even beyond the
point to which the Romantics did, but he will not assert
his individual will—he will end by shifting the field of
literature altogether, as his spokesman Axel had done the
arena of life, from an objective to a subjective world,

from an experience shared with society to an experience savored in solitude.

The heroes of the Symbolists would rather drop out of the common life than have to struggle to make themselves a place in it—they forego their mistresses, preferring dreams. And the heroes of the contemporary writers with whom I have been dealing in this book are in general as uncompromising as Axel—sometimes, indeed, the authors themselves seem almost to have patterned their lives on the mythology of the earlier generation: the Owen Aherne and Michael Robartes of Yeats, with their lonely towers and mystic chambers, their addiction to the hermetic philosophy—and Yeats himself, with his astrology and spiritualism, his own reiterated admonitions (in spite of considerable public activity) of the inferiority of the life of action to the life of solitary vision: Paul Valéry's M. Teste, sunken also in solitary brooding so far below the level where the mind is occupied in attacking particular practical problems that it is no longer interested even in thoughts which have for their objects particular fields of experience, but only in the processes of thought itself—and Teste's inventor, the great poet who can hardly bring himself to write poetry, who can hardly even bring himself to explain why he cannot bring himself to write poetry; the ineffectual fragmentary imagination, the impotence and resignation, of the poet of "Gerontion" and "The Waste Land"; the supine and helpless hero of "A la Recherche du Temps Perdu," with his application of prodigious intellectual energy to differenti-

ating the emotions and sensations which arise from his
passive contacts with life and with his preference for lying
in bed by himself and worrying about Albertine's absences
to getting up and taking her out—Proust himself, who
put into practice the regime which Huysmans had invented for his hero, keeping his shutters closed by day
and exercising his sensibility by night, whose whole elaborate work might have been based on Axel's contention
in regard to foreign travel that the reality never equals
the dream; Joyce's Bloom, with his animated consciousness and his inveterate ineptitude; Joyce's new hero who
surpasses even the feats of sleeping of Proust's narrator and
M. Teste by remaining asleep through an entire novel;
and Gertrude Stein, who has withdrawn into herself more
completely, who has spun herself a more impenetrable
cocoon, than even Michael Robartes, M. Teste, Gerontion,
H. C. Earwicker or Albertine's asthmatic lover.

There is a difference between Proust's cork-lined bedroom and Alfred de Vigny's ivory tower. Vigny was dealing, even in his art, with that active life of the world in
which he had participated, but the post-Romantic writer
who sleeps by day has lost touch with that world so completely that he no longer knows precisely what it is like.
We recognize in a Romantic like Coleridge, with his
mulling, metaphysics-weaving mind and his drugs, much
of the temperament and mentality of the author of "A la
Recherche du Temps Perdu"; but even Coleridge has more
politics than Proust.

II

One of the principal causes, of course, for this withdrawal of the *fin de siècle* poets from the general life of their time, was the fact that in the utilitarian society which had been produced by the industrial revolution and the rise of the middle class, the poet seemed to have no place. For Gautier's generation, the bourgeois had already become the enemy; but one took a lively satisfaction in fighting him. By the end of the century, however, the bourgeois's world was going so strong that, from the point of view of the poet, it had come to seem hopeless to oppose it. The artistic heroes of Thomas Mann with their abject "inferiority complex" in the presence of the good German burgher are typical of the end of the century; but certain writers with a strong Romantic strain like H. G. Wells and Bernard Shaw tried to promote through the new social sciences, in the teeth of the bourgeois world, the realization of those visions of universal happiness which had been cherished by some of the most individualistic of the Romantics, such as Shelley and Rousseau. But if one had no sociological interest and no satirical bent and so no way of turning society to account, one did not try to struggle with it or to attract attention by publishing one's grievances against it: one simply did one's best to ignore it, to keep one's imagination free of it altogether.

The poets of the end of the century, when they happened to be incapable of Naturalism or of social idealism like William Morris's, were thus peculiarly maladjusted persons. We are less conscious of this in the case of the early Symbolist writers I have mentioned because they were men who either, not possessing particularly vigorous personalities, resigned themselves easily to their special situation or, from illness or for some other reason, were not able to rebel against it long. Pater and Mallarmé were professors, living quietly and modestly among their books; Verlaine drifted with every wind; Corbière and Laforgue were dying of tuberculosis in their twenties; Ducasse was dead at twenty-four, perhaps murdered for his alliance with the Socialists; and for Villiers de l'Isle-Adam, a man of distinguished family who had plumbed the depths of poverty and misery in Paris to emerge finally, with health and disposition ruined, as a reputation of the literary cafés, it was easy to reject, in the rôle of the haughty Axel, imaginary treasures and honors. Yet both the characteristic tendency of the Symbolists to intimate rather than speak plainly and their cult of the unique personal point of view are symptomatic of the extent to which they found themselves out of touch with their fellows and thrown in upon their own private imaginations. Another hero and pioneer of Symbolism, however, was both to struggle with the world and survive—though to survive as something other than a poet; and his career reveals the whole situation in a dramatic burst of light.

Arthur Rimbaud was born in the north of France, the son of a pious and strong-willed countrywoman and of an army officer who, during the years of his campaigning, paid little attention to his family and finally abandoned them altogether. A prize scholar at his provincial school, Rimbaud had run, by the time he was nineteen, through the whole repertoire of modern ideas: he had reacted against a strict religious training into romantic atheism and paganism; had flamed up, at the fall of the Second Empire, with social-revolutionary idealism; and had finally devoured Darwin and the other evolutionary writers—as, in poems written between sixteen and nineteen (1870–73), he had, as one of his biographers has said, "lived in three years the literary evolution of modern times." Rimbaud's earliest poetry was in a familiar Romantic vein, to which, however, he soon brought fresh strong colors and new elements of irony and invective. He had already, at seventeen, attempted, in a letter to a friend, an original reëstimate of the Romantics, of whom he asserted that they had never properly been judged, and proposed at the same time a new theory of poetry which, though more violent and apocalyptic than most expressions of Symbolist doctrine, prophesied the advent of Symbolism:

"I say that one must be a *visionary*—that one must make oneself a VISIONARY.

"The poet makes himself a *visionary* through a long, immense and reasoned *derangement of all the senses*. All forms of love, of suffering, of madness; he seeks himself, he exhausts all poisons in himself to keep only their quintessences. An indescribable torture in which he has need of all faith, all superhuman force, in which he becomes, among all, the great sick man, the great criminal, the great accursed—and the supreme Scholar!—for he arrives at the *unknown*— Because he has cultivated his soul, already rich, more than anyone else! He arrives at the unknown; and even if, driven insane, he should end by losing his grasp on his visions, he has seen them! Let him perish, in his plunging, by unheard-of unnamable things: other horrible workers will come; they will begin at those horizons where their predecessors sank! . . .

"The poet is a true Stealer of Fire.

"He is charged with humanity, with the animals themselves; he must make his inventions felt, handled, heard. If what he brings back from *beyond* has form, he gives form; if it is formless, he gives the formless. To find a language;

"—All speech, furthermore, being idea, the time of a universal language will come! One has to be an academician—deader than a fossil—to make a dictionary of any language at all. The weak-minded would begin *thinking* about the first letter of the alphabet and might quickly end by going mad!—

"This language will be of the soul for the soul, summing up all, perfumes, sounds, colors, catching hold of thought with thought and drawing it out. The poet would define the quantity of unknown awakening in his time in the universal soul: he would give more than the formula of his thought, more than the annotation of his march to *Progress!* An enormity becoming a norm absorbed by all, he would be a true *multiplier of progress!* . . .

"I habituated myself," he wrote later, "to simple hallucination: I would see quite honestly a mosque instead of a factory, a school of drummers composed of angels, calashes on the roads of the sky, a drawing-room at the bottom of a lake: monsters, mysteries; the announcement of a musical comedy would cause horrors to rise before me.

"Then I explained my magical sophistries by the hallucination of words!

"I ended by finding sacred the disorder of my intelligence. . . ."

Rimbaud had apparently arrived at the point of view set forth in his letter independently of the influence of any other French poet; and, in the productions described in the later passage, had merely been giving expression to a unique personal way of seeing—though he was to know something of English literature and had probably read Poe's poetry as early as 1872. A few months after writing this letter, however, he had made the acquaintance of Paul Verlaine. Verlaine, though he published his poems in the collections of the Parnassians, was already tending toward pure musical effects and taking unauthorized metrical liberties; and he had a special predisposition toward the sort of poetry with which Rimbaud was beginning to experiment boldly. He helped and encouraged the boy; took him into his house in Paris and tried to put him in touch with the Parisian literary world.

And Rimbaud in his turn was not only profoundly to influence Verlaine's poetry, but to play havoc with his life. Verlaine, then twenty-seven, had just been married and his wife was expecting a baby; but his impressionable feminine nature, at once rakish and sentimental, was delighted and infatuated by Rimbaud. Rimbaud, who, for all the boy's blue eyes and apple-cheeks which were combined with his ungainly figure and his large bumpkin's hands and feet, for all his unsteady adolescent's voice with its northern country accent, had already his hard core and his harsh will; and he now brought to the rôle of outlaw the moral force which he had inherited from his mother, even though her narrowness and rigor, her merciless domination of his childhood, had been driving him to take the part of Satan. A provincial in Paris without a penny, as well as a man of genius at an age when most boys are only just beginning to indulge their first doubts and to hazard their first original phrases, Rimbaud's position would by no means have been easy even if his nature had not been intractable. He ran amuck in the literary circles to which Verlaine introduced him, and, after disrupting Verlaine's household, carried him off on a vagabondage of adventure through Belgium and England. Verlaine had already, presumably, become rather discontented with his bourgeois domestic life—he was obliged to live with his wife's family—and Rimbaud had quickly infected him with his own ambition to become a supreme Visionary and a supreme outlaw against bourgeois society: "I had, indeed, in all sincerity of spirit," Rimbaud writes in one of his prose poems, "undertaken to restore him to his primitive condition of child of the Sun—and we wandered, fed with the wine of thieves' dens and the hardtack of the road, I eager to find the place and the formula." But this programme was too much for Verlaine, whom Rimbaud ridiculed and bedevilled and who was made uneasy by memories of his wife: her child had been born in the meantime and she was now bringing an action for divorce. Rimbaud himself, in the abrupt ruthless confrontation of the realities of his situation which followed this hallucinated period, was aware of the extent to which he had made Verlaine a victim of his own special maladjustment—and of the extent to which he himself, in regard to that maladjustment, had been taking a line of least resistance: "Beside his dear sleeping body," he makes Verlaine say in "Une Saison en Enfer," "how many hours of the night I have watched, seeking why he should desire so furiously to escape from reality. Never before had man such an ambition. I recognized—without fearing for him —that he might be a serious danger to society. Has he perhaps secrets to change life?" Rimbaud had always been given to seeing himself in the rôle of a criminal: "Even as a child," he writes, "I used to admire the incorrigible convict on whom the jail is always closing again. . . . He had for me more strength than a saint, more good sense than a traveller—and himself, himself alone! for witness of his glory and his reason." And now he makes Verlaine play at this game with him: on one occasion, they both get arrested for discussing imaginary robberies and murders in the railway station at Arras.

The literary results of this expedition were Verlaine's "Romances sans Paroles" and Rimbaud's "Illuminations."

Their titles indicate the wide difference between the temperaments and geniuses of the two men; yet the poems represent a sort of collaboration which was to be as important as Mallarmé's cénacle in making the new poetry self-conscious and in giving it the courage of its convictions.

At last, after several quarrels and separations, Verlaine and Rimbaud parted definitively—though not until Verlaine had been sentenced to two years in prison at Brussels for shooting Rimbaud in the wrist, and Rimbaud, meeting Verlaine at Stuttgart after the latter's release and finding that he had while in jail repented of his former errors and found repose in the bosom of the Church, had first proceeded to get Verlaine drunk and make him blaspheme his faith, "cause" as Rimbaud wrote in a letter, "the ninety-eight wounds of Our Lord to bleed," and then—according, at least, to the legend—as they were walking through the Black Forest and another altercation arose, knocked him down with a club and left him unconscious.

In the meantime, while Verlaine was in jail, Rimbaud had returned to his mother's house in the Ardennes, where, during the spring and summer of 1873, he composed that extraordinary masterpiece "Une Saison en Enfer," in which the hysteria of the late nineteenth century in France, not very different from that of our own time—an age recently deprived of religious faith, demoralized and embittered by war and already becoming dissatisfied with social utopianism, science and the cult of art as an end in itself—was crystallized in the sharp and dazzling fragments of what Verlaine called a "diamond prose." But now, not merely unreconciled to the bourgeois world and at the centre of the conflict of its intellectual currents, but disillusioned at last with all these, disgusted with his own incoherence and even with the brilliant literature which he had created to give it expression, he had planned an escape from the European reality by a more effective means than self-hallucination. Rimbaud had always thought of himself as a peasant, as a member of "the inferior race," the blue-eyed Gauls whom the Romans had conquered—and he had always longed for some life that would take the place of the lost brutality and innocence of Europe, for the non-Christian, non-middle-class life of the Orient, of Africa:

"Priests, professors, masters," he now writes, "you are wrong to give me up to justice. I have never belonged to these people; I have never been a Christian; I am of the race who sang in torture; I do not understand the laws; I haven't the moral sense, I am a brute; you are doing wrong. Yes, my eyes are closed to your light. I am a nigger, a beast. But I may be saved. You yourselves are false niggers, savage and grasping madmen. Tradesman, you are a nigger; magistrate, you are a nigger; general, you are a nigger; emperor, old itching palm, you are a nigger: you have drunk of a contraband liquor from Satan's distillery. This people is inspired by fever and cancer. Invalids and old men are so respectable that they ought to be boiled. The wisest course is to quit this continent, where madness prowls to provide these wretches with hostages. I am entering into the true kingdom of Shem.

"Do I know Nature? do I know myself?— *No more words.* I bury the dead in my belly. Shouts, drums, dance, dance, dance! I do not even foresee the hour when the white men will land among us and when I shall be nothing again.

"Hunger, thirst, shouts, dance, dance, dance, dance!"

Having finished his "pagan book, nigger book," as he called it before he gave it its final name, "A Season in Hell," he went down in the autumn to Paris, where the literary men in the cafés, who had heard of his escapades with Verlaine, received him with insulting coldness. He returned to his mother's house and burnt up all the copies of "Une Saison en Enfer" which he had just received from his publisher, as well as all the other manuscripts he had.

And now he proceeded to carry out the resolution which he had announced in the work he had burnt. Shutting himself up and studying continuously, sometimes for twenty-four hours at a time, he applies himself to learning the modern languages—he had always had a linguistic gift—which are most useful for travel and trade: English, German, Spanish, Italian, Russian, Arabic and Greek. And as a few years before, just out of school, without money and almost without friends, he had kept obstinately running away to Paris—so now, determined to turn his back on Europe, as moneyless and more friendless than before, he tries repeatedly to reach the East. First, after teaching for a year in Germany, he sells his trunk and makes his way to Italy, with the intention of joining

a friend who has a soap-factory in the Cyclades; but, un-
dertaking to travel to Brindisi on foot, he gets a sunstroke
and is repatriated by the French consul. At Marseilles, he
manages to live by unloading cargo and helping truck-
drivers, and then enlists in the Carlist army, but finally
returns to his mother's house. Next, in order to get passage
to Java, he enlists for six years in the Dutch army—lands
at Batavia, deserts, joins the crew of an English sailing-
vessel, goes back to France and home again. The next
year, under the pretext of wanting to go to Austria for the
purpose of learning German, he succeeds in getting some
money out of his mother; but immediately upon arriving
in Vienna, he takes his cabman out for a drink and in
return is robbed of his coat with all his money, and finds
himself obliged to sell key-rings and shoe-laces in the street
till he gets into a row with the Austrian police and is sent
back again to France. Soon, however, he sets out on foot
for Hamburg, whence he hopes to find some way of getting to the East, but where, instead, he falls in with a
circus, with which he travels as interpreter and barker on
a tour of the Scandinavian countries, finally getting himself sent back by the consul from Stockholm to Charleville again. On his next attempt, after earning a little
money unloading cargo at Marseilles, he buys passage to
Alexandria, but on the ship develops gastric fever from a
rubbing of his ribs against his abdomen, caused by too
much walking—and goes back to Charleville.

Three months afterwards, however—in the spring of
1878—by way of Switzerland, Italy and Egypt, he suc-

ceeds in reaching the island of Cyprus and gets a job as
foreman in one of the quarries. But he catches typhoid
and by the spring of the next year is at home with his
family once more. When a friend asks him whether he is
writing nowadays, he replies with annoyance and scorn:
"I don't do anything with that any more"; and when, on
the eve of his departure the next spring, he hears one of
his friends congratulate another on having just bought
some Lemerre editions—Lemerre had been the publisher
of the Parnassians—he bursts out: "That's a lot of money
wasted. It's absolutely idiotic to buy books—and especially
books like that. You've got a ball between your shoulders
that ought to take the place of books. When you put
books on your shelves, the only thing they do is cover up
the leprosies of the old walls." He looks for work in
Cyprus, in Egypt, in Abyssinia, in all the ports of the
Red Sea, and finally finds a job at Aden working at twelve
francs a day for a firm of French coffee importers. This
company presently sends him to Harrar, where it is starting a new branch, and later makes Rimbaud the director
of all its expeditions into Galla and Somaliland. Rimbaud
was the first European to penetrate into the country of
Ogadain; and on his return from an extremely dangerous
expedition to one of the native potentates, he traced for
the first time the itinerary afterwards taken by the Ethio-
pian railway. At last, however, he quarrels with his employers and, after adventures of various kinds, sets up at
Harrar a trading-post of his own, where he traffics in
sugar, rice, silk, cotton-goods and arms, sending out his

own caravans, intriguing with the local kings, entertaining European travellers with enchanting and cynical conversation and maintaining a harem of native women carefully selected as coming from different parts of the country so that they may teach him their different languages. During this period, he wrote to a friend on *Le Temps* asking to be sent as war correspondent to cover the Italo-Abyssinian campaign. This proposal was declined, but in answering his letter the friend informed him that his poems, preserved by Verlaine, were being published and read in Paris, and that, in the circles of the new Symbolist school, he had become a legendary figure, an attempt having even been made to found a new literary system on a sonnet in which he had assigned different colors to the vowels. But at this period, Rimbaud's only literary concern was to supply reports to the Geographical Society, and, when he refers to his poetry at all, it is to dismiss it as "absurd" or "disgusting." "I couldn't go on with it," he told his sister later. "I should have gone mad —and besides it was bad stuff." The only ambition he now admits is to make enough money to marry a French girl and retire from his present business—"to have at least one son whom I could spend the rest of my life bringing up according to my own ideas, cultivating and arming him with the completest education that one can get in this age, and whom I could see become a famous engineer, powerful and rich through science."

One winter, however, after Rimbaud had been twelve years in the East, he found himself suffering from what

he took at first to be varicose veins; but he refused to go
to a doctor, kept on walking and riding, as if he could
dominate even disease by his stubborn and brutal will—
and presently found that his leg was so swollen that he
was obliged to direct his business from bed. At last the
pain had become so severe that he was compelled to give
up altogether and have himself carried on a litter to Aden,
a terrible journey of twelve days, on the second of which
he spent sixteen hours without shelter under pouring rain.

The English doctor at Aden told Rimbaud that he
would be unable to treat him properly, and shipped him
back to France, where, in the hospital at Marseilles, they
amputated his leg. For the last time Rimbaud returned
to his mother's: he tried to get about on a crutch, but the
infection had spread through his whole system. He spent
an agonizing summer of pain and fever, and then, with
a fixed idea of returning to the East, had himself sent
back to Marseilles. There he died, attended only by his
sister. It was harvest-time on the family farm, and the
daughter's absence was bitterly resented by her mother,
who when Arthur had been away, had refused to get for
him instruments and books which he had sent her the
money to buy. Isabelle, Rimbaud's sister, had never known
till after her brother's death, when she read about it in
the papers, that Arthur had been a poet, but she heard
him "end his life in a sort of continual dream, saying
strange things very gently in a voice that would have
charmed me if it had not pierced my heart. What he was
saying was all dreams, yet it was not the same thing at all

as when he had had the fever. It was as if he did it on purpose. . . . He mixed all sorts of things up, and with art." But Rimbaud, in his final delirium, was still obsessed by the idea of the East: on his death-bed, he insisted upon dictating a letter to a steamship company, asking how much the passage would cost and when he should have himself carried aboard.

One is likely to be guilty of over-simplification in using people's personal careers to point the morals of general social situations. Rimbaud, in his rôle of African trader, had obviously succeeded at last in emulating his father and his mother both at once—repeating the career of the former, who had campaigned in Italy, Algiers and the Crimea, by his wanderings and his intolerant independence at the same time that, by his sound character as a trader and his concentration upon making money, he was achieving the only sort of success which his mother could understand. Yet Rimbaud's life has a typical significance: it moves us, it seems to put before us an acute phase of the human predicament, as if it were a great play. The other poets of whom I have been writing were as little at home in their nineteenth-century world as Rimbaud, and they were mostly as disillusioned with its enthusiasms; but they had remained in it and managed to hold their places in it by excreting, like patient molluscs, iridescent shells of literature—whereas Rimbaud, with genius equal to any's, with genius perhaps superior to any's, had rejected Europe altogether—not merely its society and ideas, but even the kind of sensibility which one cultivated when one tried to live at odds with it and the kind of literature this sensibility supplied—getting away to a life of pure action and a more primitive civilization.

And if actions can be compared with writings, Rimbaud's life seems more satisfactory than the works of his Symbolist contemporaries, than those even of most of his Symbolist successors, who stayed at home and stuck to literature. Rimbaud was far from finding in the East that ideal barbarous state he was seeking; even at Harrar during the days of his prosperity he was always steaming with anxieties and angers—but his career, with its violence, its moral interest and its tragic completeness, leaves us feeling that we have watched the human spirit, strained to its most resolute sincerity and in possession of its highest faculties, breaking itself in the effort to escape, first from humiliating compromise, and then from chaos equally humiliating. And when we turn back to consider even the masterpieces of that literature which Rimbaud had helped to found and which he had repudiated, we are oppressed by a sullenness, a 'ethargy, a sense of energies ingrown and sometimes festering. Even the poetry of the noble Yeats, still repining through middle age over the emotional miscarriages of youth, is dully weighted, for all its purity and candor, by a leaden acquiescence in defeat.

III

What then is to be the future of this literature? Will the poets become more and more esoteric as the world be-

comes more and more difficult for them, diverging further
and further from the methods and the language of popular literature in proportion as popular literature approxi-
mates more and more closely to journalism? Will the
sciences dominate the future, as Pierre de Massot has suggested in a book which traces the development of Symbolism from Mallarmé to Dadaism, "smothering the last
works of the past, until the day when literature, music
and painting have become the three principal branches of
ˌneurology"? Paul Valéry has recently predicted that as
radio, moving picture and television come to take the
place of books as means of affecting people's feelings and
ideas, literature, as we have known it in the past, may
become "as obsolete and as far removed from life and
practice as geomancy, the heraldic art and the science of
falconry." Literature, according to Valéry, has become
"an art which is based on the *abuse of language*—that is,
it is based on language as a creator of illusions, and not
on language as a means of transmitting realities. Everything which makes a language more precise, everything
which emphasizes its practical character, all the changes
which it undergoes in the interests of a more rapid trans-
mission and an easier diffusion, are contrary to its function as a poetic instrument." As language becomes more
international and more technical, it will become also less
capable of supplying the symbols of literature; and then,
just as the development of mechanical devices has compelled us to resort to sports in order to exercise our muscles,
so literature will survive as a game—as a series of spe-

cialized experiments in the domain of "symbolic expression and imaginative values attained through the free combination of the elements of language."

I agree with Valéry that "the development in Europe, since 1852, of literary works which are extremely difficult, subtle and refined, which are written in a complicated style, and which, for that reason, are forbidden to most readers, bears some relation to the increase in number of literates," and to the consequent "intensive production of mediocre or average works." But I am by no means sure that the future destiny of this difficult and subtle art is to be practised only as a sort of game and with no relation to other intellectual activities. The truth is, I believe, that Valéry's pessimism arises itself from the special point of view which, as I have said, has been associated from the beginning with the school of literature that Valéry represents.

The disillusion and weariness which we recognize as characteristic of the eighties and nineties were in reality the aspects of a philosophy which, implicit in the writings of the Symbolists, was to come to its full growth and exert its widest influence during the period that followed the War. I do not mean that Symbolism as an organized movement went on becoming more and more powerful until it triumphed over all rival movements: the eminence at this particular time of a set of writers—such writers as I have discussed in this book—all stemming more or less directly from Symbolism, was unexpected and rather sudden, and it was due largely to extra-literary accidents. The

period immediately before the War had been character-
ized, on the whole, by a predominance of Naturalistic
and social-idealistic literature—the great reputations in
England and France had been those of writers like Shaw,
Wells, and Bennett, Romain Rolland and Anatole France.
But when the prodigious concerted efforts of the War had
ended only in impoverishment and exhaustion for all the
European peoples concerned, and in a general feeling of
hopelessness about politics, about all attempts to organize
men into social units—armies, parties, nations—in the service of some common ideal, for the accomplishment of
some particular purpose, the Western mind became peculiarly hospitable to a literature indifferent to action and
unconcerned with the group. Many of the socially-minded
writers, besides, had been intellectually demoralized by
the War and had irreparably lost credit in consequence;
whereas these others—Yeats, Valéry, Joyce, Proust—had
maintained an unassailable integrity and now fell heir to
the prestige which had been sacrificed by other poets and
novelists who had abandoned the detached study of human motives and the expression of those universal emotions which make all classes and peoples one, to become
intolerant partisans. It had required a determined independence and an overmastering absorption in literature
to remain unshaken by the passions and fears of that
time—and in the masterpieces which these scattered and
special writers had been producing in isolation, and, as it
were, secretly, while pandemonium raged without, their
justification was plain. These books revealed new discov-

eries, artistic, metaphysical, psychological: they mapped the labyrinths of human consciousness as they seemed never to have been mapped before, they made one conceive the world in a new way. What wonder that for those who survived the War these writers should have become heroes and leaders?

There are, as I have said, in our contemporary society, for writers who are unable to interest themselves in it either by studying it scientifically, by attempting to reform it or by satirizing it, only two alternative courses to follow—Axel's or Rimbaud's. If one chooses the first of these, the way of Axel, one shuts oneself up in one's own private world, cultivating one's private fantasies, encouraging one's private manias, ultimately preferring one's absurdest chimeras to the most astonishing contemporary realities, ultimately mistaking one's chimeras for realities. If one chooses the second, the way of Rimbaud, one tries to leave the twentieth century behind—to find the good life in some country where modern manufacturing methods and modern democratic institutions do not present any problems to the artist because they haven't yet arrived. In this book, I have been occupied with writers who have, in general, taken Axel's course; but the period since the War has furnished almost as many examples of writers who have gone the way of Rimbaud—without usually, however, like him, getting to the point of giving up literature altogether. All our cult, which Wyndham Lewis has denounced, of more primitive places and peoples is really the manifestation of an impulse similar to Rimbaud's—D. H. Lawrence's mornings in Mexico and his explorations of Santa Fé and Australia; Blaise Cendrars's negro anthology, the negro masks which bring such high prices in Paris, André Gide's lifelong passion for Africa which has finally led him to navigate the Congo, Sherwood Anderson's exhilaration at the "dark laughter" of the American South, and the fascination for white New Yorkers of Harlem; and even that strange infatuation with the infantile—because our children are more barbarous than we—which has allowed the term Expressionism to be applied at once to drawings done by the pupils in German schools and to the dramas of German playwrights, which caused Nathalia Crane to be taken seriously and made Daisy Ashford all the rage; that hysterical excitement over modern "primitives" which has led the generation of Jean Cocteau to talk about the douanier Rousseau as their fathers did about Degas—all this has followed in the wake of Rimbaud.

Yet Lawrence, for all his rovings, must come back to the collieries again; and for Anderson, though he may seek in New Orleans the leisure and ease of the old South, it is the factories of Ohio which still stick in his crop. The Congo masks in Paris are buried in galleries or in the houses of private collectors almost as completely as if they were sunk among the ruins of their vanished dynasties in the African wilderness; and when white New Yorkers, obstreperous and drunken, visit the Harlem cabarets at night, they find the negroes in American business suits, attempting modestly and drearily to conform to the requirements of Western civilization. Our shocking children soon grow up into adults as docile as their mothers and fathers. And as for those that choose Axel's course, the price paid by the man of imagination who, while remaining in the modern world, declines to participate in its activities and tries to keep his mind off its plight, is usually to succumb to some monstrosity or absurdity. We feel it in Proust's hypochondriac ailments and his fretting self-centred prolixities; in Yeats's astrology and spirit-tappings and in the seventeenth-century cadence which half puts to sleep his livest prose; in the meagreness of the poetic output of Paul Valéry and T. S. Eliot contrasted with their incessant speculations as to precisely what constitutes poetry, precisely what function it performs and whether there is any point in writing it; even in the mystifications by which Joyce, "forging," just behind that screen, "the uncreated consciousness" not merely of the Irish but of the western man of our time, has made his books rather difficult of access to a public for whom a few chapter headings or a word of explanation might have enabled them to recognize more readily a mirror for the study of their own minds. (The philosophical mathematicians and physicists whose work these novelists and poets parallel seem to have developed, no doubt from the same social and political causes, a similar metaphysical hypertrophy: consider the disproportionate size of the shadow-structure of speculation which such a writer as Eddington tries to base on some new modification of physical theory, itself suggested on most uncertain evidence.)

It is true of these later writers that they have not dissociated themselves from society so completely as the
original group of Symbolists: they have supplied us, as a
matter of fact, with a good deal of interesting social criticism; but it is usually a criticism which does not aim at
anything, it is an exercise—Proust is the great example—
of the pure intelligence playing luminously all about but
not driven by the motor power of any hope and not directed by any creative imagination for the possibilities of
human life. If these writers ever indicate a preference for
any social order different from the present one, it is in-
variably for some society of the past as they have read of
it in its most attractive authors—as Yeats likes to imagine
himself in the rôle of some great lord and patron of arts
of the Renaissance, or as Eliot dedicates his credo to a
seventeenth-century Anglican bishop. And this tendency
to look to the past, in spite of the revolutionary character
of some of their methods, has sometimes given even to
their most original work an odd Alexandrian aspect: the
productions of Eliot, Proust and Joyce, for example, are
sometimes veritable literary museums. It is not merely
that these modern novelists and poets build upon their
predecessors, as the greatest writers have done in all times,
but that they have developed a weakness for recapitu-
lating them in parodies.

When these writers do turn their attention to the contemporary world and its future, it is usually with strange,
and even eerie, results. Eliot has recently—explaining
by the way, in regard to causes in general, that "we fight

rather to keep something alive than in the expectation that anything will triumph"—put forward, or announced his intention of putting forward, a programme of classicism, royalism and Anglo-Catholicism; and Yeats, in his astrological "Vision," has predicted the future of Europe as follows:

"A decadence will descend, by perpetual moral improvement, upon a community which may seem like some woman of New York or Paris who has renounced her rouge pot to lose her figure and grow coarse of skin and dull of brain, feeding her calves and babies somewhere upon the edge of the wilderness. The decadence of the Greco-Roman world with its violent soldiers and its mahogany dark young athletes was as great, but that suggested the bubbles of life turned into marbles, whereas what awaits us, being democratic and *primary*, may suggest bubbles in a frozen pond—mathematical Babylonian starlight. . . .

"It is possible that the ever increasing separation from the community as a whole of the cultivated classes, their increasing certainty, and that falling in two of the human mind which I have seen in certain works of art is preparation. During the period said to commence in 1927, with the 11th gyre, must arise a form of philosophy which will become religious and ethical in the 12th gyre and be in all things opposite of that vast plaster Herculean image, final *primary* thought. It will be concrete in expression, establish itself by immediate experience, seek no general agreement, make little of God or any exterior unity, and it will call that good which a man can contemplate himself as doing always and no other doing at all. It will make a cardinal truth of man's immortality that its virtue may not lack sanction, and of the soul's reëmbodiment that it may restore to virtue that long preparation none can give and hold death an interruption. The supreme experience, Plotinus's ecstasy of the Saint, will recede, for men—finding it difficult—substituted dogma and idol, abstractions of all sorts of things beyond experience; and man may be long content with those more trivial supernatural benedictions as when Athena took Achilles by his yellow hair. Men will no longer separate the idea of God from that of human genius, human productivity in all its forms."

I believe therefore that the time is at hand when these writers, who have largely dominated the literary world of the decade 1920–30, though we shall continue to admire them as masters, will no longer serve us as guides. Axel's world of the private imagination in isolation from the life of society seems to have been exploited and explored as far as for the present is possible. Who can imagine this sort of thing being carried further than Valéry and Proust have done? And who hereafter will be content to inhabit a corner, though fitted out with some choice things of one's own, in the shuttered house of one of these writers—where we find ourselves, also, becoming conscious of a lack of ventilation? On the other hand, it seems equally unsatisfactory, equally impossible, to imitate Rimbaud: we carry with us in our own minds and habits the civilization of machinery, trade, democratic education and standardization to the Africas and Asias to which we flee, even if we do not find them there before us. Nor can we keep ourselves up very long at home by any of the current substitutes for Rimbaud's solution—by occupying ourselves exclusively with prize-fighters or with thugs or by simply remaining drunk or making love all the time. In the meantime, western Europe has been recovering from the exhaustion and despair of the War; and in America the comfortable enjoyment of what was supposed to be American prosperity, which since the War has made it possible for Americans to accept with a certain complacency the despondency as well as the resignation of European books, has given way to a sudden disquiet. And Americans and Europeans are both becoming more and more conscious of Russia, a country where a central social-political idealism has been able to use and to inspire the artist as well as the engineer. The question begins to press us again as to whether it is possible to make a practical success of human society, and whether, if we continue to fail, a few masterpieces, however profound or noble, will be able to make life worth living even for the few people in a position to enjoy them.

The reaction against nineteenth-century Naturalism which Symbolism originally represented has probably now run its full course, and the oscillation which for at least three centuries has been taking place between the poles of objectivity and subjectivity may return toward objectivity again: we may live to see Valéry, Eliot and Proust displaced and treated with as much intolerance as those writers—Wells, France and Shaw—whom they have themselves displaced. Yet as surely as Ibsen and Flaubert brought to their Naturalistic plays and novels the sensibility and language of Romanticism, the writers of a new reaction in the direction of the study of man in his relation to his neighbor and to society will profit by the new intelligence and technique of Symbolism. Or—what would be preferable and is perhaps more likely—this oscillation may finally cease. Our conceptions of objective and subjective have unquestionably been based on false dualisms; our materialisms and idealisms alike have been derived from mistaken conceptions of what the researches of science implied—Classicism and Romanticism, Naturalism and Symbolism are, in reality, therefore false alternatives. And so we may see Naturalism and Symbolism combine to provide us with a vision of human life and its universe, richer, more subtle, more complex and more complete than any that man has yet known—indeed, they have already so combined, Symbolism has already rejoined Naturalism, in one great work of literature, "Ulysses."

I cannot believe, then, with Paul Valéry that Symbolism is doomed to become more and more highly specialized until it has been reduced to the status of an intellectual pastime like anagrams or chess. It seems to me far more likely that it will be absorbed and assimilated by the general literature and thought. All the exponents of Symbolism have insisted that they were attempting to meet a need for a new language. "To find a tongue!" Rimbaud had cried. "One has to be an academician—deader than a fossil—to make a dictionary of any language at all." And Valéry himself had followed Mallarmé in an effort to push to a kind of algebra the classical language of French poetry; Gertrude Stein has explained that her later writings are intended to "restore its intrinsic meaning to literature"; and Joyce, in his new novel, has been attempting to create a tongue which shall go deeper than conscious spoken speech and follow the processes of the unconscious. It is probably true, as Pater has suggested, that there is something akin to the scientific instinct in the efforts of modern literature to render the transitory phases of "a world of fine gradations and subtly linked conditions, shifting intricately as we ourselves change." In any case, the experiments of men who in their lifetimes have been either received with complete indifference or denounced as practical jokers or lunatics may perhaps prove of equal importance with those scattered researches in mathematics and physics which seemed at first merely whimsical exercises on the margins of their subjects, but which have been laid under contribution by the great modern physical systems—without which these could scarcely have been constructed. Mallarmé's poetry, in its time, seemed no more gratuitous and abstruse than Gauss's fourth-dimensional coördinates—yet it has been built upon by writers as considerable in their own field as Einstein is in his.

As I have pointed out in connection with Gertrude Stein, our ideas about the "logic" of language are likely to be superficial. The relation of words to what they convey—that is, to the processes behind them and the processes to which they give rise in those who listen to or read them—is still a very mysterious one. We tend to assume that being *convinced* of things is something quite different from having them *suggested* to us; but the suggestive language of the Symbolist poet is really performing the same sort of function as the reasonable language of the realistic novelist or even the severe technical languages of science. The most, apparently, we can say of language is that it indicates relations, and a Symbolist poem does this just as much as a mathematical formula: both suggest imaginary worlds made up of elements abstracted from our experience of the real world and revealing relations which we acknowledge to be valid within those fields of experience. The only difference between the language of Symbolism and the literary languages to which we are more accustomed is that the former indicates relations which, recently perceived for the first time, cut through or underlie those in terms of which we have been in the habit of thinking; and that it deals with them by means of what amounts, in comparison with conventional language, to a literary shorthand which makes complex ideas more easily manageable. This new language may actually have the effect of revolutionizing our ideas of syntax, as modern philosophy seems to be tending to discard the notion of cause and effect. It is evidently working, like modern scientific theory, toward a totally new conception of reality. This conception, as we find it to-day in much Symbolist literature, seems, it is true, rather formidably complicated and sometimes even rather mystical; but this complexity may presently give rise to some new and radical simplification, when the new ideas which really lie behind these more and more elaborate attempts to recombine and adapt the old have finally begun to be plain. And the result may be, not, as Valéry predicts, an infinite specialization and divergence of the sciences and arts, but their finally falling all into one system. He himself suggests such a possibility by constantly reminding us of the single "method" common to all departments of thought. And who can say that, as science and art look more and more deeply into experience and achieve a wider and wider range, and as they come to apply themselves more and more directly and expertly to the needs of human life, they may not arrive at a way of thinking, a technique of dealing with our perceptions, which will make art and science one?

The writers with whom I have here been concerned have not only, then, given us works of literature which, for intensity, brilliance and boldness as well as for an architectural genius, an intellectual mastery of their materials, rare among their Romantic predecessors, are probably comparable to the work of any time. Though it is true that they have tended to overemphasize the importance of the individual, that they have been preoccupied with introspection sometimes almost to the point of insanity, that they have endeavored to discourage their readers, not only with politics, but with action of any kind—they have yet succeeded in effecting in literature a revolution analogous to that which has taken place in science and philosophy: they have broken out of the old mechanistic routine, they have disintegrated the old materialism, and they have revealed to the imagination a new flexibility and freedom. And though we are aware in them of things that are dying—the whole belle-lettristic tradition of Renaissance culture perhaps, compelled to specialize more and more, more and more driven in on itself, as industrialism and democratic education have come to press it closer and closer—they none the less break down the walls of the present and wake us to the hope and exaltation of the untried, unsuspected possibilities of human thought and art.

APPENDICES

APPENDIX I

THREE VERSIONS OF A PASSAGE FROM JAMES JOYCE'S NEW NOVEL

1. Navire D'Argent: 1925.

Tell me, tell me, how could she cam through all her fellows, the daredevil? Linking one and knocking the next and polling in and petering out and clyding by in the eastway. Who was the first that ever burst? Someone it was, whoever you are. Tinker, tailor, soldier, sailor, Paul Pry or polishman. That's the thing I always want to know. She can't put her hand on him for the moment. It's a long long way, walking weary! Such a long way backwards to row! She says herself she hardly knows who her graveller was or what he did or how young she played or when or where or how often he jumped her. She was just a young thin pale soft shy slim slip of a thing then, sauntering, and he was a heavy trudging lurching lieabroad of a Curraghman, making his hay for the sun to shine on, as tough as the oaktrees (peats be with them!) used to rustle that time down by the dykes of killing Kildare, that forestfellfoss with a plash across her. She thought she'd sink under the ground with shame when he gave her the tiger's eye!

2. Transition: 1927.

Tell me, tell me, how could she cam through all her fellows, the neckar she was, the diveline? Linking one and knocking the next, tapping a flank and tipping a jutty and palling in and petering out and clyding by on her eastway. Wai-whou was the first that ever burst? Someone he was, whoever they were, in a tactic attack or in single combat. Tinker, tailor, soldier, sailor, Paul Pry or polishman. That's the thing I always want to know. Push up and push upper and come to headquarters! Was it waterlows year, after Grattan or Flood, or when maids were in Arc or when three stood hosting? Faith will find where the Doubt arises like Nemo from Nirgends found the Nihil. Worry you sighin foh, Albern, O Anser? Untie the gemman's fistiknots, Qwic and Nuancee? She can't put her hand on him for the moment. It's a long long way, walking weary! Such a long way backwards to row! She says herself she hardly knows whuon the annals her graveller was, a dynast of Leinster, a wolf of the sea, or what he did or how young she played or when and where and how often he jumnped her. She was just a young thin pale soft shy slim slip of a thing then, sauntering, and he was a heavy trudging lurching lieabroad of a Curraghman, making his hay for the sun to shine on, as tough as the oaktrees (peats be with them!) used to rustle that time down by the dykes of killing Kildare, that forstfellfoss with a plash across her. She thought she'd sink under the ground with nymphant shame when he gave her the tigris eye!

3. "Anna Livia Pluribelle," a small book published in 1928.

Tell me, tell me, how cam she camlin through all her fellows, the neckar she was the diveline? Linking one and knocking the next, tapting a flank and tipting a jutty and palling in and pietaring out and clyding by on her eastway. Waiwhou was the first thurever burst? Someone he was, whuebra they were, in a tactic attack or in single combat. Tinker, tilar, souldrer, salor, Pieman Peace or Polistaman. That's the thing I always want to know. Push up and push upper and come to headquarters! Was it waterlows year, after Grattan or Flood, or when maids were in Arc or when three stood hosting? Fidaris will find where the Doubt arises like Nieman from Nirgends found the Nihil. Worry you sighin foh, Albern, O Anser? Untie the gemman's fistiknots, Qvic and Nuancee? She can't put her hand on him for the moment. Tez thelon langlo, walking weary! Such a loon way backwards to row! She says herself she hardly knows whuon the annals her graveller was, a dynast of Leinster, a wolf of the sea, or what he did or how blyth she played or how, when, why, where and who offon he jumnpad her. She was just a young thin pale soft shy slim slip of a thing then, sauntering, by silvamoonlake,

and he was a heavy trudging lurching lieabroad of a Curraghman, making his hay for whose sun to shine on, as tough as the
oaktrees (peats be with them!) used to rustle that time down by
the dykes of killing Kildare, for forstfellfoss with a plash across
her. She thought she's sankh neathe the ground with nymphant
shame when he gave her the tigris eye!

APPENDIX II

MEMOIRS OF DADAISM*

BY TRISTAN TZARA

At the beginning of the year 1920, I arrived back in Paris, extremely glad to see my friends again. I took part in the demonstrations which aroused the rage of the Parisian public, in company with Aragon, Breton, Dermée, Eluard, Ribemont-Dessaignes, Picabia, Péret, Soupault, Rigaut, Marguerite Buffet and others. The début of Dadaism in Paris took place on the twenty-third of January, at the matinée organized by the Dadaist review *Littérature*. Louis Aragon, a slender young man with feminine features, A. Breton, whose behavior displays the stigmata of the religious sectarians, G. Ribemont-Dessaignes, a man whose simple appearance conceals the fiery temper of the great accusers of humanity, and Philippe Soupault, whose facility of expression flows forth in bizarre images, gave readings from their works. Picabia, who has undergone so many influences, particularly those of the clear and powerful mind of Marcel Duchamp, exhibited a number of pictures, one of which was a drawing done in chalk on a blackboard and erased on the stage; that is to say, the picture was valid for only two hours. As for me, announced as "Dada," I read aloud a newspaper article while an electric bell kept ringing so that no one could hear what I said. This was very badly received by the public, who became exasperated and shouted: "Enough! Enough!" An attempt was made to give a futuristic interpretation to this act, but all that I wanted to convey was simply that my presence on the stage, the sight of my face and my movements, ought to satisfy people's curiosity and that anything I might have said really had no importance.

At the Grand Palais des Champs Elysées, thousands of persons

* A partial translation of these appeared in *Vanity Fair*, to which I am indebted for permission to republish them.

of all classes manifested very uproariously it is impossible to say exactly what—their joy or their disapproval, by unexpected cries and general laughter, which constituted a very pretty accompaniment to the manifestoes read by six people at once. The newspapers said that an old man in the audience gave himself up to behavior of a character more or less intimate, that somebody set off some flashlight powder and that a pregnant woman had to be taken out. It is true that the papers had also announced that Charlie Chaplin was going to deliver a lecture on Dada. Although we denied the rumor, there was one reporter who followed me everywhere. He thought that the celebrated actor was up to some new stunt and was planning a surprise entrance. I remember with tenderness that Picabia, who was to have taken part in the demonstration, disappeared as soon as it began. For five hours it was impossible to find him. The séance ended with a speech by "The King of the Fakirs," M. Buisson, who has a curious occupation: he predicts the future every day to those who wish to listen to him, on the Boulevard de la Madeleine. In the evening he sells papers at the Metro exits.

Several days afterwards, there took place in a church which had been transformed into a cinema—premises of the Club du Faubourg—at the invitation of that association, which includes more than three thousand workers and intellectuals, an explanation of the Dadaist Movement. There were four of us on the stage: Ribemont-Dessaignes, Aragon and Breton; and I. M. Léo Poldès presided. On this occasion, the audience were more serious: they listened to us. Their disapproval was expressed in shrill cries. Raymond Duncan, the philosopher who walks about Paris in the costume of Socrates, was there with all his school. He came to our defense and quieted the audience. A debate followed. The very best Socialist orators took sides and spoke for or against us. We replied to the attacks and the audience boiled in unison. Aragon wrote a moving article on that memorable matinée in *Les Ecrits Nouveaux.*

A week later, a public debate on Dada took place at the Université Populaire. Eluard, Fraenkel, Dermée, Breton, Ribemont-Dessaignes, Soupault and I participated with all the force of our temperaments in a séance torn by political passions. All the manifestoes of the presidents appeared in the Dadaist review, *Littérature*—it is well known that the Dadaist Movement has three hundred and ninety-one presidents and that anyone can become a president without the slightest trouble.

391 was also the name of a review which several of us started; it expanded and became a periodical of world-wide reputation. People finally became afraid of it, because it described things as they really were without any attempt to soften them. How many critics came to regret having uttered so many imbecilities!

A scandal provoked by the hypocrisy of certain Cubists in the bosom of a modern art society brought on the complete schism between the Cubists and the Dadas—an event which gave great force of cohesion to the nineteen dissenting Dadaists.

Paul Eluard, whom we call the inventor of a new metal of darkness, began to publish his review *Proverbe* in which all the Dadaists collaborated and which contributed a vein of its own. It was chiefly a matter of contradicting logic and language. This is how Soupault characterizes the collaborators of *Proverbe:*

> Louis Aragon, the Glass Syringe.
> Arp, Clean Wrinkles.
> André Breton, the Glass of Water in a Storm.
> Paul Eluard, the Nurse of the Stars.
> Th. Fraenkel, the Great Earth Serpent.
> Benjamin Péret, the Lemon Mandarin.
> G. Ribemont-Dessaignes, the Steam Man.
> Jacques Rigaut, the Hollow Plate.
> Philippe Soupault, the Musical Urinal.
> Tristan Tzara, the Man with the Pearl Head.

Dadaist hand-bills and books were spreading the agitation through Paris and the whole world.

In the month of May, the demonstration at the Théâtre de l'Œuvre, that courageous enterprise directed by Lugné-Poe, showed the vitality of Dada at its height. Twelve hundred people were turned away. There were three spectators for every seat; it was suffocating. Enthusiastic members of the audience had brought musical instruments to interrupt us. The enemies of Dada threw down from the balconies copies of an anti-Dada paper called *Non* in which we were described as lunatics. The scandal reached proportions absolutely unimaginable. Soupault proclaimed: "You are all idiots! You deserve to be presidents of the Dadaist Movement!" Breton, with the house completely dark, read in his thunderous voice a manifesto far from gentle toward the audience. Then Ribemont-Dessaignes read a soothing and complimentary manifesto. Paul Eluard presented some "examples." I will give one: the curtain goes up; two people, one of them with a letter in his hand, appear from opposite sides of the stage and meet in the centre; the following dialogue takes place:

> *"Le bureau de poste est en face."*
> *"—Que voulez vous que ça me fasse?"*
> *"Pardon, je vous voyais une lettre à la main. Je croyais . . ."*
> *"—Il ne s'agit pas de croire, mais de savoir."*

After which, each goes his way, and the curtain falls. There were six of these examples, very widely varied, in which the mixture of humanity, idiocy and unexpectedness contrasted curiously with the brutality of the other numbers. I invented on the occasion of this performance a diabolical machine composed of a klaxon and three successive invisible echoes, for the purpose of impressing on the minds of the audience certain phrases describing the aims of Dada. The ones which created the most sensation were: "Dada is against the high cost of living," and "Dada is a virgin microbe." We also produced three short plays by Soupault, Breton and Ribemont-Dessaignes and "La Première Aventure Céleste de M. Antipyrine," which I had written in 1916. This play is a boxing match with words. The characters, confined in sacks and trunks, recite their parts without moving, and one can easily imagine the effect this produced—performed in a greenish light—on the already excited public. It was impossible to hear a single word of the play. Mlle. Hania Routchine was to have sung at the end of the play a sentimental song by Duparc. The audience either took this for a sacrilege or considered that a thing so simple—it was intended to produce a contrast—was out of place on this occasion; in any case, they did not restrain their language. Mlle. Routchine, who was accustomed to the great successes of the Vaudeville, did not understand the situation and, after exchanging some amenities with the public, refused to finish the song. For two hours we could hardly calm her, for she wept wildly.

At the Salle Gaveau, at the Dada Festival, the scandal was also great. For the first time in the history of the world, people threw at us, not only eggs, salads and pennies, but beefsteaks as well. It was a very great success. The audience were extremely Dadaist. We had already said that the true Dadaists were against Dada. Philippe Soupault appeared as a magician. As he called the names of the Pope, Clemenceau and Foch, children's balloons came out of a large box and floated up to the ceiling. Paul Souday in his notice in *Le Temps* said that really, at a certain distance, the faces of the persons summoned actually appeared on the surfaces of the balloons. The audience was so excited and the atmosphere so overcharged that a number of other ideas merely suggested took on the appearance of reality. Ribemont-Dessaignes did a motionless dance and Mlle. Buffet interpreted some Dadaist music. A flashlight taken by the newspaper *Comœdia* during a performance of a play by me shows everybody in the house waving their arms and with their mouths open shouting.

All the Paris celebrities were present. Mme. Rachilde had written an article in a newspaper inviting some *poilu* to shoot us with a revolver. This did not prevent her a year later from appearing on the stage and defending us. She no longer regarded us as a danger to the *esprit français*. They did not kill us in the Salle Gaveau, but all the journalists tried to do so in their notices. Columns were written declaring that Dada wasn't to be talked about any more—which suggested this observation to Jean Paulhan [the following is in English in the original]:

"If you must speak of Dada you must speak of Dada.

If you must not speak of Dada you must still speak of Dada."

Among the other Dadaist reviews, *Cannibale* had a great success: it developed the absolutely anti-literary point of view which will be the relativist point of view of future generations. The superabundance of life of these future generations will find its place in the movement, and they will forget the rigid conventions, the paralyzed ideas, of a tradition which is nothing but laziness.

* * *

After France, the country tormented most by this impulse which knows no frontiers has been Germany. Already in 1918, Huelsenbeck, a vigorous and intelligent man and a poet of talent, who had assisted at the foundation of Dada in Zurich, brought the Dadaist verities into Germany with the zeal of a true apostle. He found there enthusiastic friends: George Grosz, who had lived in America, and who expressed in his drawings the tumultuous life of the great American cities, W. Heartfield, a sensitive poet, and Raoul Hausmann, who interests himself only in life. They had long been convinced of the guilt of the Kaiser in bringing on the war, and their relations with Liebknecht, Professor Nicolai and the pacifists were a secret to no one. The many demonstrations which they organized had a great influence and they can boast of having helped to bring on the German revolution.

They have their newspapers, their publishing house and a Dada Club, which soon brought to light great talents—the song writer, W. Mehring, for example; the painter, Mlle. H. Hoech; the philosopher, Daimonides, etc., etc. They have organized international expositions, and tours of the principal German cities. These tours came to a very bad end: if it had not been for the intervention of the police, the Dadaists would have been killed by their audiences. At Hanover, where the crowd took possession of their baggage, they had to get out of town as fast as possible. At Dresden, their cash-box was confiscated. When an opera singer who had nothing to do with Dada made an attempt to calm the audience, she was beaten up by the angry mob. At Prague, the scandal took on such proportions that the Czecho-Slovak government was forced to drive the Dadaists out and to forbid any Dadaist demonstration on Czecho-Slovakian territory.

I have not yet spoken of Baader, who is the head of the Dadaist religion. He has had visions: Jesus Christ has appeared to him several times. The number of his adepts is enormous. He has also played a political rôle. At Weimar he threw proclamations into the parliament and interrupted the sitting by accusing the new revolutionary Germany of being inspired by the reactionary ideas of Goethe and Schiller. Baader, who calls himself the President of the World, is the father of three children. He has twice been locked up by mistake in a lunatic asylum. He is not an especially interesting man, but certainly a very genial one. On the occasion of the death of his wife, he delivered a long oration to the three thousand people at the funeral, contending that death is essentially a Dadaist affair. He was wearing a smile on his lips. He had, none the less, been very fond of his wife. The same day he cut off his beard, which had been that of a true apostle.

Huelsenbeck is at present a doctor and journalist at Danzig. He is a great lover of America, whose praises he has sung in three books: "Dada the Conqueror," "Forward Dada!" and "Germany Must Go." The last Dadaist exposition at Berlin came to a very bad end: the Minister of War brought an indictment against the men who had organized it for having insulted the German officers "by deformations and tendencious inscriptions." The defenses of some of the Dadaists are masterpieces of malice and irony.

Another group lives in Cologne, Dada W. 3. Max Ernst, painter and poet, has made a great many Dadaist discoveries. His paintings bear the same relation to painting that the moving-pictures do to photography—fresh and direct realizations of a mind which owes nothing to the researches of its predecessors. His intelligence is fine and distinguished; it is plain that he is an enthusiastic Alpine climber. We call him the inventor of the mystery on rollers. Baargeld, a young millionaire, was a Bolshevist before being converted to Dadaism. His specialty is methodology. He was brought up in the love of Stendhal, for whom his father has more than admiration. The "Rosa Bonheur of the Dadaists" has done some very amusing things in painting. Job Haubrich contributes to their efforts with a sincere enthusiasm. Their organ is called *Die Schammade*. They have obtained from the city of Cologne two very important concessions: they have been allowed to hold an exposition in a public urinal, with free admission; and the city has published at its own expense a handsome album of Dada lithographs by Max Ernst. Ernst has founded with Arp, of whom I shall speak in a moment, a society for the manufacture of "Fatagaga" pictures. The dissenting Dadaists have grouped themselves under the name of "Stupid" [sic]. K. Schwitters is not an absolutely pure Dadaist. He lives in Hanover—it seems that he has quite an original turn of mind. The publisher Stegemann at Hanover has sold more than four hundred thousand little Dada books.

Dada has no adepts in England, but it is very well known there. M. A. Binnyon has given a lecture on Dadaism and F. S. Flint has written a brochure about us.

In Russia, the Dadaists call themselves "41°": Zdanevitch, Krutchony and Terentiev. They are abstract and very productive. The first-mentioned is professor of Dadaism at the University of Tiflis.

In Holland, Dada has fervent adherents: J. K. Bonset at Leyden and Th. van Doesburg, who will come to the defense of Dada in a forthcoming book. Their review appears in several languages and is called *Mécano*. P. Citroen and Bloomfield have made Amsterdam their base of operations.

Dada has received much attention in Spain. Its promoters are Jacques Edwards, Guillermo de Torre, Lasso de la Vega and Cansino d'Assens.

In Rome, Dada is philosophical, distinguished, fastidious and skeptical with the Baron J. Evola; in Milan and Mantua, determined and trenchant with Cantarelli, Fiozzi and Bacchi grouped about the *Blue Review*. Tired of the single-track ideas of Marinetti, these young men are getting away from Futurism and from the other artistic formulas.

Arp still lives in Switzerland, at Zurich: he is Alsatian, his mother is French. He is one of my best friends. He has illustrated two books of my poems. He is one of the most sympathetic men I have ever met. He wears shoes specially made for him at Ascona. They look like hippopotamuses' feet and have a pretty design in leather. The stories that he tells have an irresistible gaiety. The reliefs he has done represent imaginary solidified vegetations, and his drawings: embroidery, rain and the sleep of marine insects and crystal fingers. Mlle. Teuber has made for a marionette theatre puppets representing Dadaists and psychoanalysts like Dr. Jung. The painter Augusto Giacometti is too old to be a genuine Dadaist. He has declared that Dada is the sole joy of his life. Dada is known throughout the world. I have been able to observe for myself in the course of a trip that Dada is as well known in Switzerland as at Milan, Venice, Belgrade, Vincovtch, Bucharest, Jassy, Constantinople, Athens, Messina, Naples and Rome. On the Acropolis, a professor of theology was telling me, as he shook his fists toward the Wingless Victory, that God would avenge himself on Dada and all these newfangled ideas. I had good reason to know he spoke truly: I caught a cold which made me miserable for three weeks.

At Constantinople, I talked with a Greek doctor who had lived in Paris, and who didn't know who I was. He told me that he knew Tristan Tzara very well. Calmly, in spite of my amazement, I asked him what Tzara looked like. "He is tall and blond," he replied. I couldn't keep from laughing, because I am small and dark.

INDEX

INDEX

315

INDEX

INDEX

INDEX

INDEX